M000224352

STORIES OF
PEOPLE & CIVILIZATION

JAPANESE

ANCIENT ORIGINS

FLAME TREE PUBLISHING
6 Melbray Mews, Fulham,
London SW6 3NS, United Kingdom
www.flametreepublishing.com

First published and copyright © 2023
Flame Tree Publishing Ltd

23 25 27 26 24
1 3 5 7 9 10 8 6 4 2

ISBN: 978-1-80417-575-0

Cover and pattern art was created by Flame Tree Studio, with elements courtesy
of Shutterstock.com/svekloid/AQ_taro_neo. Additional interior decoration courtesy
of Shutterstock.com/Christos Georghiou.

Special thanks to Liz Wyse.

Judith John (lists of Ancient Kings & Leaders) is a writer and editor specializing in
literature and history. A former secondary school English Language and Literature
teacher, she has subsequently worked as an editor on major educational projects,
including *English A: Literature* for the Pearson International Baccalaureate series.
Judith's major research interests include Romantic and Gothic literature, and
Renaissance drama.

The text in this book is compiled and edited, with a new introduction, from *A History of
the Japanese People*, by F. Brinkley and Dairoku Kikuchi (The Encyclopedia
Britannica Company, 1915).

A copy of the CIP data for this book is available
from the British Library.

Designed and created in the UK | Printed and bound in China

COLLECTOR'S EDITIONS

STORIES OF
PEOPLE & CIVILIZATION
JAPANESE
ANCIENT ORIGINS

With a New Introduction by
JAKE LEIGH-HOWARTH
Further Reading and
Lists of Ancient Kings & Leaders

FLAME TREE PUBLISHING

CONTENTS

CONTENTS

STORIES OF
PEOPLE & CIVILIZATION
JAPANESE
ANCIENT ORIGINS

SERIES FOREWORD

Stretching back to the oral traditions of thousands of years ago, tales of heroes and disaster, creation and conquest have been told by many different civilizations, in ways unique to their landscape and language. Their impact sits deep within our own culture even though the detail in the stories themselves are a loose mix of historical record, the latest archaeological evidence, transformed narrative and the unwitting distortions of generations of storytellers.

Today the language of mythology lives around us: our mood is jovial, our countenance is saturnine, we are narcissistic and our modern life is hermetically sealed from others. The nuances of the ancient world form part of our daily routines and help us navigate the information overload of our interconnected lives.

The nature of a myth is that its stories are already known by most of those who hear or read them. Every era brings a new emphasis, but the fundamentals remain the same: a desire to understand and describe the events and relationships of the world. Many of the great stories are archetypes that help us find our own place, equipping us with tools for self-understanding, both individually and as part of a broader culture.

For Western societies it is Greek mythology that speaks to us most clearly. It greatly influenced the mythological heritage of the ancient Roman civilization and is the lens through which we still see the Celts, the Norse and many of the other great peoples and religions. The Greeks themselves inherited much from their neighbours, the Egyptians, an older culture that became weary with the mantle of civilization.

Of course, what we perceive now as mythology had its own origins in perceptions of the divine and the rituals of the sacred. The earliest civilizations, in the crucible of the Middle East, in the Sumer of the third millennium BCE, are the source to which many of the mythic archetypes can be traced. Over five thousand years ago, as humankind collected together in cities for the first time, developed writing and industrial scale agriculture, started to irrigate the rivers and attempted to control rather than be at the mercy of its environment, humanity began to write down its tentative explanations of natural events, of floods and plagues, of disease.

Early stories tell of gods or god-like animals who are crafty and use their wits to survive, and it is not unreasonable to suggest that these were the first rulers of the gathering peoples of the earth, later elevated to god-like status with the distance of time. Such tales became more political as cities vied with each other for supremacy, creating new gods, new hierarchies for their pantheons. The older gods took on primordial roles and became the preserve of creation and destruction, leaving the new gods to deal with more current, everyday affairs. Empires rose and fell, with Babylon assuming the mantle from Sumeria in the 1800s BCE, in turn to be swept away by the Assyrians of the 1200s BCE; then the Assyrians and the Egyptians were subjugated by the Greeks, the Greeks by the Romans and so on, leading to the spread and assimilation of common themes, ideas and stories throughout the world.

The survival of history is dependent on the telling of good tales, but each one must have the 'feeling' of truth, otherwise it will be ignored. Around the firesides, or embedded in a book or a computer, the myths and legends of the past are still the living materials of retold myth, not restricted to an exploration of historical origins. Now we have devices and global communications that give us unparalleled access to a diversity of traditions. We can find out about Indigenous American, Indian, Chinese and tribal African mythology in a way that was denied to our ancestors, we can find connections, plot the archaeology, religion and the mythologies of the world to build a comprehensive image of the human experience that is both humbling and fascinating.

The books in this series introduce the many cultures of ancient humankind to the modern reader. From the earliest migrations across the globe to settlements along rivers, from the landscapes of mountains to the vast Steppes, from woodlands to deserts, humanity has adapted to its environments, nurturing languages and observations and expressing itself through records, mythmaking stories and living traditions. There is still so much to explore, but this is a great place to start.

Jake Jackson
General Editor

STORIES OF
PEOPLE & CIVILIZATION

JAPANESE
ANCIENT ORIGINS

INTRODUCTION
& FURTHER READING

INTRODUCTION TO
JAPANESE ANCIENT ORIGINS

FIRST ENCOUNTERS

Driven **off course** by violent storms, on 23 September 1543 a battered Chinese ship approached an unfamiliar coastline. Anchoring in a cove, the Chinese captain Gohō – accompanied by two strange-looking men with unusually light complexions – alighted on the beach. So it was observed by a nearby group of startled peasants, who called upon village chief and scholar Nishimura Oribenojō to investigate.

Scrawling written Chinese in the sand with a stick to communicate, Nishimura asked Gohō about the origins of his peculiar shipmates. The captain explained that they were southern barbarians and merchants hailing from a distant land with primitive traditions called Portugal, where it was the custom to eat food with the hands and to drink without the use of cups. The new arrivals would likely have been similarly curious, inquisitively asking for information about the alien locale in which they found themselves. They would soon learn they had sailed to the southernmost tip of Tanegashima Island, located in the outer archipelago of the fabled kingdom of Japan.

THE LAND OF GOLD

Before 1543 the realm of Japan was an enigma representing the very furthest reaches of the known world. Doubtless those Chinese and Portuguese privileged to set foot on it for the first time would have been on the lookout for the glimmers and flashes of its most coveted of minerals.

For almost a millennium Japan had been well known in China as a producer of gold, a belief that stemmed from early Japanese visits to the Chinese mainland. In 804, for example, Chinese officials were amazed when a Japanese delegation delivered 13 kg of gold to the Japanese ambassador for his living expenses. The island's reputation as a repository of precious treasure was crystallized by the booming gold trade that later took place between the Song Dynasty and Japan.

It was because of this bustling commerce that the Portuguese and other civilizations had a similar conception of Japan to the Chinese. In the thirteenth century Marco Polo (1254–1324) famously traversed the vast expanse of territory that lay between Europe and Asia before ending up at the court of Mongolian chieftain Kublai Khan. Here he also picked up on whispers of Japan's extraordinary wealth.

Over three chapters that would stir the imagination of even Christopher Columbus as he set sail for the New World in 1492, Polo told of a realm so rich that even the roofs of Japanese palaces were lined with gold while bedroom floors were covered with a layer of gold two fingers thick. It was a belief also shared by the Arab geographer Muhammad al-Idrisi (1100–1165), who thought that gold was so cheap in Japan that even dog collars were made from it.

EARLY CHRISTIAN PERSPECTIVES

Encouraged by the cooperation of the natives and the peaceful nature of the first encounter, it was not long before European vessels were making arduous journeys across vast oceans. The aim of those on board was either to barter with the Japanese or to spread word of the Christian God. Emerging from this initial wave of immigration was the earliest European eyewitness account of Japan, released in 1585 and penned by Portuguese Jesuit missionary Luis Frois (1532–1597). In his chronicle *Striking Contrasts in the Customs of Europe*, Frois wrote of Japan's societal and martial customs with the traditional disdain that Europeans felt for cultures not their own. Written largely so that incoming Jesuits could understand Japanese behaviour through comparison to European mores, Frois's work is unmistakably infused with the perspective of an outsider.

A product of his time, Frois writes disparagingly about liberal Japanese attitudes to female chastity and judgementally about the tendency of Japanese men to grow out their nails so they look like the talons of a bird, among other things; he also constantly refers to fellow Europeans as 'us' and 'ours'. Yet with the expulsion of Europeans from the 1630s following a failed uprising of Japanese Christians against the ruling elite, the narrative of Frois and other Christian works would largely inform European knowledge of Japan for the next 250 years or so. Entering into a period of deliberate, self-imposed isolation that lasted well into the mid-nineteenth century, Japan once again became enshrouded in mystery.

MORE ACCURACY

Over the next few centuries Japan became inaccessible to European powers with the notable exception of the Dutch, who were permitted to establish a small trading post in Nagasaki. Information pertaining to Japan's history and culture now almost exclusively originated from a smattering of irregular accounts written by employees of the Dutch East India Company stationed in this single commercial hub.

Surprisingly, however, it was in this period of seclusion that the most accurate picture of the Japanese thus far emerged. Englebert Kaempfer (1651–1716) was a German adventurer who from 1683 had set out on a remarkable world tour. He started in Sweden and travelled through Russia, Persia and Siam, then finally on to Japan in 1690, where he lived for two years.

A man of the Enlightenment, Kaempfer provided a much-needed counterbalance to the Christian depictions that had dominated the discourse for so long. Supplied with Japanese chronicles, maps and other sources procured for him by his faithful servant and translator Imamura Gen'emon, Kaempfer pieced together the most precise record of Japanese history to date. First released in 1727 as *The History of Japan*, Kaempfer's magnum opus was hailed as a major contribution to the nascent field of Japanology and remained influential right up until the end of the nineteenth century.

JAPAN OPENS UP

On the other hand, the growing pantheon of literature spearheaded by Kaempfer that aimed to demythologize Japan had little effect on the general perception of the island. In continuing to be a hermit state, cut off from the rest of the world, Japan was still viewed as a land of legend and fairytale even as late as the mid-nineteenth century.

In an article published in the journal *Christian Remembrance* in 1852, one writer rhapsodized how Japan was like 'some Atlantis of the East', its peculiar isolation the source of an enduring fascination, 'like the fabled river of antiquity, it is a people which flows through the ocean of society but never mingles with the common stream of humanity'.

Economic turmoil and the growing dissension of the peasantry, however, meant that two years later all this would change. In 1854 the Japanese came to an agreement with the United States of America, allowing the Americans to access the ports of Nagasaki, Hakodate and Shimoda. By the end of the decade, after the brokering of similar treaties with Britain, Russia, the Netherlands and France, Japan was once again open to foreigners, enabling a second wave of curious Europeans to flock to its shores.

JAPAN HYSTERIA

Following the country's entry on to the international stage, Western society became infatuated with all things Japanese. Imported silk kimonos embroidered with dragons, cranes and other symbolic creatures represented the heights of genteel fashion. Whimsical Japanese gardens and ponds commissioned by the well-to-do became the ultimate status symbol, while Japanese-influenced plays and productions such as Gilbert and

Sullivan's comic opera *The Mikado; or The Town of Titpitu* – which ran for nearly 300 performances at New York's Fifth Avenue Theatre – became overnight sensations.

A profusion of exotic travel accounts such as *Unbeaten Tracks in Japan*, published in 1880 by Isabella Bird (1831–1904), and *Glimpses of Unfamiliar Japan*, published in 1894 by Lafcadio Hearn (1950–1904), further burnished orientalist images of Japan. The avalanche of titles on Japan would lead the early British Japanologist Basil Hall Chamberlain (1850–1935) wryly to comment in his *Things Japanese: Being Notes on Various Subjects Connected with Japan* that 'not to have written a book about Japan is fast becoming a title to distinction'.

But while others were content with sketching out only a superficial understanding of Japan to please admiring audiences back home, others like Chamberlain – who lived in Japan for 38 years and wrote extensively on the Japanese – felt compelled to go deeper, just as Englebert Kaempfer had done over 150 years before. Francis Brinkley, one of the authors of the present text, was similarly inclined.

FRANCIS BRINKLEY AND KIKUCHI DAIROKI

Brinkley (1841–1912) was born in Leinster to an aristocratic Irish family. In 1866 he was in Nagasaki, preparing for his new appointment as adjutant to his cousin, the governor of Hong Kong. It was in Nagasaki that he witnessed a rare duel between samurai warriors. In the aftermath he was taken aback by the actions of the victor who, after covering his felled opponent with his *haori* – a type of Japanese half-coat – clasped his hands in solemn prayer. So impressed was Brinkley by the samurai's conduct that a year later he moved permanently to Japan, never to return to his homeland.

A skilled grammatician, Brinkley's earliest achievement was to bridge the linguistic gulf with his *Guide to English Self-Taught*, released in 1875. It became the standard textbook for beginners in the English language throughout the country. In his next major work, *Japan: Described and Illustrated by the Japanese*, published between 1887 and 1898, Brinkley's guiding principles became even more apparent. He believed – perhaps more deeply than any other writer – that the story of Japanese civilization had to be told from a Japanese perspective rather than a Western one. Brinkley approached *A History of the Japanese People* with the same mentality, writing it in collaboration with the Japanese polymath Kikuchi Dairoki (1855–1917).

The son of a distinguished Japanese scholar of Western studies, Dairoki was one of the first Japanese students sent overseas for his education. Having graduated from University College London in 1874, he then graduated top of the year at St John's College, Cambridge University, in 1875. A mathematician by trade, Dairoki also played an integral role in modernizing education in Japan and was in many ways the perfect co-author. Like Brinkley, he was armed with a complex understanding of both the English and Japanese worlds, and was driven by a deep desire to educate. There was thus no duo better equipped to communicate the ancient origins of Japan to an English audience through a sober, balanced and careful approach – a welcome contrast to previous overemphasis on the exotic and primitive.

IN THIS BOOK

Beginning with the prehistoric origins of Japan's mythological roots, primeval inhabitants and archaeological record, Brinkley and Dairoki next trace the outlines of the island's earliest culture, society and economic structures. Moving into the realm of history, the third chapter discusses Japan's first generation of emperors – starting with Emperor Jimmu and ending with Nintoku – and their role in the creation, organization and definition of the original Japanese polity. The fourth section explores the protohistoric sovereigns, the beginning of foreign influence from China and Japan's initial colonial foray into nearby Korea. Following on from this, the narrative traces the historic introduction of Buddhism to the island, along with the violence and struggle that accompanied it, and the calamitous loss of Japan's foothold in Korea that took place between the reigns of Kinmei and Takara.

The text goes on to reveal the importance of the Daika Reforms, an attempt to re-exert the Emperor's waning authority in response to an increasingly disobedient noble class. In the penultimate chapter the characteristics of the Nara Epoch – marked by notable artistic accomplishments and the further integration of Buddhism and Chinese influence into almost every crevice of Japanese society – are clearly described. Concluding this comprehensive exposition of formative Japanese history is the Heian Epoch. This was an epic period, almost four centuries in length, during which the destiny of Shogunate Japan, its artistic direction, international relations and form of governance were shaped by a bitter and protracted civil war.

FINAL WORDS

The importance of *A History of the Japanese People* today should not be understated. Written from the perspectives of an Anglophile and a Japanophile, its contents represent a fine equilibrium of both extremes that was unique for its time. Unlike the Jesuit priest Luis Frois, who had so comprehensively presented Japan as the Other, or even Englebert Kaempfer, who despite honourable intentions only had a limited, two-year access to the island, Brinkley and Dairoki wrote from a truly insider's perspective that should be celebrated by the modern reader.

FURTHER READING

Bowers, John, 'Engelbert Kaempfer: Physician, Explorer, Scholar, and Author', *Journal of the History of Medicine and Allied Sciences* 21:3 (1966): 237–59

Brown, Delmer, *The Cambridge History of Japan: Volume 1 Ancient Japan* (Cambridge University Press, 2008)

Farris, William, *Daily Life and Demographics in Ancient Japan* (University of Michigan Press, 2020)

Farris, William, *Sacred Texts and Buried Treasures: Issues in the Historical Archaeology of Ancient Japan* (University of Hawaii Press, 1998)

Hoare, James, 'Captain Francis Brinkley (1841–1912): Yatoi, Scholar and Apologist', in *Britain & Japan: Biographical Portraits, Vol. III*, edited by J. Hoare (Routledge, 1999)

Korniki, Peter, 'European Japanology at the End of the Seventeenth Century', *Bulletin of the School of Oriental and African Studies* 56:3 (1993): 502–24

Lidin, Olof, *Tanegashima: The Arrival of Europe in Japan* (NIAS Press, 2002)

Lowe, Bryan, *Ritualized Writing: Buddhist Practice and Scriptural Cultures in Ancient Japan* (University of Hawaii Press, 2017)

Morris, Ivan, *The World of the Shining Prince: Court Life in Ancient Japan* (first ed. Oxford University Press, 1964; Kodansha America, 2000)

Ooms, Herman, *Imperial Politics and Symbolics in Ancient Japan: The Tenmu Dynasty, 650–800* (University of Hawaii Press, 2009)

Reff, Daniel; Danford, Richard; and Gill, Robin (eds.), *The First European Description of Japan, 1585: A Critical English-Language Edition of Striking Contrasts in the Customs of Europe and Japan* (Routledge, 2014)

Ruxton, Ian; and Noboru Koyama, *Japanese Students at Cambridge University in the Meiji Era, 1868–1912: Pioneers for the Modernization of Japan* (Lulu Press, 2010)

Polo, Marco (introduction and translation by Nigel Cliff), *The Travels* (Penguin Classics, 2015)

Jake Leigh-Howarth is a freelance history writer. He holds an MA in Modern History from the University of Leeds where he focused on the accounts of Western travellers to Soviet Central Asia and Eastern Siberia. Devoted to making history more accessible to the general public and a regular contributor to Ancient Origins.net, he has penned numerous articles online and in print on everything from the history of Japan and Greece to the Second World War. He also writes scripts for some of the most popular history YouTube channels such as Simple History, where his videos have millions of views.

PREHISTORIC ORIGINS

For most civilizations the ancient origins of their past are sacred, helping to define an unknowable world at the same time as binding together the fabric of their societies. This opening chapter considers the fundamental elements that make up Japan, including its foundational myth and the journey that its fledgling settlers may have taken to reach it. In addition, the sepulchres, weaponry, artefacts and pottery left behind by the Yamato culture paint a vivid picture· of Japan's very earliest human habitation. Later on the genesis of the Japanese language – a true outlier with very little resemblance to other tongues – is explored.

THE MYTHOLOGICAL ORIGINS OF JAPAN

The term *Kami*, often translated as "god", has no exact translation in English. Of the hundreds of families into which Japanese society came to be divided, each had its *Kami*, and he was nothing more than the head of the household. Fifty years ago, the Government was commonly spoken of as *O Kami* (the Honourable Head), and a feudatory frequently had the title of *Kami* of such and such a locality. Thus to translate *Kami* by "deity" or "god" is misleading, and as the English language furnishes no exact equivalent, the best plan is to adhere to the original expression.

Japanese mythology opens at the beginning of "the heaven and the earth." But it makes no attempt to account for the origin of things. It introduces us at once to a "plain of high heaven," the dwelling place of these invisible *Kami*, one of whom is the great central being, and the other two derive their titles from their productive attributes. Thereafter two more *Kami* are born from an elementary reedlike substance that sprouts on an inchoate earth. This is the first reference to organic matter. The two newly born *Kami* are invisible like their predecessors, and like them are not represented as taking any part in the creation. They are solitary, unseeable, and functionless, but the evident idea is that they have a more intimate connexion with cosmos than the *Kami* who came previously into existence, for one of them is named after the reed-shoot from which he emanated, and to the other is attributed the property of standing eternally in the heavens.

Now the record begins to speak of "generations." Two more solitary and invisible beings are born, one called the *Kami* who stands eternally on earth, the other the "abundant integrator." Each of these represents a generation, now the record begins to speak of "generations.". Five generations ensue, each consisting of two *Kami*, a male and a female, and thus the epithet "solitary" as applied to the first seven *Kami* becomes intelligible. All these generations are represented as gradually approximating to the exercise of creative functions, for the names become more and more suggestive of earthly relations (the *Kami* of mud-earth; the *Kami* of germ-integration; the *Kami* of the great place; the *Kami* of the perfect exterior, etc). The last couple, forming the fifth generation, are Izanagi and Izanami, appellations signifying the male and female *Kami* of desire. By all the other *Kami* these two are commissioned to "make, consolidate, and give birth to the drifting land," a jewelled spear being given to them as a token of authority, and a floating bridge being provided to carry them to earth. Izanagi and Izanami thrust the spear downwards and stir the "brine" beneath, with the result that it coagulates, and, dropping from the spear's point, forms the first of the Japanese islands, Onogoro. This island they take as the basis of their future operations, and here they beget, by ordinary human processes – which are described without any reservations – first, "a great number of islands, and next, a great number of *Kami*."

Three of these newly created beings act a prominent part in the sequel of the story. They are the "heaven-shining *Kami*" (*Amaterasu-o-mi-Kami*), commonly spoken of as the "goddess of the Sun;" the *Kami* of the Moon, and the *Kami* of force (Susanoo). Izanagi expresses much satisfaction at the begetting of these three. He hands his necklace to the *Kami* of the Sun and commissions her to rule the "plain of heaven;" he confers upon the *Kami* of the Moon the dominion of night, and he appoints the *Kami* of force (Susanoo) to rule the sea-plain.

The dividing line between mythological tradition and historical legend is now reached. Susanoo, the insubordinate *Kami*, was expelled from heaven for his destructive violence. After the descent of Susanoo, the *Kami* on the "plain of high heaven" took no further part in "making" or "ruling" the "ever fruitful land of reed-covered moors, and luxuriant rice-fields," as Japan was called.

Various *Kami* were sent from heaven to the land of Japan where they vied for supremacy. It had been originally intended that the dominion of Japan should be given to the senior of the five *Kami* born of the five-hundred-jewel string of the Sun goddess. But during the interval devoted to bringing the land to a state of submission, this *Kami*'s spouse, had borne a son, Hikoho no Ninigi (Rice-Ears of Ruddy Plenty), and this boy having now grown to man's estate, it was decided to send him as ruler of Japan. A number of *Kami* were attached to him as guards and assistants. The *Records* and the *Chronicles* agree in stating that he descended on Kirishimayama in Tsukushi, which is the ancient name of the island of Kyushu. This is one of the first eight islands begotten by Izanagi and Izanami. Hence the alternative name for Japan, "Land of the Eight Great Islands."

At all events he built for himself a palace and presently he encountered a beautiful girl. She gave her name as Brilliant Blossom, and described herself as the daughter of the *Kami* of mountains. According to legend their son Hohodemi was said to have lived for 580 years. His son, called Fuki-ayezu (Unfinished Thatch), married Princess Good Jewel, his own aunt, and by her had four sons. The first was named Itsuse (Five Reaches) and the youngest, Iware (a village in Yamato province). This latter ultimately became Emperor of Japan, and is known in history as Jimmu (Divine Valour), a posthumous name given to him many centuries after his death. Iware and his three brothers engaged in a celebrated journey from Kyushu to Yamamoto, a distance of about 350 miles, where they experienced many vicissitudes and conquests. Iware (Jimmu), who founded a ruling dynasty, was eventually buried in a tumulus (*misasagi*) on the northeast of Mount Unebi. The site is officially recognized to this day, and on the 3rd of April every year it is visited by an Imperial envoy, who offers products of mountain, river, and sea.

THE GEOGRAPHY OF JAPAN

The group of islands forming Japan may be said to have routes of communication with the continent of Asia at six places: two in the north; two in the southwest, and two in the south. The principal connexion in the north is across the narrow strait of Soya from the northwest point of Yezo to Saghalien and thence to the Amur region of Manchuria. The secondary connexion is from the northeast point of Yezo via the long chain of the Kuriles to Kamchatka. The first of the southwestern routes is from the northwest of Kyushu via the islands of Iki and Tsushima to the southeast of Korea; and the second is from the south of the Izumo promontory in Japan, by the aid of the current which sets up the two southern routes. One of these is from the southwest of Kyushu via the Goto Islands to southeastern China; the other is from the south of Kyushu via the Ryukyu Islands, Formosa, and the Philippines to Malaysia and Polynesia. It has also been proved geologically that the islands now forming Japan must at one time have been a part of the Asiatic continent. Evidently these various avenues may have given access to immigrants from Siberia, from China, from Malaysia, and from Polynesia.

The southwestern extremity of the main island of Japan is embraced by two large islands, Kyushu and Shikoku, the former lying on the west of the latter and being, in effect, the southern link of the island chain which constitutes the empire of Japan. Sweeping northward from Formosa and the Philippines is a strong current known as the Kuro-shio (Black Tide), a name derived from the deep indigo colour of the water. This tide, on reaching the vicinity of Kyushu, is deflected to the east, and passing along the southern coast of Kyushu and the Kii promontory, takes its way into the Pacific. Evidently boats carried on the bosom of the Kuro-shio would be likely to make the shore of Japan at one of three points, namely, the south, or southeast, of Kyushu, the south of Shikoku or the Kii promontory.

Now, according to the *Records*, the first place "begotten" by Izanagi and Izanami was an island called Awa, supposed to be in the vicinity of Awaji. The latter is a long, narrow island stretching from the northeast of Shikoku towards the shore of the main island – which it approaches very closely at the Strait of Yura – and forming what may be called a gate, closing the eastern entrance to the Inland Sea. After the island of Awa, the producing couple gave birth to Awaji and subsequently to Shikoku, which is described as an island having four faces, namely, the provinces of Awa, Iyo, Tosa, and Sanuki.

Rejecting the obviously allegorical fantasy of "procreation," we may reasonably suppose ourselves to be here in the presence of an emigration from the South Seas or from southern China, which debarks on the coast of Awaji and thence crosses to Shikoku. Thereafter, the immigrants touch at a triplet of small islands, described as "in the offing," and thence cross to Kyushu, known at the time as Tsukushi. This large island is described in the *Records* as having, like Shikoku, one body and four faces, and part of it was inhabited by Kumaso, of whom much is heard in Japanese history. From Kyushu the invaders pass to the islands of Iki and Tsushima, which lie between Kyushu and Korea, and thereafter they sail northward along the coast of the main island of Japan until they reach the island of Sado.

All this lends itself easily to the supposition of a party of immigrants coming originally from the south, voyaging in a tentative manner round the country described by them, and establishing themselves primarily on its outlying islands.

The immigrants would naturally have proceeded from Awaji to the Kii promontory, where the province of Yamato lies. Thereafter – on their "return," say the *Records*, and the expression is apposite – they explored several small islands not identifiable by their names but said to have been in Kibi, which was the term then applied to the provinces of Bingo, Bitchu, and Bizen, lying along the south coast of the Inland Sea and thus facing the sun, so that the descriptive epithet "sun-direction" applied to the region was manifestly appropriate.

THE ANCIENT PEOPLES OF JAPAN

Archaeology, while it discloses to us the manners and customs of the ancient inhabitants of Japan, does not afford material for clearly differentiating more than three cultures: namely, the neolithic culture of the Yemishi; the iron culture of the Yamato, and the intermediate bronze culture of a race not yet identified. There is no tangible evidence that several races co-existed with the Yemishi and that a very mixed population carried on the neolithic culture.

In considering the question of the origin of the Japanese nation four guides are available; namely, written annals, archaeological relics, physical features, and linguistic affinities.

The annals, that is to say, the *Records* and the *Chronicles*, speak of six peoples; namely, first, Izanagi and his fellow *Kami*, who, as shown above, may reasonably be identified with the original immigrants represented in the story of the so-called "birth" of the islands; secondly, Jimmu and his followers, who re-conquered the islands; thirdly, the Yemishi, who are identical with the modern Ainu; fourthly, the Kumaso; fifthly, the Sushen; and sixthly the Tsuchi-gumo (earth-spiders).

The Sushen were Tungusic ancestors of the Manchu. They are first mentioned in Japanese annals in 549 CE, when a number of them arrived by boat on the north of Sado Island and settled there, living on fish caught during spring and summer and salted or dried for winter use. The people of Sado regarded them as demons and carefully avoided them, a reception which implies total absence of previous intercourse.

The Yemishi are identified with the modern Ainu. The Yemishi are a moribund race. Only a remnant, numbering a few thousands, survives, now in the northern island of Yezo. Nevertheless it would appear that in early times the Yemishi extended from the north down the eastern section of Japan as far as the region where the present capital (Tokyo) stands, and on the west to the province now called Echizen; and that, when the *Nihongi* was written, they still occupied a large part of the main island. They were a rebellious people, who led many uprising against the Emperor.

There has been some dispute about the appellation "Kumaso." One high authority thinks that Kuma and So were the names of two tribes inhabiting the extreme south of Japan; that is to say, the provinces now called Hyuga, Osumi, and Satsuma. Others regard the term as denoting one tribe only. The question is not very material. Among all the theories formed about the Kumaso, the most plausible is that they belonged to the Sow race of Borneo and that they found their way to Japan Many similarities of custom have been traced between the two peoples. According to Japanese annals, the Kumaso must have arrived in Japan at a date prior to the advent of the immigrants represented by Izanagi and Izanami; and it would further follow that they did not penetrate far into the interior, but remained in the vicinity of the place of landing, which may be supposed to have been some point on the southern coast of Kyushu.

In ancient Japan there was a class of men to whom the epithet "Tsuchi-gumo" (earth-spiders) was applied. Their identity has been a subject of much controversy. According to the annals, the chiefs of the Tsuchi-gumo had Japanese names and their presence in Yamato preceded the arrival of Jimmu's expedition.

Thus the conclusion suggested by historical evidence is that the Japanese nation is composed of four elements: the Yamato; the Yemishi (modern Ainu); the Kumaso (or Hayato), and the Sushen. As to the last of these, there is no conclusive indication that they ever immigrated in appreciable numbers.

NEOLITHIC JAPAN

Archaeological research indicates the existence of two distinct cultures in Japan together with traces of a third. One of these cultures has left its relics chiefly in shell-heaps or embedded in the soil, while the remains of another are found mainly in sepulchral chambers or in caves. The relics themselves are palpably distinct except when they show transitional approach to each other.

The older culture is attested by more than four thousand residential sites and shell-heaps. Its most distinctive features are the absence of all metallic objects and the presence of pottery not turned on the wheel. Polished, finely chipped, and roughly hewn implements and weapons of stone are found, as are implements of bone and horn.

It was, in short, a neolithic culture. The vestiges of the other culture do not include weapons of stone. There are imitations of sheath-knives, swords, and arrow-heads, and there are some models of stone articles. But the alien features are iron weapons and hard pottery always moulded on the wheel. Copper is present mainly in connexion with the work of the goldsmith and the silversmith, and arrow-heads, jingle-bells, mirrors, etc., are also present. The former culture is identified as that of the aboriginal inhabitants, the Yemishi; the latter belongs to the Yamato race, or Japanese proper. Finally, "there are indications that a bronze culture intervened in the south between the stone and the iron phases.

The neolithic sites occur much more frequently in the northern than in the southern half of Japan. They are, indeed, six times as numerous on the north as on the south of a line drawn across the main island from the coast of Ise through Orai. The neighbourhood of the sea, at heights of from thirty to three hundred feet, and the alluvial plains are their favourite positions. So far as the technical skill shown by the relics – especially the pottery – is concerned, it grows higher with the latitude. The inference is that the settlements of the aborigines in the south were made at an earlier period than those in the north; which may be interpreted to mean that whereas the stone-using inhabitants were driven back in the south at an early date, they held their ground in the north to a comparatively modern era.

In fact, in these ancient times, the Yamato race and the aboriginal peoples had their headquarters in the same localities, respectively, as the Imperial and Feudal governments had in mediaeval and modern times. But there are no distinct traces of palaeolithic culture; the neolithic alone can be said to be represented. Its relics are numerous – axes, knives, arrow-heads, arrow-necks, bow-tips, spear-heads, batons, swords, maces, sling-stones, needles, drill-bows, drill and spindle weights, mortars and pestles, paddles, boats, sinkers, fishing-hooks, gaffs, harpoons, mallets, chisels, scrapers, hoes, sickles, whetstones, hammers, and drills.

It must be premised that though so many kinds of implements are here enumerated, the nomenclature cannot be accepted as universally accurate. The so-called "hoe," for example, is an object of disputed identity, especially as agriculture has not been proved to have been practised among the primitive people of Japan, nor have any traces of grain been found in the neolithic sites. On the other hand, the modern Ainu, who are believed to represent the ancient population, include in their religious observances the worship of the first cakes made from the season's millet, and unless that rite be supposed to have been borrowed from the Yamato, it goes to indicate agricultural pursuits. It may reasonably be assumed that the neolithic aborigines were in more or less intimate contact with the invading Yamato for something like twenty-five centuries, an interval quite sufficient to have produced many interactions and to have given birth to many new traditions.

It is true that the wheel was not employed, and that the firing was imperfect, but the variety of vessels was considerable, and the shapes and decorations were often very praiseworthy. Thus, among the braziers are found shapes obviously the originals of the Japanese *choji-buro* (clove-censer) and the graceful rice-bowl, while community of conception with Chinese potters would seem to be suggested by some of the forms of these ancient vases. Particularly interesting are earthenware images obtained from these neolithic sites. Many of them have been conventionalized into mere anthropomorphs and are rudely moulded. But they afford valuable indications of the clothing and personal adornments of the aborigines.

What end these effigies were intended to serve remains an unsettled question. Some suggest that they were used as substitutes for human sacrifices, and that they point to a time when wives and slaves were required to follow their husbands and masters to the grave. They may also have been suggested by the example of the Yamato, who, at a very remote time, began to substitute clay images for human followers of the dead; or they may have been designed to serve as mere mementoes – the images are found, not in graves or tombs, but at residential sites

Traces of a culture occupying a place intermediate between the neolithic culture and that of the Yamato are not conclusive. They are seen in pottery which, like the ware of the neolithic sites, is not turned on the wheel, and, like the Yamato ware, is decorated in a very subdued and sober fashion. It is found from end to end of the main island and even in Yezo, and in pits, shell-heaps, and independent sites as well as in tombs, burial caves, and cairns of the Yamato.

Bronze Vestiges

There are also some bronze vestiges to which considerable interest attaches, for evidently people using bronze weapons could not have stood against men carrying iron arms, and therefore the people to whom the bronze implements belonged must have obtained a footing in Japan prior to the Yamato, unless they came at the latter's invitation or as their allies. Moreover, these bronze relics – with the exception of arrow-heads – though found in the soil of western and southern Japan, do not occur in the Yamato sepulchres, which feature constitutes another means of differentiation. Daggers, swords, halberds, and possibly spear-heads constitute the hand-weapons. The daggers have a certain resemblance to the Malay *kris*, and the swords and halberds are generally leaf-shaped. But some features, as overshort tangs and unpierced loops, suggest that they were manufactured, not for service in battle but for ceremonial purposes. The bronze hand-weapons have been found in twelve provinces of southern and western Japan: namely, five provinces of northwest Kyushu; three on the Inland Sea; one facing Korea and China, and the rest on the islands of Iki and Tsushima.

These localities and the fact that similar swords have been met with in Shantung, suggest that the bronze culture came from central and eastern Asia, which hypothesis receives confirmation from the complete absence of bronze vestiges in the southern provinces of Kyushu, namely, Osumi and Satsuma. Bronze bells, of which there are many, belong to a separate page of archaeology. Though they have been found in no less than twenty-four provinces, there is no instance of their presence in the same sites with hand-weapons of bronze. In Kyushu, Higo is the only province where they have been seen, whereas in the main island they extend as far east as Totomi, and are conspicuously numerous in that province and its neighbour, Mikawa, while in Omi they are most abundant of all. They vary in height from about one foot four inches to four and a half feet, and are of highly specialized shape, the only cognate type being bells used in China during the Chou dynasty (1122–225 BCE) for the purpose of giving military signals. Given the abundance of the bells in districts where the Yamato were most strongly established, there seems to be warrant for attributing these curious relics to the Yamato culture. A reasonable hypothesis would be that the Yamato migrated from China in the days of the Chou dynasty (1122–225 BCE), and that, having landed in the province of Higo, they conquered the greater part of Tsukushi (Kyushu), and subsequently passed up the Inland Sea to Yamato.

YAMATO CULTURE

The ancient Yamato are known chiefly through the medium of relics found in their sepulchres. Residential sites exist in comparatively small numbers, so far as research has hitherto shown, and such sites yield nothing except more or less scattered potsherds and low walls enclosing spaces of considerable area. Occasionally Yamato pottery and other relics are discovered in pits, and these evidences, combined with historical references, go to show that the Yamato themselves sometimes used pit-dwellings.

The tombs yield much more suggestive relics of metal, stone, and pottery. Some four thousand of such sepulchres have been officially catalogued, but it is believed that fully ten times that number exist. The most characteristic is a tomb of larger dimensions enclosing a dolmen which contains a coffin hollowed out from the trunk of a tree, or a sarcophagus of stone, the latter being much more commonly found, as might be expected from its greater durability. Burial-jars were occasionally used, as were also sarcophagi of clay or terracotta, the latter chiefly in the provinces of Bizen and Mimasaka, probably because suitable materials existed there in special abundance. Moreover, not a few tombs belonged to the category of cists; that is to say, excavations in rock, with a single-slabbed or many-slabbed cover; or receptacles formed with stone clubs, cobbles, or boulders.

The dolmen is regarded by archaeologists as the most characteristic feature of the Yamato tombs. It was a chamber formed by setting up large slabs of stone, inclined slightly towards each other, which served as supports for another slab forming the roof. Seen in plan, the dolmens presented many shapes: a simple chamber or gallery; a chamber with a gallery, or a series of chambers with a gallery. Above the dolmen a mound was built, sometimes of huge dimensions, as, for example, the *misasagi* (the name given to all imperial tombs) of the Emperor Tenchi – d. 671 CE – which with its embankments, measured 5040 feet square), and within the dolmen were deposited many articles dedicated to the service of the deceased. Further, around the covering-mound there are generally found, embedded in the earth, terracotta cylinders (*haniwa*), sometimes surmounted with figures or heads of persons or animals.

According to the *Chronicles*, incidents so shocking occurred in connexion with the sacrifice of the personal attendants of

Prince Yamato at his burial (2 CE) that the custom of making such sacrifices was thenceforth abandoned, clay images being substituted for human beings. The *Records* speak of a "hedge of men set up round a tumulus," and it would therefore seem that these terracotta figures usually found encircling the principal *misasagi*, represented that hedge and served originally as pedestals for images. Within the dolmen, also, clay effigies are often found, which appear to have been substitutes for retainers of high rank.

Had the ancient custom been effectually abolished in the year 3 CE, when the Emperor Suinin is recorded to have issued orders in that sense, a simple and conclusive means would be at hand for fixing the approximate date of a dolmen, since all tombs containing clay effigies or encircled by terracotta *haniwa* would necessarily be subsequent to that date, and all tombs containing skeletons other than the occupants of the sarcophagi would be referable to an earlier era. But although compulsory sacrifices appear to have ceased from about the first century of the Christian era, it is certain that voluntary sacrifices continued through many subsequent ages. This clue is therefore illusory. Neither does the custom itself serve to connect the Yamato with any special race, for it is a wide-spread rite of animistic religion, and it was practised from time immemorial by the Chinese, the Manchu Tatars, and many other nations of northeastern Asia.

The dolmen also existed in China in very early times, but had been replaced by a chamber of finished masonry not later than the ninth century BCE In the Korean peninsula the dolmen with a megalithic roof is not uncommon, and the sepulchral pottery bears a close resemblance to that of the Yamato tombs.

The contents of the sepulchres, however, are more distinctive. They consist of "noble weapons and armour, splendid horse-trappings, vessels for food and drink, and various objects de luxe," though articles of wood and textile fabrics have naturally perished. Iron swords are the commonest relics. They are found in all tombs of all ages, and they bear emphatic testimony to the warlike habits of the Yamato, as well as to their belief that in the existence beyond the grave weapons were not less essential than in life. Arrow-heads are also frequently found and spear-heads sometimes. The swords are all of iron. Occasionally these swords have, at the end of the tang, a disc with a perforated design of two dragons holding a ball, a decorative motive which already betrays Chinese origin. Other swords have pommels surmounted by a bulb set at an angle to the tang, and have been suspected to be Turanian origin. These latter weapons were the so called "mallet-headed swords" said to have been used by Keiko's soldiers (82 CE). The name, *kabutsuchi*, derives from *kabu*, which is the term for turnip.

Yet another form – found mostly in the Kwanto provinces and to the north of them, from which fact its comparatively recent use may be inferred – was known in western Asia and especially in Persia, whence it is supposed to have been exported to the Orient in connexion with the flourishing trade carried on between China and Persia from the seventh to the tenth century. That a similar type is not known to exist in China proves nothing conclusive, for China's attitude towards foreign innovations was always more conservative than Japan's.

Yamato armour affords little assistance to the archaeologist: it bears no particularly close resemblance to any type familiar elsewhere. There was a corset made of sheet iron, well rivetted.

It fastened in front and was much higher behind than before, additioned protection for the back being provided by a lattice-guard which depended from the helmet and was made by fastening strips of sheet iron to leather or cloth. The helmet was usually of rivetted iron, but occasionally of bronze, with or without a peak in front. There were also guards of copper or iron for the legs, and there were shoulder-curtains constructed in the same manner as the back-curtain pendant from the helmet. Shoes of copper complete the panoply.

The workmanship of these weapons and armour is excellent: it shows an advanced stage of manufacturing skill. This characteristic is even more remarkable in the case of horse-trappings. The saddle and stirrups, the bridle and bit, are practically the same as those that were used in modern times, even a protective toe-piece for the stirrup being present. A close resemblance is observable between the ring stirrups of old Japan and those of mediaeval Europe, and a much closer affinity is shown by the bits, which had cheek-pieces and were usually jointed in the centre precisely like a variety common in Europe; metal pendants, garnished with silver and gold and carrying globular jingle-bells in their embossed edges, served for horse decoration. These facts are learned, not from independent relics alone, but also from terracotta steeds found in the tumuli and moulded so as to show all their trappings.

Other kinds of expert iron-work have also survived; as chains, rings and buckles, which differ little from corresponding objects in Europe at the present day; and the same is true of nails, handles, hinges, and other fittings. Tools used in working metal are rarely found, a fact easily accounted for when we remember that such objects would naturally be excluded from sepulchres.

There is another important relic which shows that the Yamato were indebted to China in the field of decorative art. This is a round bronze mirror, of which much is heard in early Japanese annals from the time of Izanagi downwards. In China the art of working in bronze was known and practised during twenty centuries prior to the Christian era; but although Japan seems to have possessed the knowledge at the outset of the dolmen epoch, (c. 600 BCE), it possessed no copper mine until thirteen centuries later, and was obliged to rely on Korea for occasional supplies. This must have injuriously affected its progress in the art of bronze casting.

Nevertheless, in almost all the dolmens and later tombs mirrors of bronze were placed. Japan certainly procured many Chinese mirrors, which are easily distinguished by finely executed and beautiful decorative designs in low relief on their backs; whereas mirrors manufactured in Japan – occasionally of iron – did not show equal skill of technique or ornamentation. Comparative roughness distinguished them, and they had often a garniture of jingle-bells (suzu) cast around the rim, a feature not found in Chinese mirrors. They were, in fact, an inferior copy of a Chinese prototype.

Prominent among personal ornaments were *magatama* (curved jewels) and *kudatama* (cylindrical jewels). It is generally supposed that the *magatama* represented a tiger's claw, which is known to have been regarded by the Koreans as an amulet. But the ornament may also have taken its comma-like shape from the Yō and the Yin, the positive and the negative principles which by Chinese cosmographists were accounted the great primordial factors, and which occupy a prominent place in Japanese decorative art as the *tomoye*. The cylindrical jewels evidently owed their shape to facility for stringing into necklaces or chaplets. A sword, a mirror, and a *magatama* may be called the regalia of Japan. But these jewels afford little aid in identifying the Yamato. Some of them – those of jade, chrysoprase, and nephrite – must have been imported, these minerals never having been found in Japan. But the latter fact, though it may be held to confirm the continental origin of the Yamato, gives no indication as to the part of Asia whence they emigrated.

Yamato Pottery

The pottery found in the Yamato tombs is somewhat more instructive than the personal ornaments. It seems to have been specially manufactured, or at any rate selected, for purposes of sepulture (interment), and it evidently retained its shape and character from very remote if not from prehistoric times. Known in Japan as *iwaibe* (sacred utensils), it resembles the pottery of Korea so closely that identity has been affirmed by some archaeologists and imitation by others. It has comparatively fine paste – taking the primitive pottery as standard – is hard, uniformly baked, has a metallic ring, varies in colour from dark brown to light gray, is always turned on the wheel, has only accidental glaze, and is decorated in a simple, restrained manner with conventionalized designs. The shapes of the various vessels present no marked deviation from Chinese or Korean models, except that the *tazzas* and occasionally other utensils are sometimes pierced in triangular, quadrilateral, and circular patterns, to which various meanings more or less fanciful have been assigned.

There is, however, one curious form of *iwaibe* which does not appear to have any counterpart in China or Korea. It is a large jar, or *tazza*, having several small jars moulded around its shoulder, these small jars being sometimes interspersed with, and sometimes wholly replaced by, figures of animals. It is necessary to go to the Etruscan "black ware" to find a parallel to this most inartistic kind of ornamentation.

THE JAPANESE LANGAUGE

However **numerous** may have been the races that contributed originally to the people of Japan, the languages now spoken there are two only, Ainu and Japanese. They are altogether independent tongues. The former undoubtedly was the language of the Yemishi; the latter, that of the Yamato. From north to south all sections of the Japanese nation – the Ainu of course excepted – use practically the same speech. Varieties of local dialects exist, but they show no traits of survival from different languages. On the contrary, in few countries of Japan's magnitude does corresponding uniformity of speech prevail from end to end of the realm. It cannot reasonably be assumed that, during a period of some twenty-five centuries and in the face of steady extermination, the Yemishi preserved their language quite distinct from that of their conquerors, whereas the various languages spoken by the other races peopling the island were fused into a whole so homogeneous as to defy all attempts at differentiation. The more credible alternative is that from time immemorial the main elements of the Japanese nation belonged to the same race, and whatever they received from abroad by way of immigration became completely absorbed and assimilated in the course of centuries.

The Japanese language has come to embody a very large number of Chinese words, though they are not pronounced as the Chinese pronounce the corresponding ideographs. Yet in spite of this intimate relation, re-enforced as it is by a common script, the two languages remain radically distinct; whereas between Japanese and Korean the resemblance of structure and accidence amounts almost to identity. Japanese philologists allege that no affinity can be traced between their language and the tongues of the Malay, the South Sea islanders, the natives of America and Africa, or the Eskimo, whereas they do find that their language bears a distinct resemblance to Manchu, Persian, and Turkish. Some go so far as to assert that Latin, Greek, and Sanskrit are nearer to Japanese than they are to any European language. These questions await fuller investigation.

THE CULTURE OF PREHISTORIC JAPAN

Having established an identity, the inhabitants of Japan now sought to build on its foundations to develop the social hierarchy, religion, administration and rituals of an evolving culture. It was at this time that the embryonic structures and practices that shaped authority and prosperity, namely the military and the economy, as well as agriculture, fishing and industry, also blossomed. Food, drink and fashion, which so often provide the most tantalizing of glimpses into the lives of ancient peoples, are examined in detail. Lastly, this chapter reveals the revered position of women in ancient Japanese society – and their capacity to rule and fight in the same fashion as their male counterparts.

THE SOCIAL STRUCTURE

At the basis of the social structure stand the trinity of *Kami*, mythologically called the Central Master (*Naka-Nushi*) and the two Constructive Chiefs (*Musubi no Kami*). The Central Master was the progenitor of the Imperial family; the Constructive Chiefs were the nobility, the official class. What was originally involved in the conception of official functions, we learn from incidents prefatory to the expedition conducted by Ninigi for the subjugation of Japan. Amaterasu (the Sun goddess) attached to the person of her grandson four chiefs and one chieftainess. To two of the former (Koyane and Futodama) she entrusted all matters relating to religious rites, and they became respectively the ancestors of the *Nakatomi* and the *Imibe* families. To the female *Kami* (Usume) was entrusted the making of sacred music and she founded the Sarume family. Finally, all military functions were committed to the chiefs, Oshihi and *Kume*, whose descendants constituted the *Otomo* and *Kume* families.

In every case these offices were hereditary for all time, and the families of their holders constitute the aristocracy of the nation, marrying among themselves and filling the highest offices from generation to generation. Their members bore the title of *hiko* (son of the Sun) and *hime* (daughter of the Sun), and those that governed towns and villages were called *tomo no miyatsuko*, while those that held provincial domains were entitled *kuni no miyatsuko*.

This was the origin of the Japanese polity. The descendants of Amaterasu, herself a descendant of the Central Master, occupied the throne in unbroken succession, and the descendants of the two Constructive Chiefs served as councillors, ministers, and generals. But the lineage of all being traceable to three chiefs who originally occupied places of almost equal elevation, they were united by a bond of the most durable nature. At the same time it appears that this equality had its disadvantage; it disposed the members of the aristocratic families to usurp the administrative power while recognizing its source, the Throne, and it encouraged factional dissensions, which sometimes resulted disastrously. As to the middle and lower classes, no evidence bearing on their exact composition is forthcoming. It is plain, however, that they accepted a subordinate position without active protest, for nothing like a revolt on their part is alluded to, directly or indirectly, in the *Records* or the *Chronicles*. The term for all subjects was *tomobe*.

DWELLINGS

The palace of the sovereign – called *miya* or *odono* – corresponded in appearance and construction with the shrines of the deities. It was built by erecting central pillars – originally merely sunk in the ground but in later times having a stone foundation – from which rafters sloped to corner posts, similarly erected, the sides being clapboarded. Nails were used, but the heavy timbers were tied together with ropes made by twisting the fibrous stems of climbing plants. A conspicuous feature was that the upper ends of the rafters projected across each other, and in the V-shaped receptacle thus formed, a ridge-pole was laid with a number of short logs crossing it at right angles. This disposition of timbers was evidently devised to facilitate tying and to impart stability to the thatch, which was laid to a considerable thickness.

It is not certain whether in the earliest times floors were fully boarded, or whether boarding was confined to a dais running round the sides, the rest of the interior being of beaten mud. Subsequently, however, the whole floor was boarded. Chimneys were not provided; charcoal being the principal fuel, its smoke did not incommode, and when firewood was employed, the fumes escaped through openings in the gable. For windows there were holes closed by shutters which, like the doors, swung upon hooks and staples. Rugs of skin or of rush matting served to spread on the boarded floor, and in rare cases silk cushions were employed.

The areas on which buildings stood were generally surrounded by palisades, and for a long time no other kind of defence save these palings seems to have been devised. Indeed, no mention of castles occurs until the first century BCE, when the strange term "rice-castle" (*ina-ki*) is found; the reference being apparently to a palisade fortified with rice-bags, or to a rice-granary used as a fortress. The palace of the sovereign towered so high by comparison that it was termed *Asahi-no-tada-sasu-miya* (*miya* on which the morning sun shines direct), or *Yuhi-no-hiteru-miya* (*miya* illumined by the evening sun), or some other figurative epithet, and to the Emperor himself was applied the title *O-mikado* (Great August Gate). The dwellings occupied by the nobility were similarly built, though on a less pretentious scale, and those of the inferior classes appear to have been little better than huts, not a few of them being partially sunk in the ground, as is attested by the fact that the term "enter" took the form of "creep in" (*hairu*).

ADMINISTRATION AND WORSHIP

In the instruction said to have been given by Amaterasu to her grandson Ninigi, on the eve of his expedition to Japan, the words are recorded: "My child, regard this mirror as you regard me. Keep it in the same house with yourself, and make it the mirror of purity." Accordingly the insignia – the mirror, the jewel, and the sword – were always kept in the main hall of the palace under the care of the *Nakatomi* and the *Imibe* families. An ancient volume (*Kogo-shui*) records that when the palace of Kashihara was reached by Jimmu's army, the grandson of the founder of the *Imibe* family – cutting timber with a consecrated axe (*imi-ono*) and digging foundations with a consecrated spade (*imi-suki*) – constructed a palace in which he placed the mirror, the jewel, and the sword, setting out offerings and reciting prayers to celebrate the completion of the building and the installation of the insignia. In remote antiquity religious rites and administrative functions were not distinguished. The sovereign's residence was the shrine of the *Kami*, and the term for "worship" (*matsuri*) was synonymous with that for "government."

The ceremony spoken of above – the Odono *matsuri*, or consecration of the palace – is the earliest religious rite mentioned. Next in importance was the "harvest festival." In the records of the mythological age it is related that Amaterasu obtained seeds of the "five cereals," and, recognizing their value as food, caused them to be cultivated, offering a part to the *Kami* when they were ripe and eating some herself. This became a yearly custom, and when Ninigi set out to conquer Japan, his grandmother gave rice seed to the ancestors of the *Nakatomi* and the *Imibe* families, who thenceforth conducted the harvest festival (*nii-name*, literally "tasting the new rice") every autumn, the sovereign himself taking part, and the head of the *Nakatomi* reciting a prayer for the eternity of the Imperial line and the longevity of the Emperor. Other important rites were the "great purification" (*Oharai*) performed twice a year, on the last day of the sixth month and the last day of the twelfth month; the "fire-subduing fete," the "spirit-tranquillizing fete," etc.

Of all these rites the principal features were the recitation of rituals and the offering of various objects, edible or otherwise useful. The rituals (*norito*) being, in several cases, set formulas, lent themselves with special facility to oral transmission from generation to generation.

The Shinto Religion

In the year 927 CE, seventy-five of the norito were transcribed into a book (*Yengi-shiki*, or Ceremonial Law) which contains, in addition to these rituals, particulars as to the practice of the Shinto religion; as to the organization of the priesthood – which included ten virgin princesses of the Imperial family, one each for the two great temples of Watarai in Ise and Kamo in Yamashiro – and as to the Shinto shrines qualified to receive State support. These shrines totalled 3132, among which number 737 were maintained at the Emperor's charges. Considering that the nation at that time (tenth century) did not comprise more than a very few millions, the familiar criticism that the Japanese are indifferent to religion is certainly not proved by any lack of places of worship. The language of the rituals is occasionally poetic, often figurative and generally solemn, but they are largely devoted to enumeration of *Kami*, to formulae of praise for past favours, to petitions for renewed assistance, and to recapitulations of the offerings made in support of these requests. As for the offerings, they comprise woven stuffs, and their raw materials, models of swords, arrows, shields, stags' antlers, hoes, fish (dried and fresh), salt, sake, and, in some cases, a horse, a cock, and a pig. In short, the things offered were essentially objects serviceable to living beings.

DIVINATION

As is usually the case in a nation where a nature religion is followed, divination and augury were practised largely in ancient Japan. The earliest method of divination was by roasting the shoulder-blade of a stag and comparing the cracks with a set of diagrams. The *Records* and the *Chronicles* alike represent Izanagi and Izanami as resorting to this method of presaging the future, and the practice derives interest from the fact that a precisely similar custom has prevailed in Mongolia from time immemorial. Subsequently this device was abandoned in favour of the Chinese method, heating a tortoise-shell; and ultimately the latter, in turn, gave way to the Eight Trigrams of Fuhi. The use of auguries seems to have come at a later date. They were obtained by playing a stringed instrument called *koto*, by standing at a cross-street and watching the passers, by manipulating stones, and by counting footsteps.

MILITARY FORCES

It has been related that when the "heavenly grandson" undertook his expedition to Japan, the military duties were entrusted to two *mikoto* who became the ancestors of the *Otomo* and the *Kume* families. There is some confusion about the subsequent differentiation of these families, but it is sufficient to know that, together with the *Mononobe* family, they, were the hereditary repositories of military authority. They wore armour, carried swords, spears and bows, and not only mounted guard at the palace but also asserted the Imperial authority throughout the provinces. No exact particulars of the organization of these forces are on record, but it would seem that the unit was a battalion divided into twenty-five companies, each company consisting of five sections of five men per section, a company being under the command of an officer whose rank was *miyatsuko*.

It has already been stated that archaeological research shows the Yamato race to have been in possession of iron swords and spears, as well as metal armour and shields, from a very early period, probably the date of these colonists' first coming to Japan. They also used saddles, stirrups, bridles, and bits for horses, so that a Yamato warrior in full mail and with complete equipment was perhaps as formidable a fighting man as any contemporary nation could produce. Bows and arrows were also in use. The latter, tipped with iron or stone and feathered, were carried in a quiver. The swords employed by men were originally double-edged. There was also a small single-edged sword carried by women and fastened inside the robe.

Sometimes a spear was decorated with gems. It is curious that gems should have been profusely used for personal adornment in ancient times by people who subsequently eschewed the custom well-nigh altogether, as the Japanese did. Apart from imported minerals, the materials with which the early artisans worked were coral, quartz, amber, gold, silver, and certain pebbles found in Izumo.

FINANCE AND ADMINISTRATION

No mention is made of such a thing as currency in prehistoric Japan. Commerce appears to have been conducted by barter only. In order to procure funds for administrative and religious purposes, officers in command of forces were despatched to various regions, and the inhabitants were required to contribute certain quantities of local produce. Steps were also taken to cultivate useful plants and cereals and to promote manufactures. The *Kogo-shui* states that a certain *mikoto* inaugurated the fashioning of gems in Izumo, and that his descendants continued the work from generation to generation, sending annual tribute of articles to the Court every year. It is plain that, whatever may have been the case at the outset, this assignment of whole regions to the control of officials whose responsibility was limited to the collection of taxes for the uses of the Court, could not but tend to create a provincial nobility and thus lay the foundations of a feudal system. Yet Chinese history shows that at about the beginning of the Christian era the Island Empire was in a very uncentralized state and that the sway of the Yamato was still far from receiving general recognition.

CLOTHING

The principal material of wearing apparel was cloth woven from threads of hemp and mulberry bark. According to the annals, the arts of spinning, weaving, and dyeing were known and practised from the earliest age. The Sun goddess herself is depicted as seated in the hall of the sacred loom, reeling silk from cocoons held in her mouth, and at the ceremony of enticing her from her retirement, the weaving of blue-and-white stuffs constituted an important adjunct. Terms are used (*akarurtae* and *teru-tae*) which show that colour and lustre were esteemed as much as quality. *Ara-tae* and *nigi-tae* were the names used to designate coarse and fine cloth respectively; striped stuff was called *shidori*, and the name of a princess, Taku-hata-chiji, goes to show that corrugated cloth was woven from the bark of the taku. Silken fabrics were manufactured, but the device of boiling the cocoons had not yet been invented. They were held in the mouth for spinning purposes, and the threads thus obtained being coarse and uneven, the loom could not produce good results. Silk stuffs therefore did not find much favour: they were employed chiefly for making cushions, cloth woven from cotton, hemp, or mulberry bark being preferred for clothing.

Pure white was the favourite colour; red, blue, and black being placed in a lower rank in that order. It has been conjectured that furs and skins were worn, but there is no explicit mention of anything of the kind. It would seem that their use was limited to making rugs and covering utensils. Sewing is not explicitly referred to, but the needle is; and there is no valid reason to doubt that the process of sewing was familiar.

As to the form of the garments worn, the principal were the *hakama* and the *koromo*. The *hakama* was a species of divided skirt, used by men and women alike. It has preserved its shape from age to age, and is to-day worn by school-girls throughout Japan. The *koromo* was a tunic having tight sleeves reaching nearly to the knees. It was folded across the breast from right to left and secured by a belt of cloth or silk tied round the loins. Veils also were used by both sexes, one kind (the *katsugi*) having been voluminous enough to cover the whole body. Combs are mentioned, and it is evident that much attention was devoted to the dressing of the hair. Men divided theirs in the middle and bound it up in two bunches, one over each ear. Youths tied theirs into a top-knot; girls wore their locks hanging down the back but bound together at the neck, and married ladies apparently combined the last two methods. Decoration of the head was carried far on ceremonial occasions, gems, veils, and even coronets being used for the purpose.

FOOD AND DRINK

Rice was the great staple of diet in ancient, as it is in modern, times. The importance attaching to it is shown by the fact that the Sun goddess herself is represented as engaging in its cultivation and that injuring a rice-field was among the greatest offences. Barley, millet, wheat, and beans are mentioned, but the evidence that they were grown largely in remote antiquity is not conclusive. The flesh of animals and birds was eaten, venison and wild boar being particularly esteemed. Indeed, so extensively was the hunting of deer practised that bows and arrows were often called *kago-yumi* and KAGO-YA (*kago* signifies "deer"). Fish, however, constituted a much more important staple of diet than flesh, and fishing in the abundantly stocked seas that surround the Japanese islands was largely engaged in. Horses and cattle were not killed for food. Vegetables occupied a large space in the list of articles of food. There were the radish, the cabbage, the lotus, the melon, and the wild garlic, as well as as several kinds of seaweed. Salt was used for seasoning, the process of its manufacture having been familiar from the earliest times. Only one kind of intoxicating liquor was ever known in early Japan, it was a kind of beer brewed from rice and called *sake*.

From time immemorial there were among the officials at the Imperial Court men called *kashiwa-de*, or oak-leaf hands. They had charge of the food and drink, and their appellation was derived from the fact that rice and other edibles were usually served on oak leaves. Earthenware utensils were used, but their surface, not being glazed, was not allowed to come into direct contact with the viands placed on them. In this practice another example is seen of the love of cleanliness that has always characterized and distinguished the Japanese nation. Edibles having been thus served, the vessels containing them were ranged on a table, one for each person, and chop-sticks were used. Everything was cooked, with the exception of certain vegetables and a few varieties of fish. Friction of wood upon wood provided fire, a fact attested by the name of the tree chiefly used for the purpose, *hi-no-ki*, or fire-tree. To this day the same method of obtaining a spark is practised at the principal religious ceremonials. Striking metal upon stone was another device for the same purpose.

AGRICULTURE, FISHING AND INDUSTRY

It appears that when the Yamato immigrants reached Japan, the coast lands were overgrown with reeds and the greater part of the island was covered with primeval forests. Large districts were often submerged by the overflow of rivers. The country was, for the most part, in a state of natural wilderness.

Under the sway of the Yamato, however, a great change was gradually effected. Cereals and rice were cultivated, and mulberry trees were planted for the purpose of sericulture. In the reign of Jimmu, hemp is said to have been cultivated, and timber from various trees was exploited, as pine and *hinoki* (ground-cypress) for house building, *maki* (*podocarpus Chinensis*) for coffin making, and camphor-wood for constructing boats.

In the matter of farming implements, however, neither archaeology nor history indicates anything more than iron spades, wooden hoes shod with bronze or iron, hand-ploughs, and axes. As to manufacturing industries, there were spinners and weavers of cotton and silk, makers of kitchen utensils, polishers of gems, workers in gold, silver, copper, and iron, forgers of arms and armour, potters of ornamental vessels, and dressers of leather. In later eras the persons skilled in these various enterprises formed themselves into guilds (*be*), each of which carried on its own industry from generation to generation.

The be may be described as a corporated association having for purpose the securing of efficiency by specialization. Its members seem to have been at the outset men who independently pursued some branch of industry. These being ultimately formed into a guild, carried on the same pursuit from generation to generation under a chief officially appointed. "Potters, stone coffin-makers, manufacturers of shields, of arrows, of swords, of mirrors, saddlers, painters, weavers, seamstresses, local recorders, scribes, farmers, fleshers, horse-keepers, bird-feeders, and palace attendants were all organized into be under special chiefs who were probably responsible for their efficient services.

No information is obtainable as to the nature of the boats used in very early times, but it may reasonably be inferred that the Yamato and other immigrant races possessed craft of some capacity. The presence of neolithic remains on the islands around Japan proves that the boats of the primitive people were large enough to traverse fifty miles, or more, of open sea. The *Chronicles* quote an Imperial decree issued 81 BCE, which says: "Ships are of cardinal importance to the Empire. At present the people of the coast, not having ships, suffer grievously by land transport. Therefore let every province be caused to have ships built;" and it is related that, a few months later, the building of ships was begun. Again, in 274 CE, a vessel (the Karano) one hundred feet in length, was constructed in the province of Izu.

It would seem that there was always an abundance of fishing-boats, for fishing by traps, hooks, and nets was industriously carried on. A passage in the *Records* speaks of a thousand-fathom rope of paper-mulberry which was used to draw the net in perch fishing. Spearing was also practised by fishermen, and in the rivers cormorants were used just as they are to-day.

RITES OF PASSAGE

It does not appear that the marriage tie possessed any grave significance in ancient Japan, or that any wedding ceremony was performed. There did not exist in Japan, as in China, a veto on marriages between people of the same tribe. However, under the Japanese system brothers and sisters might intermarry provided that they had not been brought up together. To understand this condition it is necessary to observe that a bride generally continued to live in her family dwelling where she received her husband's visits, and since there was nothing to prevent a husband from contracting many such alliances, it was possible for him to have several groups of children, the members of each group being altogether unknown to the members of all the rest. In a later, but not definitely ascertained era, it became customary for a husband to take his wife to his own home, and thereafter the veto upon such unions soon became imperative.

In all eras sisters might marry the same man, and polygamy was common– a desire for abundant progeny was primarily the cause. It is notable that although the line between nobles and commoners was strictly drawn and rigidly observed, it did not extend to marriage in one sense: a nobleman could always take a wife or a concubine from the family of an inferior. In fact, orders were commonly issued to this or that province to furnish so many ladies-in-waiting (*uneme*) – a term having deeper significance than it suggests – and several instances are recorded of sovereigns summoning to Court girls famed for beauty. That no distinction was made between wives and concubines has been alleged, but is not confirmed by the annals. Differentiation by rank appears to have been always practised, and the offspring was certainly thus distinguished.

A child in ancient Japan was born under considerable difficulties: its mother had to segregate herself in a parturition hut (*ubuya*), whence even light was excluded and where she was cut off from all attendance. This strange custom was an outcome of the Shinto canon of purity. Soon after birth, a child received from its mother a name generally containing some appropriate personal reference. In the most ancient times each person (so far as we can judge) bore one name, or rather one string of words compounded together into a sort of personal designation. But already at the dawn of the historical epoch we are met by the mention of surnames bestowed by the sovereign as a recompense for some noteworthy deed.

To what we should call education, whether mental or physical, there is absolutely no reference made in the histories. All that can be inferred is that, when old enough to do so; the boys began to follow one of the callings of hunter or fisherman, while the girls stayed at home weaving the garments of the family. There was a great deal of fighting, generally of a treacherous kind, in the intervals of which the warriors occupied themselves in cultivating patches of ground.

Burial rites were important ceremonials. The house hitherto tenanted by the deceased was abandoned – a custom exemplified in the removal of the capital to a new site at the commencement of each reign – and the body was transferred to a specially erected mourning-hut draped inside with fine, white cloth. The relatives and friends then assembled, and for several days performed a ceremony which resembled an Irish wake, food and *sake* being offered to the spirit of the dead, prayers put up, and the intervals devoted to weird singing and solemn dancing. Wooden coffins appear to have been used until the beginning of the Christian era, when stone is said to have come into vogue.

At the obsequies of nobles there was considerable organization. Men (*mike-hito*) were duly told off to take charge of the offerings of food and liquor; others (*kisari-mochi*) were appointed to carry the viands; others (*hahaki-mochi*) carried brooms to sweep the cemetery; there were females (*usu-me*) who pounded rice, and females (*naki-me*) who sung dirges interspersed with eulogies of the deceased. It appears, further, that those following a funeral walked round the coffin waving blue-and-red banners, carrying lighted torches, and playing music.

In the sepulchres the arms, utensils, and ornaments used daily by the deceased were interred, and it was customary to bury alive around the tombs of Imperial personages and great nobles a number of the deceased's principal retainers. The latter inhuman habit was nominally abandoned at the close of the last century before Christ, images of baked clay being substituted for human sacrifices, but the spirit which informed the habit survived, and even down to modern times there were instances of men and women committing suicide for the purpose of rejoining the deceased beyond the grave.

WOMEN IN ANCIENT JAPAN

There is evidence to show that in the prehistoric age a high position was accorded to women and that their rights received large recognition. The facts that the first place in the Japanese pantheon was assigned to a goddess; that the throne was frequently occupied by empresses; that females were chiefs of tribes and led armies on campaign; that jealous wives turned their backs upon faithless husbands; that mothers chose names for their children and often had complete charge of their upbringing – all these things go to show that the self-effacing rank taken by Japanese women in later ages was a radical departure from the original canon of society. It is not to be inferred, however, that fidelity to the nuptial tie imposed any check on extra-marital relations in the case of men: it had no such effect.

THE PREHISTORIC SOVEREIGNS

From the violent conquests of Emperor Jimmu to the human sacrifices of Emperor Nintoku, the first generation of Japanese sovereigns were as brutal as they were innovative. These powerful figures were also responsible for the reorganization and redefinition of many of the earlier religious, governmental and socio-hierarchical systems put in place by their ancestors.

Most significantly, it was this pantheon of emperors and empresses that first established relations with China and Korea. Cultural and diplomatic exchanges between these kingdoms not only created the earliest form of the Japanese written word, but also foreshadowed the colonial ambitions of later monarchs. This era also witnessed the rise of an influential class of nobles that in time would start to undermine imperial authority, auguring many later episodes of violent internal strife.

JIMMU AND HIS DESCENDANTS

It is held by eminent Japanese historians that the Emperor Jimmu, when he set out for Yamato (the country of Japan), did not contemplate an armed campaign but merely intended to change his capital from the extreme south to the centre of the country. But the perception he would have to fight for the territory, led him to amass a mighty army. Subsequently he encountered strongest resistance at the hands of Prince Nagasune, whose title of *Hiko* (Child of the Sun) showed that he belonged to the Yamato race, and who exercised military control under the authority of Nigihayahi, elder brother of Jimmu's father. The annals relate that Nigihayahi, having been convinced by a comparison of weapons of war that Jimmu was of his own lineage, surrendered the authority to him and caused Prince Nagasune to be put to death.

Thus, while it is evident that to consolidate Jimmu's conquest and to establish order among the heterogeneous elements of his empire he must have been followed by rulers of character and prowess, the annals show nothing of the kind. On the contrary, the reigns of his eight immediate successors are barren of all striking incident. The opening page in the life of Jimmu's immediate successor, Suisei, shows that the latter reached the throne by assassinating his elder brother. For the rest, the annals of the eight sovereigns who reigned during the interval between 561 and 98 BCE recount mainly the polygamous habits of these rulers and give long genealogies of the noble families founded by their offspring.

A Japanese tradition assigns to the seventy-second year of the reign of Korei the advent of a Chinese Taoist, by name Hsu Fuh. Korei, seventh in descent from Jimmu, held the sceptre from 290 to 215 BCE, and the seventy-second year of his reign fell, therefore, in 219 BCE Now, to the east of the town of Shingu in Kii province, at a place on the seashore in the vicinity of the site of an ancient castle, there stands a tomb bearing the inscription "Grave of Hsu Fuh from China," and near it are seven tumuli said to be the burial-places of Hsu's companions.

Chinese history states that Hsu Fuh was a learned man who served the first Emperor of the Chin dynasty (255–206 BCE), and that he obtained his sovereign's permission to sail to the islands of the east in search of the elixir of life.

The reign of the tenth Emperor, *Sujin* (97–30 BCE) is the first eventful period since the death of Jimmu. It is memorable for the reorganization of religious rites; for the extension of the effective sway of the Throne, and for the encouragement of agriculture. When the first Emperor installed the sacred insignia in the palace where he himself dwelt, the instinct of filial piety and the principle of ancestor worship were scarcely distinguishable. But as time passed and as the age of the *Kami* became more remote, a feeling of awe began to pervade the rites more strongly than a sense of family affection, and the idea of residing and worshipping in the same place assumed a character of sacrilege.

An attack of pestilence decimated the nation, bringing an aftermath of lawlessness and produced much unrest in the regions remote from Yamato. *Sujin* therefore organized a great military movement, the campaign of the Shido *shogun*, or "Generalissimo of the four Circuits." The leaders chosen for this task were all members of the Imperial family – a great-uncle, an uncle, a younger brother, and a first cousin of the Emperor – and the fields of operation assigned to them were: first, to the west along the northern shore of the Inland Sea; secondly, to the northwest into Tamba, Tango, and Tajima; thirdly, to the north along the sea of Japan, and finally to the east along the route now known as the Tokaido.

Thus in the provinces of Omi, of Suruga, of Mutsu, of Iwashiro, of Iwaki, of Echigo, of Etchu, of Echizen, of Bizen, of

Bitchu, of Bingo, of Harima, of Tamba, and elsewhere, there are found in later ages noble families all tracing their descent to one or another of the Shido *shoguns* despatched on the task of pacifying the country in the days of the Emperor Sujin.

The first direct reference made by Japanese annals to Korea occurs in the reign of Sujin, 33 BCE when an envoy from Kara arrived at the Mizugaki Court, praying that a Japanese general might be sent to compose a quarrel which had long raged between Kara and Shiragi, and to take the former under Japan's protection. The Emperor Sujin received the envoy courteously and seemed disposed to grant his request, but his Majesty's death (30 BCE) intervened, and not until two years later was the envoy able to return.

The Eleventh Sovereign, Suinin

Suinin (299 BCE–70 CE), second son of his predecessor, obtained the throne by a process which frankly ignored the principle of primogeniture. For Sujin, having an equal affection for his two sons, confessed himself unable to choose which of them should be his successor and was therefore guided by a comparison of their dreams, the result being that the younger was declared Prince Imperial, and the elder became duke of the provinces of *Kamitsuke* (now Kotsuke) and Shimotsuke. Suinin, like all the monarchs of that age, had many consorts: nine are catalogued in the *Records* and their offspring numbered sixteen, many of whom received local titles and had estates conferred in the provinces.

There are in the story of this sovereign some very pathetic elements. Prince Saho, elder brother of the Empress, plotted to usurp the throne. Having cajoled his sister into an admission that her brother was dearer than her husband, he bade her prove it by killing the Emperor in his sleep. But when an opportunity offered to perpetrate the deed as the sovereign lay sleeping with her knees as pillow, her heart melted, and her tears, falling on the Emperor's face, disturbed his slumber. He sought the cause of her distress, and learning it, sent a force to seize the rebel. Remorse drove the Empress to die with Prince Saho. Carrying her little son, she entered the fort where her brother with his followers had taken refuge. The Imperial troops set fire to the fort – which is described as having been built with rice-bags piled up – and the Empress emerged with the child in her arms; but having thus provided for its safety, she fled again to the fort and perished with her brother.

Two events specially memorable in this reign were the transfer of the shrine of the Sun goddess to Ise, where it has remained ever since, and the abolition of the custom of *junshi*, or following in death. The latter shocking usage, a common rite of animistic religion, was in part voluntary, in part compulsory. In its latter aspect it came vividly under the notice of the Emperor Suinin when the tomb of his younger brother, Yamato, having been built within earshot of the palace, the cries of his personal attendants, buried alive around his grave, were heard, day and night, until death brought silence.

The name of Nomi-no-Sukune is associated with the first mention of wrestling in Japanese history. By the *Chronicles* a brief account is given of a match between Nomi and Taema-no-Kuehaya. The latter was represented to be so strong that he could break horns and straighten hooks. His frequently expressed desire was to find a worthy competitor. Nomi-no-Sukune, summoned from Izumo by the Emperor, met Kuehaya in the lists of the palace of Tamaki and kicked him to death.

Wrestling thereafter became a national pastime, but its methods underwent radical change, kicking being abolished altogether.

During this period, Chinese historians wrote: "The Wa (Japanese) dwell southeast of Han (Korea) on a mountainous island in midocean. Their country is divided into more than one hundred provinces. Since the time when Wu-Ti (140–86 BCE) overthrew Korea, they (the Japanese) have communicated with the Han (Korean) authorities by means of a postal service. There are thirty-two provinces which do so, all of which style their rulers 'kings' who are hereditary. The sovereign of Great Wa resides in Yamato, distant 12,000 li (4000 miles) from the frontier of the province of Yolang (the modern Pyong-yang in Korea). In the second year of Chung-yuan (57 CE), in the reign of Kwang-wu, the Ito country sent an envoy with tribute, who styled himself Ta-fu. He came from the most western part of the Wa country. Kwang-wu presented him with a seal and ribbon."

The Twelfth Sovereign, Keiko

According to the *Records*, Keiko (71–130 CE) was ten feet two inches high, and his shank measured four feet one inch. His nomination as Prince Imperial was an even more arbitrary violation of the right of primogeniture than the case of his predecessor had been, for he was chosen in preference to his elder brother merely because, when the two youths were casually questioned as to what they wished for, the elder said, "a bow and arrows," and the younger, "the empire." Keiko appointed his sons, with three exceptions, to the position of provincial or district viceroy, preserving their Imperial connexion by calling them *wake*, or branch families.

One of the most memorable events in this epoch was the Emperor's military expedition in person to quell the rebellious Kumaso in Kyushu. There had not been any instance of the sovereign taking the field in person since Jimmu's time, and the importance attaching to the insurrection is thus shown. Allowance has to be made, however, for the fact that the territory held by these Kumaso in the south of Kyushu was protected by a natural rampart of stupendous mountain ranges which rendered military access arduous, and which, in after ages, enabled a great feudatory to defy the Central Government for centuries. Keiko's reign is remarkable chiefly for this expedition to the south, which involved a residence of six years in Hyuga, and for the campaigns of one of the greatest of Japan's heroes, Prince Yamato-dake. The military prowess of the sovereign, the fighting genius of Yamato-dake, and the administrative ability of Takenouchi-no-Sukune, the first "prime minister" mentioned in Japanese history, combined to give signal *éclat* to the reign of Keiko.

Yamato-dake overran the whole region stretching from the provinces along the Eastern Sea as far as Iwaki; crossed westward through Iwashiro to Echigo on the west coast, and turning southward, made his way through Shinano and Mino to Owari, whence, suffering from a wound caused by a poisoned arrow, he struggled on to Ise and died there. This campaign seems to have occupied ten years, and Yamato-dake was only thirty at the time of his death. He had marched against the Kumaso in the south at the age of sixteen. The *Chronicles* relate that when crossing the Usui Pass and looking down on the sea where his loved consort had cast herself into the waves to quell their fury, the great warrior sighed thrice and exclaimed, "My wife, my wife, my wife!" (*Ago, tsuma haya*), whereafter the provinces east of the mountain were designated Azuma.

Another custom inaugurated by this sovereign was to require that the rulers of provinces should send to the Yamato Court female hostages. The first example of this practice took place on the occasion of an Imperial visit to the regions overrun by Yamato-dake's forces. Each of twelve *kuni-yatsuko* (provincial rulers) was required to send one damsel for the purpose of serving in the culinary department of the palace. They were called *makura-ko* (pillow-child) and they seem to have been ultimately drafted into the ranks of the *uneme* (ladies-in-waiting).

The Thirteenth Emperor, Seimu

The thirteenth Emperor, Seimu (131–190 CE), occupied the throne for fifty-nine years, according to the *Chronicles*, but the only noteworthy feature of his reign was the organization of local governments. Speaking broadly, the facts are these: Imperial princes who had distinguished themselves by evidences of ability or courage were despatched to places of special importance in the provinces, under the name of *wake*, a term conveying the signification of "branch of the Imperial family." There is reason to think that these appointments were designed to extend the prestige of the Court rather than to facilitate the administration of provincial affairs. The latter duty was entrusted to officials called *kuni-no-miyatsuko* and *agata-nushi*, which may be translated "provincial governor" and "district headman."

In Seimu's reign almost the whole of the southern and central regions were included in the administrative circle, but the northern provinces, some of the western, and certain regions in the south (Kyushu) were not yet fully wrested from the Yemishi and the Kumaso. In subsequent reigns the rate of growth was as follows: Chuai (192–200 CE), two provinces; Ojin (270–310), twenty-one; Nintoku (313–399), seven; Hansho (406–411) and Inkyo (412–453), one each; Yuryaku (457–459), three; Keitai (507–531), one; and eight others at untraceable periods, the total being one hundred thirty-five.

The Fourteenth Emperor, Chuai, and the Empress Jingo

Whereas Chuai's predecessors, while invariably changing their residences on mounting the throne, had always chosen a site for the new palace in Yamato or a neighbouring province, the *Records*, without any explanation, carry Chuai (192–200 CE) to the far south after his accession. The *Chronicles* are more explicit. From them we gather that Chuai – who was the second son of Yamato-dake and is described as having been ten feet high with "a countenance of perfect beauty" – was a remarkably active sovereign. He commenced his reign by a progress to Tsuruga (then called Tsunuga) on the west coast of the mainland, and, a month later, he made an expedition to Kii on the opposite shore. While in the latter province he received news of a revolt of the Kumaso, and at once taking ship, he went by sea to Shimonoseki, whither he summoned the Empress from Tsuruga. An expedition against the Kumaso was then organized and partially carried out, but the Emperor's force was beaten and he himself received a fatal arrow-wound. On the eve of this disastrous move against the Kumaso, the Empress had a revelation urging the Emperor to turn his arms against Korea as the Kumaso were not worthy of his steel. But Chuai rejected the advice with scorn, and the *Kojiki* alleges that the outraged deities punished him with death, though doubtless a Kumaso arrow was the instrument. His demise was carefully concealed, and the Empress, mustering the troops, took vengeance upon the Kumaso.

Thereafter her Majesty became the central figure in a page of history – or romance -- which has provoked more controversy than any incident in Japanese annals. A descendant of the Korean prince, Ama-no-Hihoko, who settled in the province of Tajima during the reign of the Emperor Suinin, she must have possessed traditional knowledge of Shiragi, whence her ancestor had emigrated. She was the third consort of Chuai. His first had borne him two sons who were of adult age when, in the second year of his reign, he married Jingo, a lady "intelligent, shrewd, and with a countenance of such blooming loveliness that her father wondered at it." To this appreciation of her character must be added the attributes of boundless ambition and brave resourcefulness. The annals represent her as bent from the outset on the conquest of Korea and as receiving the support and encouragement of Takenouchi-no-Sukune, who had served her husband and his predecessor as prime minister.

A military expedition oversea led by a sovereign in person had not been heard of since the days of Jimmu, and to reconcile officials and troops to such an undertaking the element of divine revelation had to be introduced. At every stage signs and portents were vouchsafed by the guardian deities. By their intervention the Empress was shown to be possessed of miraculous prowess, and at their instance troops and ships assembled spontaneously. The armada sailed under divine guidance, a gentle spirit protecting the Empress, and a warlike spirit leading the van of her forces. The god of the wind sent a strong breeze; the god of the sea ruled the waves favourably; all the great fishes accompanied the squadron, and an unprecedented tide bore the ships far inland. Fighting became unnecessary. The King of Shiragi did homage at once and promised tribute and allegiance forever, and the other monarchs of the peninsula followed his example. In short, Korea was conquered and incorporated with the dominions of Japan.

There can indeed be little doubt that the compilers of the *Nihongi* embellished the bald tradition with imaginary details. Neverthelesss, there can be no doubt that Japan, at an early period, formed an alliance with Paikche (spoken of in Japan as "Kudara," namely, the regions surrounding the modern Seoul), and laid the foundation of a controlling power over the territory known as Imna (or Mimana), which lasted for several centuries."

From early times it had been customary in Japan that whenever any lands were acquired, a portion of them was included in the Imperial domain, the produce being thenceforth stored and the affairs of the estate managed at a *miyake* presided over by a *mikoto-mochi*. Thus, on the inclusion of certain Korean districts in Japan's dominions, this usage was observed, and the new *miyake* had the syllables *uchi-tsu* ("of the interior") prefixed to distinguish it as a part of Japan. It is on record that a *mikoto-mochi* was stationed in Shiragi, and in the days of Jingo's son (Ojin) the great statesman, Takenouchi-no-Sukune, took up his residence for a time in Tsukushi to assist this *mikoto-mochi* and the *chinju-fu*, should occasion arise. An almost immediate result of the oversea relations thus established was that silk and cotton fabrics of greatly improved quality, gold, silver, iron, implements, arts, and literature were imported in increasing quantities to the great benefit of civilization.

From a period prior to the death of Suinin, the power and influence of the Imperial princes and nobles was a constantly growing quantity. But the political situation developed a new phase when the Sukune family appeared upon the scene. The first evidence of this was manifested in a striking incident. When the Emperor Chuai died, his consort, Jingo, was pregnant. But the Emperor left two sons by a previous marriage, and clearly one of them should have succeeded to the throne. Nevertheless, the prime minister, Takenouchi-no-Sukune, contrived to have the unborn child recognized as Prince Imperial. Naturally the deceased Emperor's two elder sons refused to be arbitrarily set aside in favour of a baby step-brother. The principle of primogeniture did not possess binding force in those days, but it had never previously been violated except by the deliberate and ostensibly reasonable choice of an Emperor. The two princes, therefore, called their partisans to arms and prepared to resist the return of Jingo to Yamato.

Here again Takenouchi-no-Sukune acted a great part. He carried the child by the outer sea to a place of safety in Kii, while the forces of the Empress sailed up the Inland Sea to meet the brothers at Naniwa (modern Osaka). Moreover, when the final combat took place, this same Takenouchi devised a strategy which won the day, and in every great event during the reign of the Empress Jingo (201–269 CE) his figure stands prominent. Finally, his granddaughter became the consort of the Emperor Nintoku (313–399), an alliance which opened a channel for exercising direct influence upon the Throne and also furnished a precedent adopted freely in subsequent times by other noble families harbouring similarly ambitious aims. In short, from the accession of the Empress Jingo a large part of the sovereign power began to pass into the hands of the prime minister.

SOCIAL ORGANIZATION DURING THE REIGN OF THE PREHISTORIC SOVEREIGNS

At the beginning of the previous chapter brief reference was made to the three great divisions of the inhabitants of Japan; namely, the *Shimbetsu* (*Kami* class) the *Kwobetsu* (Imperial class) and the *Bambetsu* (aboriginal class). The *Shimbetsu* consisted of the descendants of vanquished chiefs, and the fact was tacitly acknowledged by assigning to this class the second place in the social scale, though the inclusion of the *Tenjin* and the *Tenson* should have assured its precedence. The *Kwobetsu* comprised all Emperors and Imperial princes from Jimmu downwards. This was the premier class. The heads of all its families possessed as a birthright the title of *omi* (grandee), while the head of a *Shimbetsu* family was a *muraji* (group-chief). The *Bambetsu* ranked incomparably below either the *Kwobetsu* or the *Shimbetsu*. It consisted of foreigners who had immigrated from China or Korea and of aboriginal tribes alien to the Yamato race. Members of the *Ban* class were designated *yakko* (or *yatsuko*), a term signifying "subject" or "servant."

In addition to the above three-class distribution, the whole Yamato nation was divided into *uji*, or families. An *uji* founded by one of the *Tenson* took precedence of all others, the next in rank being one with an Imperial prince for ancestor, and after the latter came the families of the *Tenjin* and *Chigi*. All that could not thus trace their genealogy were attached to the various *uji* in a subordinate capacity. It is not to be supposed that one of these families consisted simply of a husband and wife, children, and servants. There were great *uji* and small *uji*, the former comprising many of the latter, and the small *uji* including several households. In fact, the small *uji* (*ko-uji*) may be described as a congeries of from fifty to ninety blood relations.

In the *uji* the principle of primogeniture was paramount. A successor to the headship of an *uji* must be the eldest son of an eldest son. Thus qualified, he became the master of the household, ruled the whole family, and controlled its entire property. The chief of an ordinary *uji* (*uji no Kami*) governed all the households constituting it, and the chief of a great *uji* (*o-uji no Kami*) controlled all the small *uji* of which it was composed. In addition to the members of a family, each *uji*, small and great alike, had a number of dependants (*kakibe* or *tomobe*). In colloquial language, an *o-uji* was the original family; a *ko-uji*, a branch family.

All complications of minor importance were dealt with by the *Kami* of the *uji* in which they occurred, consultation being held with the *Kami* of the appropriate *o-uji* in great cases. Reference was not made to the Imperial Court except in serious matters. On the other hand, commands from the sovereign were conveyed through the head of an *o-uji*, so that the chain of responsibility was well defined. An interesting feature of this ancient organization was that nearly every *uji* had a fixed occupation which was hereditary, the name of the occupation being prefixed to that of the *uji*. Thus, the *uji* of gem-polishers was designated *Tamatsukuri-uji*, and that of boat builders, *Fune-uji*.

There were also *uji* whose members, from generation to generation, acted as governors of provinces (*kuni no miyatsuko*) or headmen of districts (*agata-nushi*). In these cases the name of the region was prefixed to the *uji*; as *Munakata-uji*, *Izumo-uji*, etc. Finally, there were *uji* that carried designations given by the sovereign in recognition of meritorious deeds. These designations took the form of titles. Thus the captor of a crane, at sight of which a dumb prince recovered his speech, was called *Totori no Miyatsuko* (the bird-catching governor), and *Nomi-no-Sukune*, who devised the substitution of clay figures (*haniwa*) for human sacrifices at Imperial obsequies, was designated as *Hashi no Omi* (the Pottery Grandee).

The Tomobe

The *tomobe* (attendants) – called also *mure* (the herd) or *kakibe* (domestics) – constituted an important element of the people. They were, in fact, serfs. We find them first spoken of in an active role as being sent to the provinces to provide foodstuffs for the Imperial household, and in that capacity they went by the name of provincial *Imibe*. Perhaps the most intelligible description of them is that they constituted the peasant and artisan class, and that they were attached to the *uji* in subordinate positions for purposes of manual labour. By degrees, when various kinds of productive operations came to be engaged in as hereditary pursuits, the *tomobe* were grouped according to the specialty of the *uji* to which they wore attached, and we hear of *Kanuchibe*, or the corporation of blacksmiths; *Yumibe*, or the corporation of bow-makers; *Oribe*, or the corporation of weavers, and so on.

It is not to be supposed, however, that all the *tomobe* were thus organized as special classes. Such was the case only when the *uji* to which they belonged pursued some definite branch of productive work. Moreover, there were corporations instituted for purposes quite independent of industry; namely, to perpetuate the memory of an Imperial or princely personage who had died without issue or without attaining ancestral rank.

Such *tomobe* were collectively known as *nashiro* (namesakes) or *koshiro* (child substitutes). For example, when Prince Itoshi, son of the Emperor Suinin, died without leaving a son to perpetuate his name, the *Itoshibe* was established for that purpose; and when Prince Yamato-dake perished without ascending the throne, the *Takebe* was formed to preserve the memory of his achievements. A *be* thus organized on behalf of an Emperor had the title of *toneri* (chamberlain) suffixed. Thus, for the Emperor Ohatsuse (known in history as Yuryaku) the *Hatsuse-be-no-toneri* was formed; and for the Emperor Shiraga (Seinei), the *Shiraga-be-no-toneri*.

The *Tamibe*

Another kind of be consisted of aliens who had been naturalized in Japan or presented to the Japanese Throne by foreign potentates. These were formed into *tamibe* (corporations of people). They became directly dependent upon the Court, and they devoted themselves to manufacturing articles for the use of the Imperial household. These naturalized persons were distinguished, in many cases, by technical skill or literary attainments. Hence they received treatment different from that given to ordinary *tomobe*, some of them being allowed to assume the title and enjoy the privilege of *uji*, distinguished, however, as *uji* of the *Bambetsu*. Thus, the descendants of the seamstresses, E-hime and Oto-hime, and of the weavers, Kure-hatori and Ana-hatori, who were presented to the Yamato Court by an Emperor of the Wu dynasty in China, were allowed to organize themselves into *Kinu-nui-uji* (*uji* of Silk-robe makers). The records show that during the first four centuries of the Christian era the people presented to the Yamato Court by the sovereigns of the Wu dynasty and of Korea must have been very numerous, for no less than 710 *uji* were formed by them in consideration of their skill in the arts and crafts.

Slaves

The institution of slavery (*nuhi*) existed in ancient Japan as in so many other countries. The slaves consisted of prisoners taken in war and of persons who, having committed some serious offence, were handed over to be the property of those that they had injured. The first recorded instance of the former practice was when Yamato-dake presented to the Ise shrine the Yemishi chiefs who had surrendered to him in the sequel of his invasion of the eastern provinces. The same fate seems to have befallen numerous captives made in the campaign against the Kumaso, and doubtless wholesale acts of self-destruction committed by Tsuchi-gumo and Kumaso when overtaken by defeat were prompted by preference of death to slavery.

The story of Japan's relations with Korea includes many references to Korean prisoners who became the property of their captors, and that a victorious general's spoils should comprise some slaves may be described as a recognized custom. Of slavery as a consequence of crime there is also frequent mention, and it would appear that even men of rank might be overtaken by that fate, for when (278 CE) Takenouchi-no-Sukune's younger brother was convicted of slandering him, the culprit's punishment took the form of degradation and assignment to a life of slavery. The whole family of such an offender shared his fate. There is no evidence, however, that the treatment of the *nuhi* was inhuman or even harsh: they appear to have fared much as did the *tomobe* in general.

Land-Holdings

There are two kinds of territorial rights, and these, though now clearly differentiated, were more or less confounded in ancient Japan. One is the ruler's right – that is to say, competence to impose taxes; to enact rules governing possession; to appropriate private lands for public purposes, and to treat as crown estates land not privately owned. The second is the right of possession; namely, the right to occupy definite areas of land and to apply them to one's own ends. At present those two rights are distinct. A landowner has no competence to issue public orders with regard to it, and a lessee of land has to discharge certain responsibilities towards the lessor. It was not so in old Japan. As the Emperor's right to rule the people was not exercised over an individual direct but through the *uji no Kami* who controlled that individual, so the sovereign's right over the land was exercised through the territorial owner, who was usually the *uji no Kami*. The latter, being the owner of the land, leased a part of it to the members of the *uji*, collected a percentage of the produce, and presented a portion to the Court when occasion demanded. Hence, so long as the sovereign's influence was powerful, the *uji no Kami* and other territorial magnates, respecting his orders, refrained from levying taxes and duly paid their appointed contributions to the Court.

But in later times, when the Throne's means of enforcing its orders ceased to bear any sensible ratio to the power of the *uji no Kami* and other local lords, the Imperial authority received scanty recognition, and the tillers of the soil were required to pay heavy taxes to their landlords. It is a fallacy to suppose that the Emperor in ancient times not only ruled the land but also owned it. The only land held in direct possession by the

Throne was that constituting the Imperial household's estates and that belonging to members of the Imperial family. The private lands of the Imperial family were called *mi-agata*. The province of Yamato contained six of these estates, and their produce was wholly devoted to the support of the Court. Lands cultivated for purposes of State revenue were called *miyake*. They existed in several provinces, the custom being that when land was newly acquired, a *miyake* was at once established and the remainder was assigned to princes or Court nobles (*asomi* or *asori*). The cultivators of *miyake* were designated *ta-be* (rustic corporation); the overseers were termed *ta-zukasa* (or *mi-ta no tsukasa*), and the officials in charge of the stores were *mi-agata no obito*.

As far back as 3 BCE, according to Japanese chronology, we read of the establishment of a *miyake*, and doubtless that was not the first. Thenceforth there are numerous examples of a similar measure. Confiscated lands also formed a not unimportant part of the Court's estates. Comparatively trifling offences were sometimes thus expiated. Thus, in 350 CE, Aganoko, suzerain of the Saegi, being convicted of purloining jewels from the person of a princess whom he had been ordered to execute, escaped capital punishment only by surrendering all his lands; and, in 534 CE, a provincial ruler who, being in mortal terror, had intruded into the ladies' apartments in the palace, had to present his landed property for the use of the Empress. These facts show incidentally that the land of the country, though governed by the sovereign, was not owned by him. Lands in a conquered country were naturally regarded as State property, but sufficient allusion has already been made to that custom.

The Sphere of the Sovereign's Rule

The functions of a Japanese Emperor with regard to the people and the land in general were limited to governing (*shirasu*). His ancient prerogatives of governing were: to conduct the worship of the national deities; to declare war against foreign countries and to make peace with them, as representative of the *uji*; to establish or abolish *uji*, to nominate *uji no Kami*, and to adjudicate disputes between them.

Two thousand years have seen no change in the Emperor's function of officiating as the high priest of the nation. It was the sovereign who made offerings to the deities of heaven and earth at the great religious festivals. It was the sovereign who prayed for the aid of the gods when the country was confronted by any emergency or when the people suffered from pestilence. In short, though the powers of the Emperor over the land and the people were limited by the intervention of the *uji*, the whole nation was directly subservient to the Throne in matters relating to religion. From the earliest eras, too, war might not be declared without an Imperial rescript, and to the Emperor was reserved the duty of giving audience to foreign envoys and receiving tribute. By foreign countries, China and Korea were generally understood, but the Kumaso, the Yemishi, and the Sushen were also included in the category of aliens. It would seem that the obligation of serving the country in arms was universal, for in the reign of *Sujin*, when an oversea expedition was contemplated, the people were numbered according to their ages, and the routine of service was laid down. Contributions, too, had to be made, as is proved by the fact that a command of the same sovereign required the various districts to manufacture arms and store them in the shrines.

The sovereign's competence to adjudicate questions relating to the *uji* is illustrated by a notable incident referred to the year 415 CE, during the reign of Inkyo. Centuries had then passed since the inauguration of the *uji*, and families originally small with clearly defined genealogies had multiplied to the dimensions of large clans, so that much confusion of lineage existed, and there was a wide-spread disposition to assert claims to spurious rank. It was therefore commanded by the Emperor that, on a fixed day, all the *uji no Kami* should assemble, and having performed the rite of purification, should submit to the ordeal of boiling water (*kuga-dachi*). Numerous cauldrons were erected for the purpose, and it was solemnly proclaimed that only the guilty would be scalded by the test. At the last moment, those whose claims were willingly false absconded, and the genealogies were finally rectified.

Instances of *uji* created by the sovereign to reward merit, or abolished to punish offences, are numerously recorded. Thus, when (413 CE) the future consort of the Emperor Inkyo was walking in the garden with her mother, a provincial ruler (*miyatsuko*), riding by, peremptorily called to her for a branch of orchid. She asked what he needed the orchid for and he answered, "To beat away mosquitoes when I travel mountain roads." "Oh, honourable sir, I shall not forget," said the lady. When she became Empress, she caused the nobleman to be sought for, and had him deprived of his rank in lieu of execution. There is also an instance of the killing of all the members of an *uji* to expiate the offence of the *uji no Kami*. This happened in 463 CE, when Yuryaku sat on the throne. It was reported to the Court that Sakitsuya, *Kami* of the *Shimotsumichi-uji*, indulged in pastimes deliberately contrived to insult the occupant of the throne. For example, he would match a little girl to combat against a grown woman, calling the girl the Emperor and killing her if she won. The Emperor sent a company of soldiers, and Sakitsuya with all the seventy members of his *uji* were put to death.

ADMINISTRATIVE ORGANIZATION

The administrative organization in ancient Japan was simply a combination of the *uji*. It was purely Japanese. Not until the seventh century of the Christian era were any foreign elements introduced. From ministers and generals of the highest class down to petty functionaries, all offices were discharged by *uji no Kami*, or *kabane*. In effect, the kabane was an order of nobility. Offices were hereditary and equal. The first distribution of posts took place when five chiefs, attached to the person of the *Tenson* at the time of his descent upon Japan, were ordered to discharge at his Court the same duties as those which had devolved on them in the country of their origin. The *uji* they formed were those of the *Shimbetsu*, the official title of the *Kami* being *muraji* (group chief) in the case of an ordinary *uji*, and *o-muraji* (great *muraji*) in the case of an *o-uji*, as already stated. These were the men who rendered most assistance originally in the organization of the State, but as they were merely adherents of the *Tenson*, the latter's direct descendants counted themselves superior and sought always to assert that superiority.

Thus, the title *omi* (grandee) held by the *Kami* of a *Kwobetsu-uji* was deemed higher than that of *muraji* (chief) held by the *Kami* of a *Shimbetsu-uji*. The blood relations of sovereigns either assisted at Court in the administration of State affairs or went to the provinces in the capacity of governors. They received various titles in addition to that of *omi*, for example *sukune* (noble), *ason* or *asomi* (Court noble), *kimi* (duke), *wake* (lord), etc.

History gives no evidence of a fixed official organization in ancient times. The method pursued by the sovereign was to summon such *omi* and *muraji* as were notably influential or competent, and to entrust to them the duty of discharging functions or dealing with a special situation. Those so summoned were termed *mae-isu-gimi* (dukes of the Presence). The highest honour bestowed on a subject in those days fell to the noble, Takenouchi, who, in consideration of his services, was named *O-mae-tsu-gimi* (great duke of the Presence) by the Emperor Seimu (133 CE). It became customary to appoint an *o-omi* and an *o-muraji* at the Court, just as in later days there was a *sa-daijin* (minister of the Left) and an *u-daijin* (minister of the Right). The *o-omi* supervised all members of the *Kwobetsu-uji* occupying administrative posts at Court, and the *o-muraji* discharged a similar function in the case of members of *Shimbetsu-uji*. Outside the capital local affairs were administered by *kuni-no-miyatsuko* or *tomo-no-miyatsuko*. Among the former, the heads of *Kwobetsu-uji* predominated among the latter, those of *Shimbetsu-uji*.

It will be seen from the above that in old Japan lineage counted above everything, alike officially and socially. The offices, the honours and the lands were all in the hands of the lineal descendants of the original Yamato chiefs. Nevertheless the *omi* and the *muraji* stood higher in national esteem than the *kuni-no-miyatsuko* or the *tomo-no-miyatsuko*; the *o-omi* and the *o-muraji*, still higher; and the sovereign, at the apex of all. That much deference was paid to functions. Things remained unaltered in this respect until the sixth century when the force of foreign example began to make itself felt.

THE FIFTEENTH SOVEREIGN, OJIN

Like a majority of the sovereigns in that epoch Ojin (270–310 CE) had many consorts and many children – three of the former (including two younger sisters of the Emperor) and twenty of the latter.

One of the interesting features of Ojin's reign is that maritime affairs receive notice for the first time. It is stated that the fishermen of various places raised a commotion, refused to obey the Imperial commands, and were not quieted until a noble, Ohama, was sent to deal with them. Nothing is stated as to the cause of this complication, but it is doubtless connected with requisitions of fish for the Court. Two years later, instructions were issued that hereditary corporations (*be*) of fishermen should be established in the provinces, and, shortly afterwards, the duty of constructing a boat one hundred feet in length was imposed upon the people of Izu, a peninsular province so remote from Yamato that its choice for such a purpose is difficult to explain. There was no question of recompensing the builders of this boat: the product of their labour was regarded as "tribute."

Twenty-six years later the Karano, as this vessel was called, having become unserviceable, the Emperor ordered a new Karano to be built, so as to perpetuate her name. The timbers of the superannuated ship were used as fuel for roasting salt, five hundred baskets of which were sent throughout the maritime provinces, with orders that by each body of recipients a ship should be constructed. Five hundred Karanos thus came into existence, and there was assembled at Hyogo such a fleet as had never previously been seen in Japanese waters. A number of these new vessels were destroyed almost immediately by a conflagration which broke out in the lodgings of Korean envoys from Sinra (Shiragi), and the envoys being held responsible, their sovereign hastened to send a body of skilled shipmakers by way of atonement, who were thereafter organized into a hereditary guild of marine architects, and we thus learn incidentally that the Koreans had already developed the shipbuilding skill destined to save their country in later ages.

A portion of the Karano's timber having emerged unscathed from the salt-pans, its indestructibility seemed curious enough to warrant special treatment. It was accordingly made into a lute (*koto*). The Emperor composed a song on the subject:

> "The ship Karano
> Was burned for salt:
> Of the remainder
> A koto was made.
> When it is placed on
> One hears the saya-saya
> Of the summer trees,
> Brushing against, as they stand,
> The rocks of the mid-harbour,
> The harbour of Yura."

There was no written law during this period, unless the prohibitions in the Rituals may be so regarded; the second, that there was no form of judicial trial, unless ordeal or torture may be so regarded; the third, that the death penalty might be inflicted on purely ex-parte evidence; the fourth, that a man's whole family had to suffer the penalty of his crimes, and the fifth, that already in those remote times the code of splendid loyalty which has distinguished the Japanese race through all ages had begun to find disciples.

An incident of Ojin's reign illustrates all these things. Takenouchi, the *sukune* (noble) who had served Ojin's mother so ably, and who had saved Ojin's life in the latter's childhood, was despatched to Tsukushi (Kyushu) on State business. During his absence his younger brother accused him of designs upon the Emperor. At once, without further inquiry, Ojin sent men to kill the illustrious minister. But Maneko, suzerain (*atae*) of Iki, who bore a strong resemblance to Takenouchi, personified him, and committing suicide, deceived the soldiers who would have taken the *sukune*'s life, so that the latter was enabled to return to Yamato. Arriving at Court, he protested his innocence and the ordeal of boiling water was employed. It took place on the bank of the Shiki River. Takenouchi proving victorious, his brother with all his family were condemned to become *tomo-be* of the suzerain of Kii.

The most important feature of the Ojin era was the intercourse then inaugurated with China. It may be that after the establishment of the Yamato race in Japan, emigrants from the neighbouring continent settled, from early times, in islands so favoured by nature. If so, they probably belonged to the lowest orders, for it was not until the third and fourth centuries that men of erudition and skilled artisans began to arrive. Much probably depended on the conditions existing in China itself. The Han dynasty had fallen in 190 CE, and there ensued one of the most troubled periods of Chinese history. Many fugitives from the evils of that epoch probably made their way to Korea and even to Japan. years.

It was, however, in the days of the Tsin dynasty (265–317 CE) and in those of the Eastern Tsin (317–420 CE) that under the pressure of the Hun inroads and of domestic commotions, numbers of emigrants found their way from China to Korea and thence to Japan. In the year 283 CE, according to Japanese chronology, Koreans and Chinese skilled in useful arts began to immigrate to Japan. The first to come was a girl called Maketsu. She is said to have been sent by the monarch of Kudara, the region corresponding to the metropolitan province of modern Korea. It may be inferred that she was Chinese, but as to her nationality history is silent. She settled permanently in Japan, and her descendants were known as the *kinu-nui* (silk-clothiers) of *Kume* in Yamato. In the same year (283 CE), Yuzu (called Yutsuki by some authorities), a Chinese Imperial prince, came from Korea at the head of the inhabitants of 120 districts, he had desired to conduct them to Japan, but was unable to accomplish his purpose owing to obstruction offered by the people of Sinra (Shiragi). Ojin sent two embassies – the second accompanied by troops – to procure the release of these people, and in 285 CE they reached Japan, where they received a hearty welcome, and for the sake of their skill in sericulture and silk weaving, they were honoured by organization into an *uji* – *Hata-uji* (*hata* in modern Japanese signifies "loom," but in ancient days it designated silk fabrics of all kinds).

Again, in 289 CE, a sometime subject of the after-Han dynasty, accompanied by his son, emigrated to Japan. The names of these Chinese are given as Achi and Tsuka, and the former is described as a great-grandson of the Emperor Ling of the after-Han dynasty, who reigned from 168 CE to 190. Like Yuzu he had escaped to Korea during the troubled time at the close of the Han sway, and, like Yuzu, he had been followed to the peninsula by a large body of Chinese, who, at his request, were subsequently escorted by Japanese envoys to Japan. These immigrants also were allowed to assume the status of an *uji*, and in the fifth century the title of Aya no atae (suzerain of Aya) was given to Achi's descendants in consideration of the skill of their followers in designing and manufacturing figured fabrics (for which the general term was *aya*).

When Achi had resided seventeen years in Japan, he and his son were sent to Wu (China) for the purpose of engaging women versed in making dress materials. The title of *omi* (chief ambassador) seems to have been then conferred on the two men, as envoys sent abroad were habitually so designated. They made their way via Korea to to Loh-yang where the Tsin sovereigns then had their capital (306 CE). Four women were given to them, whom they carried back to Japan, there to become the ancestresses of an *uji* known as *Kure no kinu-nui* and *Kaya no kinu-nui* (clothiers of Kure and of Kaya), appellations which imply Korean origin, but were probably suggested by the fact that Korea had been the last continental station on their route.

THE ART OF WRITING

It is not infrequently stated that a knowledge of Chinese ideographs was acquired by the Japanese for the first time during the reign of Ojin. The basis of this belief are that, in 404 CE – the King of Kudara sent two fine horses to the Yamato sovereign, and the man who accompanied them, Atogi by name, showed himself a competent reader of the Chinese classics and was appointed tutor to the Prince Imperial. By Atogi's advice a still abler scholar, Wani (Wang-in), was subsequently invited from Kudara to take Atogi's place, and it is added that the latter received the title of *fumi-bito* (scribe), which he transmitted to his descendants in Japan. But close scrutiny does not support the inference that Chinese script had remained unknown to Japan until the above incidents. What is proved is merely that the Chinese classics then for the first time became an open book in Japan.

As for the ideographs themselves, they must have been long familiar, though doubtless to a very limited circle. In the records of the later Han (25–220 CE) we read that from the time when Wu-Ti (140–86 BCE) overthrew Korea, the Japanese of thirty-two provinces communicated with the Chinese authorities in the peninsula by means of a postal service. The Wei annals (220–265 CE) state that in 238 CE, the Chinese sovereign sent a written reply to a communication from the "Queen of Japan" – Jingo was then on the throne. In the same year, the Japanese Court addressed a written answer to a Chinese rescript forwarded to Yamato by the governor of Thepang – the modern Namwon in Chollado – and in 247 CE, a despatch was sent by the Chinese authorities admonishing the Japanese to desist from internecine quarrels. These references indicate that the use of the ideographs was known in Japan long before the reign of Ojin, but the study of the ideographs had scarcely any vogue in Japan until the coming of Atogi and Wani, nor does it appear to have attracted much attention outside Court circles.

Buddhism, introduced into Japan in 552 CE, doubtless supplied the chief incentive to the acquisition of knowledge. But had the Japanese a script of their own at any period of their history? The two oldest manuscripts which contain a reference to this subject are the *Kogo-shui*, compiled by Hironari in 808 CE, and a memorial (*kammori*) presented to the Throne in 901 CE by Miyoshi Kiyotsura. Both explicitly state that in remote antiquity there were no letters, and that all events or discourses had to be transmitted orally. The Japanese cleverly adapted the Chinese ideographs to syllabic purposes, but they never devised a script of their own.

THE SIXTEENTH SOVEREIGN, NINTOKU

Nintoku's reign (313–99 CE) is remembered chiefly on account of the strange circumstances in which he came to the throne, his benevolent charity, and the slights he suffered at the hands of a jealous consort. His father, Ojin, by an exercise of caprice not uncommon on the part of Japan's ancient sovereigns, had nominated a younger son, Waka-iratsuko, to be his heir. But this prince showed invincible reluctance to assume the sceptre after Ojin's death. He asserted himself stoutly by killing one of his elder brothers who conspired against him, though he resolutely declined to take precedence of the other brother, and the latter, proving equally diffident, the throne remained unoccupied for three years when Waka-iratsuko solved the problem by committing suicide.

Such are the simplest outlines of the story. But its details, when filled in by critical Japanese historians of later ages, suggest a different impression. When Ojin died his eldest two sons were living respectively in Naniwa (Osaka) and Yamato, and the Crown Prince, Waka-iratsuko, was at Uji. They were thus excellently situated for setting up independent claims. From the time of Nintoku's birth, the prime minister, head of the great Takenouchi family, had taken a special interest in the child, and when the lad grew up he married this Takenouchi's granddaughter, who became the mother of three Emperors. Presently the representatives of all branches of the Takenouchi family came into possession of influential positions at Court, among others that of *o-omi*, so that in this reign were laid the foundations of the controlling power subsequently vested in the hands of the Heguri, Katsuragi, and Soga houses. In short, this epoch saw the beginning of a state of affairs destined to leave its mark permanently on Japanese history, the relegation of the sovereign to the place of a ineffective figurehead and the usurpation of the administrative authority by a group of great nobles.

Nintoku had the active support of the Takenouchi magnates, and although the Crown Prince may have desired to assert the title conferred on him by his father, he found himself helpless in the face of obstructions offered by the prime minister and his numerous partisans. These suffered him to deal effectively with that one of his elder brothers who did not find a place in their ambitious designs, but they created for Waka-iratsuko a situation so intolerable that suicide became his only resource. Nintoku's first act on ascending the throne was to make Naniwa (Osaka) his capital, but instead of levying taxes and requisitioning forced labour to build his palace of Takatsu, he remitted all such burdens for three years on observing from a tower that no smoke ascended from the roofs of the houses and construing this to indicate a state of poverty. During those three years the palace fell into a condition of practical ruin, and tradition describes its inmates as being compelled to move from room to room to avoid the leaking rain.

Under Nintoku's sway flood relief and irrigation improvements took place on a large scale. Yet it is in connexion with Nintoku's repairs of the Manda river-bank that we find the first mention of a heinous custom occasionally practised in subsequent ages – the custom of sacrificing human life to expedite the progress or secure the success of some public work.

At the same time, that habits indicating a higher civilization had already begun to gain ground is proved by an incident which occurred to one of the Imperial princes during a hunting expedition. Looking down over a moor from a mountain, he observed a pit, and, on inquiry, was informed by the local headman that it was an "ice-pit." The prince, asking how the ice was stored and for what it was used, received this answer: "The ground is excavated to a depth of over ten feet. The top is then covered with a roof of thatch. A thick layer of reed-grass is then spread, upon which the ice is laid. The months of summer have passed and yet it is not melted. As to its use – when the hot months come it is placed in water or *sake* and thus used." Thenceforth the custom of storing ice was adopted at the Court. It was in Nintoku's era that the pastime of hawking, afterward widely practised, became known for the first time in Japan. Korea was the place of origin, and it is recorded that the falcon had a soft leather strap fastened to one leg and a small bell to the tail. Pheasants were the quarry of the first hawk flown on the moor of Mozu.

Light is also thrown in Nintoku's annals on the method of boatbuilding practised by the Japanese in the fourth century. They used dug-outs. The provincial governor of Totomi is represented as reporting that a huge tree had floated down the river Oi and had stopped at a bend. It was a single stem forked at one end, and the suzerain of Yamato was ordered to make a boat of it. The craft was then brought round by sea to Naniwa, "where it was enrolled among the Imperial vessels." Evidently from the days of Ojin and the Karano a fleet formed part of the Imperial possessions. This two-forked boat figures in the reign of Nintoku's successor, Richu, when the latter and his concubine went on board and feasted separately, each in one fork.

THE FAMILY OF TAKENOUCHI-NO-SUKUNE

For the better understanding of Japanese history at this stage, a word must be said about a family of nobles (*sukune*) who, from the days of Nintoku, exercised potent sway in the councils of State. It will have been observed that, in the annals of the Emperor Keiko's reign, prominence is given to an official designated *Takenouchi-no-Sukune*. The family name Takenouchi was borne by different scions in succeeding reigns. The first was a grandson of the Emperor Kogen (214–158 BCE), and the representatives of the family in Nintoku's era had seven sons, all possessing the title *sukune*. They were Hata no Yashiro, Koze no Ogara, Soga no Ishikawa, Heguri no Tsuku, Ki no Tsunu, Katsuragi no Sotsu, and Wakugo.

From these were descended the five *uji* of Koze, Soga, Heguri, Ki, and Katsuragi. Although its founder was an Emperor's grandson and therefore entitled to be called "Imperial Prince" (O), the family connexion with the Throne naturally became more remote as time passed, and from the reign of Ojin we find its members classed among subjects. Nevertheless, the Empress Iwa, whose jealousy harrassed Nintoku so greatly, was a daughter of Katsuragi no Sotsu, and, as with the sole exception of the Emperor Shomu, every occupant of the throne had taken for his Empress a lady of Imperial blood, it may be assumed that the relationship between the Imperial and the Takenouchi families was recognized at that time. The roles which the five *uji* mentioned above acted in subsequent history deserve to be studied, and will therefore be briefly set down here.

The Koze-*uji* had for its founder Koze no Ogara. The representative of the fourth generation, Koze no Ohito, held the post of *o-omi* during the reign of the Emperor Keitai (507–531 CE), and his great-grandson was minister of the Left under Kotoku (545–654 CE). Thereafter, the heads of the *uji* occupied prominent positions under successive sovereigns.

The Soga-*uji* was founded by Soga no Ishikawa. His son, Machi, shared the administrative power with Heguri no Tsuku in the reign of Richu (400–405 CE), and Machi's great-grandson, Iname, immortalized himself by promoting the introduction of Buddhism in the reign of Kinmei (540–571 CE). Iname's son, Umako, and the latter's son, Yemishi, will be much heard of hereafter. No family, indeed, affected the course of Japanese history in early days more than did the Soga-*uji*.

The Heguri-*Uji*

The Heguri-uji was founded by Heguri no Tsuku who, during the reign of the Emperor Richu (400–405 CE), shared in the administration with Soga no Machi. His son, Heguri no Matori, was minister under Yuryaku (457–459 CE), and the fate which he and his son, Shibi, brought upon their family is one of the salient incidents of Japanese history.

The Ki-*uji* was founded by Ko no Tsunu, and the representatives of this *uji* took a prominent share in the empire's foreign affairs, but served also in the capacity of provincial governor and commander-in-chief.

The Katsuragi-*uji* was founded by Katsuragi no Stotsu. Nintoku's Empress, Iwa, was a daughter of the founder, and her great-granddaughter, Hae, was the mother of two sovereigns, Kenso (485–487 CE) and Ninken (488–498 CE).

THE PROTOHISTORIC SOVEREIGNS

In this period Japan continued to be receptive to the outside influences of China and Korea. Both countries left a distinctive impression on economic institutions, the arts and architecture – even the very mannerisms and structures of the Japanese court. This earlier phase of peace was soon shattered by a series of succession disputes, however, plunging the island kingdom into a miasma of internecine violence riven with horrific acts of cruelty. Elsewhere Japan began to impose its authority abroad, establishing an early foothold in Korea and becoming a major player in the geopolitical landscape of the peninsula – although Japanese military expeditions enjoyed varying degrees of success.

THE SEVENTEENTH SOVEREIGN, RICHU

Immediately after Nintoku's death Prince Nakatsu, younger brother of the heir to the throne, who had not yet assumed the sceptre, was sent by the Crown Prince (Richu, 400–405 CE) to make arrangements for the latter's nuptials with the lady Kuro, a daughter of the Takenouchi family. Nakatsu personified Richu, debauched the girl, and to avoid the consequences of the act, sought to take the life of the man he had betrayed. At this crisis of his life, Richu received loyal assistance from a younger brother, and his gratitude induced him to confer on the latter the title of Crown Prince. In thus acting, Richu may have been influenced by the fact that the alternative was to bequeath the throne to a baby, but none the less he stands responsible for an innovation which greatly impaired the stability of the succession. It should be noted, as illustrating the influence of the Takenouchi family that, in spite of the shame she had suffered, the lady Kuro became the Emperor's concubine. In fact, among the four nobles who administered the affairs of the empire during Richu's reign, not the least powerful were Heguri no Tsuku and Soga no Machi. Moreover, Richu, as has been stated already, was a son of Iwa, a lady of the same great family, and his two successors, Hansho and Inkyo, were his brothers by the same mother.

Loyalty was paramount in Japan. A retainer of the rebellious Prince Nakatsu, Sashihire, assassinated that prince at the instance of Prince Mizuha, who promised large reward. But after the deed had been accomplished, Heguri no Tsuku advised his nephew, Mizuha, saying, "Sashihire has killed his own lord for the sake of another, and although for us he has done a great service, yet towards his own lord his conduct has been heartless in the extreme." Sashihire was therefore put to death. That this principle was always observed in Japan cannot be asserted, but that it was always respected is certain.

The annals of this reign are noteworthy as containing the earliest reference to the compilation of books. Another institution established during this era was a treasury (405 CE), and the two learned Koreans who had come from Paikche (Kudara) were appointed to keep the accounts. A work of later date than the *Chronicles* or *Records* – the *Shokuin-rei* – says that in this treasury were stored "gold and silver, jewels, precious utensils, brocade and satin, saicenet, rugs and mattresses, and the rare objects sent as tribute by the various barbarians."

In Richu's reign there is found the first clear proof that tattooing was not practised in Japan for ornamental purposes. Tattooing is first mentioned as a custom of the Yemishi when their country was inspected by Takenouchi at Keiko's orders. But in Richu's time it was employed to punish the *muraji* of Atsumi, who had joined the rebellion of Prince Nakatsu. He was "inked" on the face. It appears also that the same practice had hitherto been employed to distinguish horse-keepers, but the custom was finally abandoned in deference to an alleged revelation from Izanagi, the deity of Awaji, on the occasion of a visit by Richu to that island. In the context of this revelation it is noticeable that belief in the malign influence of offended deities was gaining ground. Thus, on the occasion of the sudden death of Princess Kuro, the voice of the wind was heard to utter mysterious words in the "great void" immediately before the coming of a messenger to announce the event, and the Emperor attributed the calamity to the misconduct of an official who had removed certain persons from serving at a shrine.

THE EIGHTEENTH SOVEREIGN, HANSHO

The Emperor Hansho's short reign of five years (406–11) is not remarkable for anything except an indirect evidence that Chinese customs were beginning to be adopted at the Japanese Court. In the earliest eras, the ladies who enjoyed the sovereign's favour were classed simply as "Empress" or "consort." But from the days of Hansho we find three ranks of concubines.

THE NINETEENTH SOVEREIGN, INKYO

Inkyo (412–53) was a younger brother of his predecessor, Hansho, as the latter had been of Richu. No formal nomination of Inkyo as Prince Imperial had taken place, and thus for the first time the sceptre was found without any legalized heir or any son of the deceased sovereign to take it. In these circumstances, the ministers held a council and agreed to offer the throne to Inkyo, the elder of two surviving sons of Nintoku. Inkyo was suffering from a disease supposed to be incurable, and, distrusting his own competence, he persistently refused to accept the responsibility. The incident responsible for his ultimate consent was the intervention of a concubine, Onakatsu, afterwards Empress. Under pretext of carrying water for the prince she entered his chamber, and when he turned his back on her entreaty that he would comply with the ministers' desire, she remained standing in the bitter cold of a stormy day of January, until the water, which she had spilled over her arm, became frozen and she fell in a faint. Then the prince yielded. A year later envoys were sent to seek medical assistance in Korea, which was evidently regarded as the home of the healing science as well as of many other arts borrowed from China. A physician arrived from Sinra, and Inkyo's malady was cured.

The annals tell this story from the reign of Inkyo, important only as illustrating the manners and customs of the time. From an early period it had been usual that Japanese ladies on festive occasions should go through the graceful performance of "woven paces and waving hands," which constituted dancing, and, in the era now occupying our attention, there prevailed in the highest circles a custom that the *danseuse* should offer a maiden to the most honoured among the guests. One winter's day, at the opening of a new palace, the Empress Onakatsu danced to the music of the Emperor's lute. Onakatsu had a younger sister, Oto, of extraordinary beauty, and the Emperor, keen to possess the girl but fearful of offending the Empress, had planned this dance so that Onakatsu, in compliance with the recognized usage, might be constrained to place her sister at his disposal. It fell out as Inkyo wished, but there then ensued a chapter of incidents which undermined the dignity of the Crown.

Again and again the beautiful Oto refused to obey her sovereign's summons, and when at length, by an unworthy ruse, she was induced to repair to the palace, it was found impossible to make her an inmate of it in defiance of the Empress' jealousy. She had to be housed elsewhere, and still the Imperial lover was baffled, for he dared not brave the elder sister's resentment by visiting the younger. Finally he took advantage of the Empress' confinement to pay the long-deferred visit, but, on learning of the event, the outraged wife set fire to the parturition house and attempted to commit suicide. "Inkyo had the grace to be "greatly shocked" and to "soothe the mind of the Empress with explanations," but he did not mend his infidelity. At Oto's request he built a residence for her at Chinu in the neighbouring province of Kawachi.

It is not, perhaps, extravagant to surmise that the publicity attending this sovereign's affairs and the atmosphere of loose morality thus created were in part responsible for a crime committed by his elder son, the Crown Prince Karu. Marriage between children of the same father had always been permitted in Japan provided the mother was different, but marriage between children of the same mother was incest. Prince Karu was guilty of this offence with his sister, Oiratsume, and so severely did the nation judge him that he was driven into exile and finally obliged to commit suicide.

THE TWENTIETH SOVEREIGN, ANKO

The records of this sovereign's reign make a discreditable page of Japanese history. Anko (454–56), having ascended the throne after an armed contest with his elder brother, which ended in the latter's suicide, desired to arrange a marriage between his younger brother, Ohatsuse, and a sister of his uncle, Okusaka. He despatched Ne no Omi, a trusted envoy, to confer with the latter, who gladly consented, and, in token of approval, handed to Ne no Omi a richly jewelled coronet for conveyance to the Emperor. But Ne no Omi, covetous of the gems, secreted the coronet, and told the Emperor that Okusaka had rejected the proposal with scorn. Anko took no steps to investigate the truth of this statement. It has been already seen that such investigations were not customary in those days. Soldiers were at once sent to slaughter Okusaka; his wife, Nakashi, was taken to be the Emperor's consort, and his sister, Hatahi, was married to Prince Ohatsuse.

Now, at the time of his death, Okusaka had a son, Mayuwa, seven years old. One day, the Emperor, having drunk heavily, confessed to the Empress, Nakashi, that he entertained some apprehension lest this boy might one day seek to avenge his father's execution. The child overheard this remark, and creeping to the side of his step-father, who lay asleep with his head in Nakashi's lap, killed him with his own sword. This tale is tole in the *Chronicles* and *Records*, but in reality it is highly unlikely that a deed of the kind would never have been conceived or committed by a child; the Empress must have been a conniving party.

To what quarter, then, is the instigation to be traced? An answer seems to be furnished by the conduct of Prince Ohatsuse. Between this prince and the throne five lives intervened; those of the Emperor Anko, of the latter's two brothers, Yatsuri no Shiro and Sakai no Kuro, both older than Ohatsuse, and of two sons of the late Emperor Richu, Ichinobe no Oshiwa and Mima. Every one of these was removed from the scene in the space of a few days. Immediately after Anko's assassination, Ohatsuse, simulating suspicion of his two elder brothers, killed the *o-omi*, who refused to give them up. Ohatsuse then turned his attention to his grand-uncles, the two sons of Richu. He sent a military force to destroy one of them without any pretence of cause; the other he invited to a hunting expedition and treacherously shot. If Ohatsuse did not contrive the murder of Anko, as he contrived the deaths of all others standing between himself and the throne, a great injustice has been done to his memory.

These shocking incidents are not without a relieving feature. They furnished opportunities for the display of fine devotion. When Prince Okusaka died for a crime of which he was wholly innocent, two of his retainers, Naniwa no Hikaga, father and son, committed suicide in vindication of his memory. When Prince Sakai no Kuro and Mayuwa took refuge in the house of the *o-omi* Tsubura, the latter deliberately chose death rather than surrender the fugitives. When Prince Kuro perished, Nie-no-Sukune took the corpse in his arms and was burned with it. When Prince Ichinobe no Oshiwa fell under the treacherous arrow of Prince Ohatsuse, one of the former's servants embraced the dead body and fell into such a paroxysm of grief that Ohatsuse ordered him to be despatched. And during this reign of Yuryaku, when Lord Otomo was killed in a fatal engagement with the Sinra troops, his henchman, Tsumaro, crying, "My master has fallen; what avails that I alone should remain unhurt?" threw himself into the ranks of the enemy and perished. Loyalty to the death characterized the Japanese in every age.

THE TWENTY-FIRST SOVEREIGN, YURYAKU

This sovereign (457–79) was the Ohatsuse of whose unscrupulous ambition so much has just been heard. Some historians have described him as an austere man, but few readers of his annals will be disposed to endorse such a lenient verdict. He ordered that a girl, whose only fault was misplaced affection, should have her four limbs stretched on a tree and be roasted to death; he slew one of his stewards at a hunt, because the man did not understand how to cut up the meat of an animal; he removed a high official – Tasa, *omi* of Kibi – to a distant post in order to possess himself of the man's wife (Waka), and he arbitrarily and capriciously killed so many men and women that the people called him the "Emperor of great wickedness."

One act of justice stands to his credit. The slanderer, Ne no Omi, who for the sake of a jewelled coronet had caused the death of Prince Okusaka, as related above, had the temerity to wear the coronet, sixteen years subsequently, when he presided at a banquet given in honour of envoys from China; and the beauty of the bauble having thus been noised abroad, Ne no Omi was required to show it at the palace. It was immediately recognized by the Empress, sister of the ill-starred prince, and Ne no Omi, having confessed his crime, was put to death, all the members of his *uji* being reduced to the rank of serfs.

In the record of Richu's reign, brief mention has been made of the establishment of a Government treasury. In early days, when religious rites and administrative functions were not differentiated, articles needed for both purposes were kept in the same store, under the charge of the *Imibe-uji*. But as the Court grew richer, owing to receipt of domestic taxes and foreign "tribute," the necessity of establishing separate treasuries, was felt and a "domestic store" (*Uchi-kura*) was formed during Richu's reign, the Koreans, Achi and Wani, being appointed to keep the accounts. In Yuryaku's time a third treasury had to be added, owing to greatly increased production of textile fabrics and other manufactures. This was called the *Okura*, a term still applied to the Imperial treasury, and there were thus three stores, *Okura*, *Uchi-kura*, and *Imi-kura*. Soga no Machi was placed in supreme charge of all three, and the power of the Soga family grew proportionately.

The reign of Yuryaku is partially redeemed by the encouragement given to the arts and crafts. It has already been related that the members of the *Hata-uji*, which had been constituted originally with artisans from China, gradually became dispersed throughout the provinces and were suffering some hardships when Yuryaku issued orders for their reassembly and reorganization. Subsequently the sovereign gave much encouragement to sericulture, and, inspired doubtless by the legend of the Sun goddess, inaugurated a custom which thereafter prevailed in Japan through all ages, the cultivation of silkworms by the Empress herself. At a later date, learning from a Korean handicraftsman (*tebito*) – whose name has been handed down as Kwan-in Chiri – that Korea abounded in experts of superior skill, Yuryaku commissioned this man to carry to the King of Kudara (Paikche) an autograph letter asking for the services of several of these experts. This request was complied with, and the newcomers were assigned dwellings at the village of Tsuno in Yamato; but as the place proved unhealthy, they were afterwards distributed among several localities.

It is also recorded that, about this time, there came from China a man called An Kiko, a descendant of one of the Wu sovereigns. He settled in Japan, and his son, Ryu afterwards – named Shinki – is reputed to have been the first exponent of Chinese pictorial art in Japan. In the year 470 CE, there was another arrival of artisans, this time from Wu (China), including weavers and clothiers. They landed in the province of Settsu, and to commemorate their coming a road called the "Kure-saka" (Wu acclivity) was constructed from that port to the Shihatsu highway. The descendants of these immigrants were organized into two hereditary corporations (*be*) of silk-clothiers, the *Asuka no Kinu-nui-be* and the *Ise no Kinu-nui-be*. Two years later (472), orders were issued for the cultivation of mulberry trees in all suitable provinces, and at the same time the previously reassembled members of the *Hata-uji* were once more distributed to various localities with the object of widening their sphere of instruction.

In the year 473 a very interesting event is recorded. The *muraji* of the Hanishi was ordered to furnish craftsmen to manufacture "pure utensils" for serving viands daily in the palace. These Hanishi are first spoken of as having been employed at the suggestion of Nomi-no-Sukune, in the days of the Emperor Suinin (3 CE), to make clay substitutes for the human beings thitherto inhumed at the sepulchres of notables. In response to this order the *muraji* summoned his own *tami-be* (private hereditary corporation) then located at seven villages in the provinces of Settsu, Yamashiro, Ise, Tamba, Tajima, and Inaba. They were organized into the *Nie no Hanishibe*, or hereditary corporation of potters of table-utensils. Ceramists had previously come from Kudara (Paikche), and there can be no doubt that some progress was made in the art from the fifth century onwards. But the art of applying glaze to ceramic manufactures was not discovered until a much later period.

RELATIONS WITH KOREA

When Yuryaku ascended the throne, Japan still enjoyed her original friendship with Paikche (Kudara), whence ladies-in-waiting were sent periodically to the Yamato Court. The Japanese military post at Mimana (Imna) was retained and a governor was kept there, but Japan's relations with Shiragi (Sinra) were somewhat strained, owing to harsh treatment of the latter's special envoys who had come to convey their sovereign's condolences on the death of the Emperor Inkyo (453). From the time of Yuryaku's accession, Shiragi ceased altogether to send the usual gifts to the Emperor of Japan. In the year 463, Yuryaku, desiring to possess himself of the wife of a high official, Tasa, sent him to be governor of Mimana, and in his absence debauched the lady. Tasa, learning how he had been dishonoured, raised the standard of revolt and sought aid of the Shiragi people. Then Yuryaku, with characteristic refinement of cruelty, ordered Tasa's son, Oto, to lead a force against his father. Oto seemingly complied, but, on reaching the peninsula, opened communication with his father, and it was agreed that while Tasa should hold Imna, breaking off all relations with Japan, Oto should adopt a similar course with regard to Paikche. This plot was frustrated by Oto's wife, Kusu, a woman too patriotic to connive at treason in any circumstances. She killed her husband, and the Court of Yamato was informed of these events.

From that time, however, Japan's hold upon the peninsula was shaken. Yuryaku sent four expeditions there, but they accomplished nothing permanent. The power of Koma in the north increased steadily, and it had the support of China. Yuryaku's attempts to establish close relations with the latter – the Sung were then on the throne – seem to have been inspired by a desire to isolate Korea. He failed, and ultimately Kudara was overrun by Koma, as will be seen by and by. It is scarcely too much to say that Japan lost its paramount status in Korea because of Yuryaku's illicit passion for the wife of one of his subjects.

MANNERS AND CUSTOMS

During this epoch the sovereigns of Japan had not yet begun to affect the sacred seclusion which, in later ages, became characteristic of them. It is true that, after ascending the throne, they no longer led their troops in war, though they did so as Imperial princes. But in other respects they lived the lives of ordinary men – joining in the chase, taking part in banquets, and mixing freely with the people.

From the time when the fierce *Kami*, Susanoo, put his thoughts into verse as he sought for a place to celebrate his marriage, great crises and little crises in the careers of men and women respectively inspire couplets. We find an Emperor addressing an ode to a dragon-fly which avenges him on a gadfly; we find a prince reciting impromptu stanzas while he lays siege to the place whither his brother has fled for refuge; we find a heartbroken lady singing a verselet as for the last time she ties the garters of her lord going to his death, and we find a sovereign corresponding in verse with his consort whose consent to his own dishonour he seeks to win.

Yet in the lives of all these men and women of old, there are not many other traces of corresponding refinement or romance. We are constrained to conjecture that many of the verses quoted in the *Records* and the *Chronicles* were fitted in after ages to the events they commemorate. Another striking feature in the lives of these early sovereigns is that while on the one hand their residences are spoken of as *muro*, a term generally applied to dwellings partially underground, on the other, we find more than one reference to high towers. Thus Yuryaku is shown as "ordering commissioners to erect a lofty pavilion in which he assumes the Imperial dignity," and the Emperor Nintoku is represented as "ascending a lofty tower and looking far and wide" on the occasion of his celebrated sympathy with the people's poverty.

THE TWENTY-SECOND SOVEREIGN, SEINEI

Succession Disputes

The era of the five sovereigns so far featured in this chapter – an era of fifty-nine years – inherited many legacies from the immediate past: a well-furnished treasury, a nation in the enjoyment of peace, a firmly established throne, and a satisfactory state of foreign relations. These comfortable conditions seem to have exercised demoralizing influence. The bonds of discipline grew slack; fierce quarrels on account of women involved fratricide among the princes of the blood, and finally the life of an Emperor was sacrificed – the only instance of such a catastrophe in Japanese history.

The Emperor Yuryaku's evil act in robbing Tasa of his wife, Waka, entailed serious consequences. He selected to succeed to the throne his son Seinei, by Princess Kara, who belonged to the Katsuragi branch of the great Takenouchi family. But Princess Waka conspired to secure the dignity for the younger of her own two sons, Iwaki and Hoshikawa, who were both older than Seinei. She urged Hoshikawa to assert his claim by seizing the Imperial treasury, and she herself with Prince Iwaki and others accompanied him thither. They underestimated the power of the Katsuragi family. Siege was laid to the treasury and all its inmates were burned, with the exception of one minor official to whom mercy was extended and who, in token of gratitude, presented twenty-five acres of rice-land to the *o-muraji*, Lord Otomo, commander of the investing force.

The Fugitive Princes

The Emperor Seinei (480–484 CE) had no offspring, and for a time it seemed that the succession in the direct line would be interrupted. For this lack of heirs the responsibility ultimately rested with Yuryaku. In his fierce ambition to sweep away every obstacle, actual or potential, that barred his ascent to the throne, he inveigled Prince Oshiwa, eldest son of the Emperor Richu, to accompany him on a hunting expedition, and slew him mercilessly on the moor of Kaya. Oshiwa had two sons, Oke and Woke, mere children at the time of their father's murder. They fled, under the care of Omi, a *muraji*, who, with his son, Adahiko, secreted them in the remote province of Inaba. Omi ultimately committed suicide in order to avoid the risk of capture and interrogation under torture, and the two little princes, still accompanied by Adahiko, calling themselves "the urchins of Tamba," became menials in the service of the obito of the Shijimi granaries in the province of Harima.

Twenty-four years had been passed in that seclusion when it chanced that Odate, governor of the province, visited the *obito* on an occasion when the latter was hosting revels to celebrate the building of a new house, it fell to the lot of the two princes to act as torch-bearers, the lowest role that could be assigned to them, and the younger counselled his brother that the time had come to declare themselves, for death was preferable to such a life. Tradition says that, being invited to dance "when the night had become profound, when the revel was at its height and when every one else had danced in turn," the Prince Woke, accompanying his movements with verses extemporized for the occasion, danced so gracefully that the governor twice asked him to continue, and at length he announced the rank and lineage of his brother and himself. The governor, astonished, "made repeated obeisance to the youths, built a palace for their temporary accommodation, and going up to the capital, disclosed the whole affair to the Emperor, who expressed profound satisfaction."

THE TWENTY-THIRD SOVEREIGN, KENSO

O ke, the elder of the two, was made Prince Imperial, and should have ascended the throne on the death of Seinei, a few months later. Arguing, however, that to his younger brother Woke it was entirely due that they had emerged from a state of abject misery, Oke announced his determination to cede the honour to Woke, who, in turn, declined to take precedence of his elder brother. This dispute of mutual deference continued for a whole year, during a part of which time the administration was carried on by Princess Awo, elder sister of Woke. At length the latter yielded and assumed the sceptre as the 23rd Emperor "Kenso" (485–487). His first care was to collect the bones of his father, Prince Oshiwa, who had been murdered and buried unceremoniously on the moor of Kaya in Omi province. It was long before the place of interment could be discovered, but at length an old woman served as guide, and the bones of the prince were found mingled in inextricable confusion with those of his loyal vassal, Nakachiko, who had shared his fate.

A double sepulchre was erected in memory of the murdered prince and his faithful follower and the old woman who had pointed out the place of their unhonoured grave was given a house in the vicinity of the palace, a rope with a bell attached being stretched between the two residences to serve as a support for her infirm feet and as a means of announcing her coming when she visited the palace. But the same benevolent sovereign who directed these gracious doings was with difficulty dissuaded from demolishing the tomb and scattering to the winds of heaven the bones of the Emperor Yuryaku, under whose hand Prince Oshiwa had fallen.

In connexion with this, the introduction of the principle of the vendetta has to be noted. Its first practical application is generally referred to the act of the boy-prince, Mayuwa, who stabbed his father's slayer, the Emperor Anko (456 CE). But the details of Anko's fate are involved in some mystery, and it is not until the time (486 CE) of Kenso that we find a definite enunciation of the Confucian doctrine, afterwards rigidly obeyed in Japan, "A man should not live under the same heaven with his father's enemy." History alleges that, by his brother's counsels, the Emperor Kenso was induced to abandon his intention of desecrating Yuryaku's tomb, but the condition of the tomb to-day suggests that these counsels were not entirely effective.

THE TWENTY-FOURTH SOVEREIGN, NINKEN

The **twenty-fourth sovereign**, Ninken (488–98), succeeded to the throne after the death of his younger brother, and occupied it for ten years of a most uneventful reign. Apart from the fact that tanners were invited from Korea to improve the process followed in Japan, the records contain nothing worthy of attention. One incident, however, deserves to be noted as showing the paramount importance attached in those early days to all the formalities of etiquette. The Empress dowager committed suicide, dreading lest she should be put to death for a breach of politeness committed towards Ninken during the life of his predecessor, Kenso. At a banquet in the palace she had twice neglected to kneel when presenting, first, a knife and, secondly, a cup of wine to Ninken, then Prince Imperial.

THE TWENTY-FIFTH SOVEREIGN, MURETSU

Muretsu (499–506) was the eldest son of his predecessor, Ninken. According to the *Chronicles*, his reign opened with a rebellion by the great Heguri family, whose representative, Matori, attempted to usurp the Imperial dignity while his son, Shibi, defiantly wooed and won for himself the object of the Emperor's affections. Matori had been Yuryaku's minister, and his power as well as his family influence were very great, but the military nobles adhered to the sovereign's cause and the Heguri were annihilated.

The *Chronicles* represent Muretsu as a monster of cruelty, the Nero of Japanese history, who plucked out men's nails and made them dig up yams with their mutilated fingers; who pulled out people's hair; who made them ascend trees which were then cut down, and who perpetrated other hideous excesses. Here again the *Records*, as well as other ancient authorities are absolutely silent, and the story in the *Chronicles* has attracted keen analyses by modern historiographers. Their almost unanimous conclusion is that the annals of King Multa of Kudara, who committed all kinds of atrocities and was finally deposed by his people, have been confused with those of the Emperor Muretsu.

THE TWENTY-SIXTH SOVEREIGN, KEITAI

The death of the Emperor Muretsu left the throne without any successor in the direct line of descent, and for the first time since the foundation of the empire, it became necessary for the great officials to make a selection among the scions of the remote Imperial families. Their choice fell primarily on the representative of the fifth generation of the Emperor Chuai's descendants. But as their method of announcing their decision was to despatch a strong force of armed troops to the provincial residence of the chosen man, he naturally misinterpreted the demonstration and sought safety in flight.

Then the *o-omi* and the *o-muraji* turned to Prince Odo, fifth in descent from the Emperor Ojin on his father's side and eighth in descent from the Emperor Suinin on his mother's. Arako, head of the horse-keepers, had secretly informed the prince of the ministers' intentions, and thus the sudden apparition of a military force inspired no alarm in Odo's bosom. He did, indeed, show seemly hesitation, but finally he accepted the insignia and ascended the throne as Keitai (507–31), confirming all the high dignitaries of State in their previous offices. From the point of view of domestic affairs his reign was uneventful, but the empire's relations with Korea continued to be much disturbed, as will be presently explained.

THE TWENTY-SEVENTH SOVEREIGN, ANKAN

The Emperor Keitai had a large family, but only one son was by the Empress, and as he was too young to ascend the throne immediately after his father's death, he was preceded by his two brothers, Ankan and Senkwa, sons of the senior concubine. This complication seems to have caused some difficulty, for whereas Keitai died in 531, Ankan's reign did not commence until 534 and lasted just a year. The most noteworthy feature of his era was the establishment of State granaries in great numbers, a proof that the Imperial power found large extension throughout the provinces. In connexion with this, the *o-muraji*, Kanamura, is quoted as having laid down, by command of the Emperor, the following important doctrine, "Of the entire surface of the soil, there is no part which is not a royal grant in fee; under the wide heavens there is no place which is not royal territory." The annals show, also, that the custom of accepting tracts of land or other property in expiation of offences was obtaining increased vogue.

Senkwa (536–39) was the younger brother of Ankan. He reigned only three years and the period of his sway was uneventful, if we except the growth of complications with Korea, and the storing of large quantities of grain in Tsukushi, as provision against "extraordinary occasions" and also a means of offering hospitality to visitors from overseas.

RELATIONS WITH KOREA

It appears to be certain that at a very early date, Japan established a foothold on the south coast of Korea at Mimana, and established there a permanent station (chinju-fu) which was governed by one of its own officials. It is also apparent that, during several centuries, the eminent military strength of Yamato received practical recognition from the principalities into which the peninsula was divided; that they sent to the Court of Japan annual presents which partook of the nature of tribute, and that they treated its suggestions, for the most part, with deferential attention. This state of affairs received a rude shock in the days of Yuryaku, whose desire for the wife of a high Korean official, Tasa, led to a revolt. From that time Japan's position in the peninsula was compromised. The Koreans perceived that its strength might be paralyzed by the sins of its sovereigns and the disaffection of its soldiers. Shiragi (Sinra), whose frontier was conterminous with that of the Japanese settlement on the north, had always been restive in the proximity of a foreign aggressor. From the time of Yuryaku's accession this region ceased to convey the usual tokens of respect to the Yamato Court, and, on the other hand, s cultivated the friendship of Koma as an ally in the day of retribution.

It may be broadly stated that Korea was then divided into three principalities: Shiragi in the south and east; Kudara in the centre and west, with its capital at the modern Seoul, and

Koma in the north, having Pyong-yang for chief city. This last had recently pushed its frontier into Manchuria as far as the Liao River, and was already beginning to project its shadow over the southern regions of the peninsula, destined ultimately to fall altogether under its sway. In response to Shiragi's overtures, the King of Koma sent a body of troops to assist in protecting that principality against any retaliatory attack on the part of the Japanese in Mimana. But the men of Shiragi, betrayed into imagining that these soldiers were destined to be the van of an invading army, massacred them, and sought Japanese aid against Koma's vengeance. The Japanese acceded, and Shiragi was saved for a time, but at the cost of incurring the lasting enmity of Koma. Shiragi still withheld its tribute to Japan and invaded the territory of Kudara, which had always maintained most friendly relations with Yamato. The Emperor Yuryaku sent two expeditions to punish this deviancy, but the result being inconclusive, he resolved to take the exceptional step of personally leading an army to the peninsula.

This design, which, had it matured, might have radically changed the history of the Far East, was checked by an oracle, and Yuryaku appointed three of his powerful nobles to go in his stead. The Shiragi men fought with desperate tenacity. One wing of their army was broken, but the other held its ground. Neither side could claim a decisive victory, but both were too much exhausted to renew the combat. This was not the limit of Japan's misfortunes. A feud broke out among the leaders of the expedition, and one of them, Oiwa, shot his comrade as they were *en route* for the Court of the Kudara monarch, who had invited them in the hope of negotiating a peace, since the existence of his own kingdom depended on Japan's intervention between Koma and Shiragi.

Owing to this feud among her generals, Japan's hold on Mimana became more precarious than ever while its prestige in the peninsula declined perceptibly. Nevertheless its military reputation still retained much of its potency. Thus, ten years later (477 CE), when the King of Koma invaded Kudara and held the land at his mercy, he declined to follow his generals' counsels of extermination in deference to Kudara's long friendship with Yamato. It is related that, after this disaster, the Japanese Emperor gave the town of Ung-chhon (Japanese, Kumanari) to the remnant of the Kudara people, and the latter's capital was then transferred from its old site in the centre of the peninsula – a place no longer tenable – to the neighbourhood of Mimana. Thenceforth Yuryaku aided Kudara zealously. He not only despatched a force of five hundred men to guard the palace of the King, but also sent (480) a flotilla of war-vessels to attack Koma from the west coast. Koma maintained at that epoch relations of intimate friendship with the powerful Chinese dynasty of the Eastern Wei, and Yuryaku's essays against such a combination were futile, though he prosecuted them with considerable vigour.

After his death the efficiency of Japan's operations in Korea was greatly impaired by factors hitherto happily unknown in her foreign affairs – treason and corruption. Lord Oiwa, whose shooting of his fellow general, Karako, has already been noted, retained his post as governor of Mimana for twenty-one years, and then (487), ambitious of wider sway, opened relations with Koma for the joint invasion of Kudara, in order that he himself might ascend the throne of the latter. A desperate struggle ensued. Several battles were fought, in all of which the victory is historically assigned to Oiwa, but if he really did achieve any success, it was purely ephemeral, for he ultimately abandoned the campaign and returned to Japan, giving another shock to his country's waning reputation in the peninsula. If the Yamato Court took any steps to punish this act of lawless ambition, there is no record.

Nothing notable took place until 509, when Keitai was on the throne. In that year, a section of the Kudara people, who, in 477, had been driven from their country by the Koma invaders and had taken refuge within the Japanese dominion of Mimana, were restored to their homes with Japanese co-operation and with renewal of the friendly relations which had long existed between the Courts of Yamato and Kudara. Three years later (512), Kudara asked that four regions, forming an integral part of the Yamato domain of Mimana, should be handed over, apparently as an act of pure benevolence. Japan consented – perhaps because it was deemed a wise policy to strengthen Kudara against the growing might of Shiragi, Yamato's perennial foe. The two officials by whose advice the throne made this sacrifice were the *o-muraji*, Kanamura, and the governor of Mimana, an *omi* called Oshiyama. They went down in the pages of history as corrupt statesmen who, in consideration of bribes from the Kudara Court, surrendered territory which Japan had won by force of arms and held for five centuries.

In the following year (513) the Kudara Court again utilized the services of Oshiyama to procure possession of another district, Imun (Japanese, Komom), which lay on the northeast frontier of Mimana. Kudara falsely represented that this region had been seized by Habe, one of the petty principalities in the peninsula, and the Yamato Court, acting at the counsels of the same *o-muraji* (Kanamura) who had previously espoused

Kudara's cause, credited Kudara's story. This proved an ill-judged policy. It is true that Japan's prestige in the peninsula received signal recognition on the occasion of promulgating the Imperial decree which sanctioned the transfer of the disputed territory. All the parties to the dispute, Kudara, Shiragi, and Habe, were required to send envoys to the Yamato Court for the purpose of hearing the rescript read, and thus Japan's pre-eminence was constructively acknowledged. But her order provoked keen resentment in Shiragi and Habe. The general whom she sent with five hundred warships to escort the Kudara envoys was ignominiously defeated by the men of Habe, while Shiragi seized the opportunity to invade Mimana and to occupy a large area of its territory.

For several years the Yamato Court made no attempt to re-assert itself, but in 527 an expedition of unprecedented magnitude was organized. It consisted of sixty thousand soldiers under the command of Keno no Omi, and its object was to chastise Shiragi and to re-establish Mimana in its original integrity. But here an unforeseeable obstacle presented itself. For all communication with the Korean peninsula, Tsukushi (Kyushu) was an indispensable base, and it happened that, just at this time, Kyushu had for ruler (*miyatsuko*) a nobleman called Iwai, who is said to have long entertained treasonable designs. A knowledge of his mood was conveyed to Shiragi, and tempting proposals were made to him if he could frustrate the expedition under Keno no Omi. Iwai thereupon occupied the four provinces of Higo, Hizen, Bungo, and Buzen, thus effectually placing his hand on the neck of the communications with Korea and preventing the embarkation of Keno no Omi's army. He established a pseudo-Court in Tsukushi and there gave audience to tribute-bearing envoys from Koma, Kudara and Shiragi.

For the space of a year this rebel remained master of the situation, but, in 528 CE, the *o-muraji*, Arakahi, crushed him after a desperate conflict in the province of Chikugo. Iwai effected his escape to Buzen and died by his own hand in a secluded valley. Although, however, this formidable rebellion was thus successfully quelled, the great expedition did not mature. Keno, its intended leader, did indeed proceed to Mimana and assume there the duties of governor, but he proved at once arrogant and incompetent, employing to an extravagant degree the ordeal of boiling water, so that many innocent people suffered fatally, and putting to death children of mixed Korean and Japanese parentage instead of encouraging unions which would have tended to bring the two countries closer together.

In its relations with Korea during this period, Japan showed more loyalty than sagacity. Itwas invariably ready to accede to proposals from Kudara, and the latter, taking astute advantage of this mood, secured Japanese endorsement of territorial transfers which brought to the Yamato Court nothing but the enmity of Kudara's rivals. By these errors of statesmanship and by the misgovernment of officials like Keno, conditions were created which, as will be seen hereafter, proved ultimately fatal to Japan's sway in the peninsula.

While Japan was palpably inferior to its Korean neighbour in civilization, in wealth, and in population, in one respect the superiority was largely on its side; namely, in the quality of Japanese soldiers. As the material development of Japan and its civilization progressed, it was liable to lose more and gain less by despatching expeditions to a land which squandered much of its resources on internecine quarrels and was deteriorating by comparison. The task of maintaining Mimana and succouring Kudara then became an obligation of prestige which gradually ceased to interest the nation.

FINANCE

In the period now under consideration no system of land taxation had yet come into existence. The requirements of the Court were met by the produce of the *mi-agata* (Imperial domains), and rice for public use was grown in the *miyake* districts, being there stored and devoted to the administrative needs of the region. Occasionally the contents of several *miyake* were collected into one district, as, for example, when (536 CE) the Emperor Senkwa ordered a concentration of foodstuffs in Tsukushi. The *miyake* were the property of the Crown, as were also a number of hereditary corporations (*be*), whose members discharged duties, from building and repairing palaces – no light task, seeing that the site of the palace was changed with each change of occupant – to sericulture, weaving, tailoring, cooking, and arts and handicrafts of all descriptions, each *be* exercising its own function from generation to generation, and being superintended by its own head-man (*obito* or *atae*).

Any insufficiency in the supplies furnished by the sovereign's own people was made good by levying on the *tomo-no-miyatsuko*. It will be seen that there was no annual tax regularly imposed on the people in general, though universal requisitions were occasionally made to meet the requirements of public works, festivals or military operations. Doubtless this special feature of

Yamato finance was due in part to the fact that all the land and all the people, except those appertaining to the Crown, were in the possession of the *uji*, without whose co-operation no general fiscal measure could be adopted. When recourse to the nation at large was necessitated to meet some exceptional purpose, orders had to be given, first, to the *o-omi* and *o-muraji*; next, by these to the *Kami* of the several *o-uji*; then, by the latter to the *Kami* of the various *ko-uji*, and, finally, by these last to every household.

The machinery was thorough, but to set it in motion required an effort which constituted an automatic obstacle to extortion. The lands and people of the *uji* were governed by the Emperor but were not directly controlled by him. On the other hand, to refuse a requisition made by the Throne was counted contumelious and liable to punishment. Thus when (534 CE) the Emperor Ankan desired to include a certain area of arable land in a *miyake* established for the purpose of commemorating the name of the Empress, and when Ajihari, suzerain (*atae*) of the region, sought to evade the requisition by misrepresenting the quality of the land, he was reprimanded and had to make atonement by surrendering a portion of his private property.

CRIMINAL LAW

Although the use of the ideographic script became well known from the fifth century, everything goes to show that no written law existed at that time, or, indeed, for many years afterwards. Neither are there any traces of Korean or Chinese influence in this realm. Custom prescribed punishments, and the solemnity of a judicial trial found no better representative than the boiling-water ordeal. If a man took oath to the deities of his innocence and was prepared to thrust his arm into boiling mud or water, or to lay a red-hot axe on the palm of his hand, he was held to have complied with all the requirements. If a man committed a crime, punishment extended to every member of his family. On the other hand, offences might generally be expiated by presenting lands or other valuables to the Throne. As for the duty of executing sentences, it devolved on the *mononobe*, who may be described as the military corporation. Death or exile were common forms of punishment, but degradation was still more frequent. It often meant that a family, noble and opulent to-day, saw all its members handed over to-morrow to be the serfs or slaves of some *uji* in whose be they were enrolled to serve thenceforth, themselves and their children, through all generations in some menial position – it might be as sepulchre-guards, it might be as scullions.

Tattooing on the face was another form of penalty. The first mention of it occurs in 400 CE when Richu condemned the *muraji*, Hamako, to be thus branded, but whether the practice originated then or dated from an earlier period, the annals do not show. It was variously called *hitae-kizamu* (slicing the brow), *me-saku* (splitting the eyes), and so on, but these terms signified nothing worse than tattooing on the forehead or round the eyes. The Emperor Richu deemed that such notoriety was sufficient penalty for high treason, but Yuryaku inflicted tattooing on a man whose dog had killed one of his Majesty's fowls.

Death at the stake appears to have been very uncommon. This terrible form of punishment seems to have been revived by Yuryaku. He caused it to be inflicted on one of the ladies-in-waiting and her paramour, who had forestalled him in the girl's affections. The first instance is mentioned in the annals of the Empress Jingo, but the victim was a Korean and the incident happened in war. To Yuryaku was reserved the infamy of employing such a penalty in the case of a woman. Highly placed personages were often allowed to expiate an offence by performing the religious rite of *harai* (purification), the offender defraying all expenses.

EVERYDAY LIFE

As **Chinese literature** became familiar and as the arts of the Middle Kingdom and Korea were imported into Japan, the latter's customs naturally underwent some changes. Tall buildings, as has been already stated, began to take the place of the partially subterranean *muro*. Apparently the fashion of high buildings was established in the reign of Anko when (456 CE) the term *ro or takadono* (lofty edifice) is, for the first time, applied to the palace of Anko in Yamato. A few years later (468), we find mention of two carpenters, Tsuguno and Mita, who, especially the latter, were famous experts in Korean architecture, and who received orders from Yuryaku to erect high buildings. It appears further that silk curtains (*tsumugi-kaki*) came into use in this age for partitioning rooms, and that a species of straw mat (*tatsu-gomo*) served for carpet when people were hunting, travelling, or campaigning.

While Yuryaku was on the throne, Korea and China sent pictorial experts to Japan. The Korean was named Isuraka, and the Chinese, Shinki. The latter is said to have been a descendant of the Emperor Wen of the Wei dynasty. His work attracted much attention in the reign of Muretsu, who bestowed on him the *uji* title of *Ooka no Obito*. His descendants practised their art with success in Japan, and from the time of the Emperor Tenchi (668–671) they were distinguished as *Yamato no eshi* (painters of Yamato).

If we credit the annals, the composition of poetry commenced in the earliest ages and was developed independently of foreign influences. From the sovereign down to the lowest subject, everyone composed verses. These were not rhymed; the structure of the Japanese language does not lend itself to rhyme. Their differentiation from prose consisted solely in the numerical regularity of the syllables in consecutive lines; the alternation of phrases of five and seven syllables each. A *tanka* (short song) consisted of thirty-one syllables arranged thus, 5, 7, 5, 7, and 7; and a *naga-uta* (long song) consisted of an unlimited number of lines, all fulfilling the same conditions as to number of syllables and alternation of phrases. No parallel to this kind of versification has been found yet in the literature of any other nation.

A favourite pastime during the early historic period was known as *uta-gaki* or *uta-kai*. In cities, in the country, in fields, and on hills, young people assembled in springtime or in autumn and enjoyed themselves by singing and dancing. Promises of marriage were exchanged, the man sending some gifts as a token, and the woman, if her father or elder brother approved, despatching her head-ornament (*oshiki no tamakatsura*) to her lover. On the wedding day it was customary for the bride to present "table-articles" (*tsukue-shiro*) to the bridegroom in the form of food and drink. There were places specially associated in the public mind with *uta-gaki* – Tsukuba Mountain in Hitachi, Kijima-yama in Hizen, and Utagaki-yama in Settsu. Sometimes men of noble birth took part in this pastime, but it was usually confined to the lower middle classes.

FORM OF GOVERNMENT

The original form of government under the Yamato seems to have been feudal. The heads of *uji* were practically feudal chiefs. Even orders from the Throne had to pass through the *uji no Kami* in order to reach the people. But from the time of Nintoku (313–349) to that of Yuryaku (457–479), the Court wielded much power, and the greatest among the *uji* chiefs found no opportunity to interfere with the exercise of the sovereign's rights. Gradually, however, and mainly owing to the intrusion of love affairs or of lust, the Imperial household fell into disorder, which prompted the revolt of Heguri, the *o-omi* of the *Kwobetsu* (Imperial families); a revolt subdued by the loyalty of the *o-muraji* of the *Shimbetsu* (*Kami* families).

From the days of the Emperor Muretsu (499–506), direct heirs to succeed to the sceptre were wanting in more than one instance, and a unique opportunity thus offered for traitrous attempts to gain the throne. There was none. Men's minds were still deeply imbued with the conviction that by the *Tenjin* alone might the Throne be occupied. But with the introduction of Buddhism (552 CE), that conviction received a shock. That the Buddha directed and controlled man's destiny was a doctrine inconsistent with the traditional faith in the divine authority of the "son of heaven." Hence from the sixth century the prestige of the Crown began to decline, and the power of the great *uji* grew to exceed that of the sovereign. During a short period (645–670) the authority of the Throne was reasserted, owing to the adoption of the Tang systems of China; but thereafter the great *Fujiwara-uji* became paramount and practically administered the empire.

It is hard to determine whether the prevailing system was feudal, or prefectural, or a mixture of both. Much depends on a knowledge of the functions discharged by the *kuni-no-miyatsuko*, who were hereditary officials, and the *kuni-no-tsukasa* (or *kokushi*) who were appointed by the Throne. The first mention of *kokushi* is made in the year 374 CE, during the reign of Nintoku, but there can be little doubt that they had existed from an earlier date. They were, however, few in number, whereas the *miyatsuko* were numerous, and this comparison probably furnishes a tolerably just basis for estimating the respective prevalence of the prefectural and the feudal systems. In short, the method of government inaugurated at the foundation of the empire appears to have been essentially feudal in practice, though theoretically no such term was recognized; and at a later period – apparently about the time of Nintoku – when the power of the hereditary *miyatsuko* threatened to grow inconveniently formidable, the device of reasserting the Throne's authority by appointing temporary provincial governors was resorted to, so that the prefectural organization came into existence side by side with the feudal, and the administration preserved this dual form until the middle of the seventh century.

From the time of Nintoku (313–399 CE) until the introduction of Buddhism (552 CE), there were four *uji* whose chiefs participated conspicuously in the government of the country. The first was that of Heguri. It belonged to the Imperial class

(*Kwobetsu*) and was descended from the celebrated Takenouchi-no-Sukune. In the days of the Emperor Muretsu (499–506), the chief of this *uji* attempted to usurp the throne and was crushed. The second was the Otomo. This *uji* belonged to the *Kami* class (*Shimbetsu*) and had for ancestor Michi no Omi, the most distinguished general in the service of the first Emperor Jimmu. The chiefs of the *Otomo-uji* filled the post of general from age to age, and its members guarded the palace gates. During the reign of Yuryaku the office of *o-muraji* was bestowed upon Moroya, then chief of this *uji*. His son, Kanamura, succeeded him. By his sword the rebellion of Heguri no Matori was quelled, and by his advice Keitai was called to the Throne. He served also under Ankan, Senkwa, and Kinmei, but the miscarriage of Japan's relations with Korea was attributed to him, and the title of *o-muraji* was not conferred on any of his descendants.

The *uji* of Mononobe next calls for notice. This *uji* also belonged to the *Kami* class, and its progenitor was Umashimade, who surrendered Yamato to Jimmu on the ground of consanguinity. Thenceforth the members of the *uji* formed the Imperial guards (*uchi-tsu-mononobe*) and its chiefs commanded them. Among all the *uji* of the *Kami* class the Mononobe and the Otomo ranked first, and after the latter's failure in connexion with Korea, the Mononobe stood alone. During the reign of Yuryaku, the *uji*'s chief became *o-muraji*, as did his grandson, Okoshi, and the latter's son, Moriya, was destroyed by the *o-omi*, Soga no Umako, in the tumult on the accession of Sushun (588 CE).

The fourth of the great *uji* was the Soga, descended from Takenouchi-no-Sukune. After the ruin of the Heguri, this *uji* stood at the head of all the Imperial class. In the reign of Senkwa (536–539), Iname, chief of the Soga, was appointed *o-omi*, and his son, Umako, who held the same rank, occupies an important place in connexion with the introduction of Buddhism. It will be observed that among these four *uji*, Heguri and Soga served as civil officials and *Otomo* and *Mononobe* as military.

There are also three other *uji* which figure prominently on the stage of Japanese history. They are the *Nakatomi*, the *Imibe*, and the *Kume*. The *Nakatomi* discharged the functions of religious supplication and divination, standing, for those purposes, between (*Naka*) the Throne and the deities. The *Imibe* had charge of everything relating to religious festivals; an office which required that they should abstain (*imi suru*) from all things unclean. The *Kume* were descended from Amatsu *Kume* no Mikoto, and their duties were to act as chamberlains and as guards of the Court.

Finally, there was the *Oga-uji*, descended from *Okuni*nushi, which makes the eighth of the great *uji*. From the time of the Emperor Jimmu to that of the Empress Suiko (593–628 CE), the nobles who served in ministerial capacities numbered forty and of that total the *Mononobe* furnished sixteen; the *Otomo*, six; the *o-omi* houses (i.e. the *Kwobetsu*), nine; the *Imibe*, one; the *Nakatomi*, six; and the *Oga*, two. Thus, the military *uji* of *Mononobe* and *Otomo* gave to the State twenty-two ministers out of forty during a space of some twelve centuries.

FROM THE REIGN OF KINMEI TO TAKARA, 540–645

It was in this period that the creed of Buddhism, having originated in India, made its way to Japan by way of a Chinese monk. Initially viewed with suspicion, it was not immediately adopted. Only after a great confrontation had taken place between the advocates of the new faith and those who believed it to be an existential threat to traditional Shinto values was Buddhism able to thrive. The glorious religious awakening of Japan embodied in the Seventeen Article Constitution, and even in the diffusion of new types of music and leisure, was contrasted by the disastrous loss of the Korean colony and the subsequent blow to Japan's international prestige.

THE INTRODUCTION OF BUDDHISM

During the reign of the Emperor Ming of the Hou-Han [later Han] dynasty, in the year 65 CE, a mission was sent from China to procure the Buddhist Sutras as well as some teachers of the Indian faith. More than three centuries elapsed before, in the year 372, the creed obtained a footing in Korea; and not for another century and a half did it find its way (522) to Japan. It encountered no obstacles in Korea. The animistic belief of the early Koreans has never been clearly studied, but whatever its exact nature may have been, it certainly evinced no bigotry in the presence of the foreign faith, for within three years of the arrival of the first image of Sakiya Muni in Koma, two large monasteries had been built, and the King and his Court were all converts.

No such reception awaited Buddhism in Japan when, in 522, a Chinese bonze, Shiba Tachito, arrived, erected a temple on the Sakata plain in Yamato, enshrined an image of Buddha there, and endeavoured to propagate the faith. At that time, Wu, the first Emperor of the Liang dynasty in China, was employing all his influence to popularize the Indian creed. Tradition says that Shiba Tachito came from Liang, and in all probability he took the overland route via the Korean peninsula, but the facts are obscure. No sensible impression seems to have been produced in Japan by this missionary. Buddhism was made known to a few, but the Japanese showed no disposition to worship a foreign god. Twenty-three years later (545), the subject attracted attention again. Song Wang Myong, King of Kudara, menaced by a crushing attack on the part of Koma and Shiragi in co-operation, made an image of the Buddha, sixteen feet high, and petitioned the Court of Yamato in the sense that as all good things were promised in the sequel of such an effort, protection should be extended to him by Japan. Tradition says that although Buddhism had not yet secured a footing in Yamato, this image must be regarded as the pioneer of many similar objects subsequently set up in Japanese temples.

Nevertheless, 552 CE is usually spoken of as the date of Buddhism's introduction into Japan. In that year the same

King of Kudara presented direct to the Yamato Court a copper image of Buddha plated with gold; several canopies (*tengai*), and some volumes of the sacred books, by the hands of Tori Shichi (Korean pronunciation, Nori Sachhi) and others. The envoys carried also a memorial which said: "This doctrine is, among all, most excellent. But it is difficult to explain and difficult to understand. Even the Duke Chou and Confucius did not attain to comprehension. It can produce fortune and retribution, immeasurable, illimitable. It can transform a man into a Bodhi. Imagine a treasure capable of satisfying all desires in proportion as it is used. Such a treasure is this wonderful doctrine. Every earnest supplication is fulfilled and nothing is wanting. Moreover, from farthest India to the three Han, all have embraced the doctrine, and there is none that does not receive it with reverence wherever it is preached. Therefore thy servant, Myong, in all sincerity, sends his retainer, Nori Sachhi, to transmit it to the Imperial country, that it may be diffused abroad throughout the home provinces, so as to fulfil the recorded saying of the Buddha, 'My law shall spread to the East.'"

It is highly probable that in the effort to win the Yamato Court to Buddhism, King Myong was influenced as much by political as by moral motives. He sought to use the foreign faith as a link to bind Japan to his country, so that he might count on his oversea neighbour's powerful aid against the attacks of Koma and Shiragi. A more interesting question, however, is the aspect under which the new faith presented itself to the Japanese when it first arrived among them as a rival of Shinto and Confucianism. There can be no doubt that the form in which it became known at the outset was the Hinayana, or

Exoteric, as distinguished from the Mahayana, or Esoteric. But how did the Japanese converts reconcile its acceptance with their allegiance to the traditional faith, Shinto? The clearest available answer to this question is contained in a book called *Taishiden Hochu*, where, in reply to a query from his father, Yomei, who professed inability to believe foreign doctrines at variance with those handed down from the age of the *Kami*, Prince Shotoku is recorded to have replied:

"Your Majesty has considered only one aspect of the matter. I am young and ignorant, but I have carefully studied the teachings of Confucius and the doctrine of the *Kami*. I find that there is a plain distinction. Shinto, since its roots spring from the *Kami*, came into existence simultaneously with the heaven and the earth, and thus expounds the origin of human beings. Confucianism, being a system of moral principles, is coeval with the people and deals with the middle stage of humanity. Buddhism, the fruit of principles, arose when the human intellect matured. It explains the last stage of man. To like or dislike Buddhism without any reason is simply an individual prejudice. Heaven commands us to obey reason. The individual cannot contend against heaven. Recognizing that impossibility, nevertheless to rely on the individual is not the act of a wise man or an intelligent. Whether the Emperor desire to encourage this creed is a matter within his own will. Should he desire to reject it, let him do so; it will arise one generation later. Should he desire to adopt it, let him do so; it will arise one generation earlier. A generation is as one moment in heaven's eyes. Heaven is eternal. The Emperor's reign is limited to a generation; heaven is boundless and illimitable. How can the Emperor struggle against heaven? How can heaven be concerned about a loss of time?"

Shinto taught about the origin of the country but did not deal with the present or the future. Confucianism discusses the present and had no concern with the past or the future. Buddhism, alone, preached about the future. That life ended with the present could not be believed by all. Many men thought of the future, and it was therefore inevitable that many should embrace Buddhism.

But at the moment when the memorial of King Myong was presented to the Emperor Kinmei (540–571 CE), the latter was unprepared to make a definite reply. The image, indeed, he found to be full of dignity, but he left his ministers to decide whether it should be worshipped or not. A division of opinion resulted. The *o-omi*, Iname, of the Soga family, advised that, as Buddhism had won worship from all the nations on the West, Japan should not be singular. But the *o-muraji*, Okoshi, of the *Mononobe-uji*, and Kamako, *muraji* of the *Nakatomi-uji*, counselled that to bow down to foreign deities would be to incur the anger of the national gods. In a word, the civil officials advocated the adoption of the Indian creed; the military and ecclesiastical officials opposed it. That the head of the *Mononobe-uji* should have adopted this attitude was natural: it is always the disposition of soldiers to be conservative, and that is notably true of the Japanese soldier (*bushi*). The *Nakatomi* were the guardians of the Shinto ceremonials: thus, their aversion to the acceptance of a strange faith is explained.

What is to be said, however, of the apparently radical policy of the Soga chief? Why should he have advocated so readily the introduction of a foreign creed? There are two apparent reasons.

One is that the Hata and Aya groups of Korean and Chinese artisans were under the control of the Soga-*uji*, and that the latter were therefore disposed to welcome all innovations coming from the Asiatic continent. The other is that between the *o-muraji* of the *Kami* class (*Shimbetsu*) and the *o-omi* of the Imperial class (*Kwobetsu*) there had existed for some time a political rivalry which began to be acute at about the period of the coming of Buddhism, and which was destined to culminate, forty years later, in a great catastrophe. The Emperor himself steered a middle course. He neither opposed nor approved but entrusted the image to the keeping of the Soga noble, who must have been singularly free from the superstitions of his age, for he not only received the image with pleasure but also enshrined it with all solemnity in his Mukuhara residence, which he converted wholly into a temple.

Very shortly afterwards, however, the country was visited by a pestilence, and the calamity being regarded as an expression of the *Kami*'s resentment, the *o-muraji* of the *Mononobe* and the *muraji* of the *Nakatomi* urged the Emperor to cast out the emblems of a foreign faith. Accordingly, the statue of the Buddha was thrown into the Naniwa canal and the temple was burned to the ground. Necessarily these events sharply accentuated the enmity between the Soga and the *Mononobe*. Twenty-five years passed, however, without any attempt to restore the worship of the Buddha. Iname, the *o-omi* of the Soga, died; Okoshi, the *o-muraji* of the *Mononobe*, died, and they were succeeded in these high offices by their sons, Umako and Moriya, respectively.

When the Emperor Bidatsu ascended the throne in 572 CE, the political stage was practically occupied by these two ministers only; they had no competitors of equal rank. In 577, the King of Kudara made a second attempt to introduce Buddhism into Japan. He sent to the Yamato Court two hundred volumes of sacred books; an ascetic; a yogi (meditative monk); a nun; a reciter of mantras (magic spells); a maker of images, and a temple architect. The annals briefly relate that ultimately a temple was built for the new-comers in Naniwa (modern Osaka). Two years later, Shiragi also sent a Buddhist eidolon, and in 584 – just sixty-two years after the coming of Shiba Tachito from Liang and thirty-two years after Soga no Iname's attempt to popularize the Indian faith – two Japanese high officials returned from Korea, carrying with them a bronze image of Buddha and a stone image of Miroku (the Sanskrit Maitreya, the expected Messiah of the Buddhist).

These two images were handed over, at his request, to the *o-omi*, Umako, who had inherited his father's ideas about Buddhism. He invited Shiba Tachito, then a village mayor, to accompany one Hida on a search throughout the provinces for Buddhist devotees. They found a man called Eben, a Korean who had originally been a priest, and he, having resumed the stole, consecrated the twelve-year-old daughter of Shiba Tachito, together with two other girls, as nuns. The *o-omi* now built a temple, where the image of Miroku was enshrined, and a pagoda on the top of whose central pillar was deposited a Buddhist relic which had shown miraculous powers.

Again the old superstitions prevailed. The plague of small-pox broke out once more. This fell disease had been carried from Cochin China by the troops of General Ma Yuan during the Han dynasty, and it reached Japan almost simultaneously with the importation of Buddhism. The physicians of the East had no skill in treating it, and its ravages were terrible, those that escaped with their lives having generally to lament the loss of their eyes. So soon as the malady made its second appearance in the immediate sequel of the new honours paid to Buddhism, men began to cry out that the *Kami* were punishing the nation's apostasy, and the *o-muraji*, Moriya, urged the Emperor (Bidatsu) to authorize the suppression of the alien religion. Bidatsu, who at heart had always been hostile to the innovation, consented readily, and the pagoda and the temple were razed and burned. But the ravages of the pestilence now grew more unsparing. The Emperor himself, as well as the *o-omi*, Umako, were attacked, and now the popular outcry took another tone: men ascribed the plague to the wrath of Buddha. Umako, in turn, pleaded with the Emperor, and was permitted to rebuild the temple and reinstate the nuns, on condition that no efforts were made to proselytize.

Thus Buddhism recovered its footing, but the enmity between the *o-muraji* and the *o-omi* grew more implacable than ever. They insulted each other, even at the obsequies of the sovereign, and an occasion alone was needed to convert their anger into an appeal to arms.

SUCCESSION DISPUTES

When the Emperor Bidatsu died (585 CE) no nomination of a Prince Imperial had taken place, and the feud known to exist between the *o-omi* and the *o-muraji* increased the danger of the situation.

Umako, the great *uji* of Soga was closely related to all the Imperial personages who figured prominently on the stage at this period of Japanese history. The Emperor Kinmei was his elder brother-in-law. The Emperors Yomei, Bidatsu and Sushun were his nephews. The Empress Suiko was his niece of Umako. Prince Shotoku was his son-in-law and Prince Anahobe was a nephew.

The Thirty-First Emperor Yomei

The Emperor Yomei (585–87) was the fourth son of the Emperor Kinmei and a nephew of the *o-omi*, Umako. The *Chronicles* say that he "believed in the law of Buddha and reverenced Shinto". Yomei's accession was opposed by his younger brother, Prince Anahobe, who had the support of the *o-muraji*, Moriya; but the Soga influence was exerted in Yomei's behalf. Anahobe did not suffer his discomfiture patiently. He attempted to procure admission to the mourning chamber of the deceased Emperor for some unexplained purpose, and being resisted by Miwa Sako, who commanded the palace guards, he laid a formal complaint before the *o-omi* and the *o-muraji*. In the sequel Sako was killed by the troops of the *o-muraji*, though he merited rather the latter's protection as a brave soldier who had merely done his duty, who opposed Buddhism, and who enjoyed the confidence of the Empress Dowager. To Umako, predicting that this deed of undeserved violence would prove the beginning of serious trouble, Moriya insultingly retorted that small-minded men did not understand such matters. Moriya's mind was of the rough military type. He did not fathom the subtle unscrupulous intellect of an adversary like Umako, and was destined to learn the truth by a bitter process.

Umayado, eldest son of the Emperor Yomei, is one of the most distinguished figures in the annals of Japan. He has been well called "the Constantine of Buddhism." From his earliest youth he evinced a remarkable disposition for study. A learned man was invited from China to teach him the classics, and priests were brought from Koma to expound the doctrine of Buddhism, in which faith he ultimately became a profound believer. In fact, to his influence, more than to any other single factor, may be ascribed the final adoption of the Indian creed by Japan. He never actually ascended the throne, but as regent under the Empress Suiko he wielded Imperial authority. In history he is known as Shotoku Taishi (Prince Shotoku).

In the second year of his reign, the Emperor Yomei was seized with the malady which had killed his father. In his extremity he desired to be received into the Buddhist faith to which he had always inclined, and he ordered the leading officials to consider the matter. A council was held. Moriya, *o-muraji* of the *Mononobe*, and Katsumi, *muraji* of the *Nakatomi*, objected resolutely. They asked why the *Kami* of the country should be abandoned in a moment of crisis. But Umako, *o-omi* of the Soga, said: "It is our duty to obey the Imperial commands and to give relief to his Majesty. Who will dare to suggest contumely?" Buddhist priests were then summoned to the palace. It was a moment of extreme tension. Prince Umayado (Shotoku) grasped the hands of the *o-omi* and exclaimed, "If the minister had not believed in Buddhism, who would have ventured to give such counsel?" Umako's answer is said to have been: "Your Imperial Highness will work for the propagation of the faith. I, a humble subject, will maintain it to the death." Moriya, the *o-muraji*, made no attempt to hide his resentment, withdrawing to a safe place and there concentrating his forcesth. Meanwhile the Emperor's malady ended fatally. His reign had lasted only one year. At the point of death he was comforted by an assurance that the son of Shiba Tachito would renounce the world to revere his Majesty's memory and would make an image of the Buddha sixteen feet high.

Buddhism had now gained a firm footing at the Yamato Court, but its opponents were still active. Their leader, the o-muraji, thought that his best chance of success was to contrive the accession of Prince Anahobe, whose attempt to take precedence of his elder brother, the Emperor Yomei, has been already noted. The conspiracy was discovered, and the Soga forces, acting under the nominal authority of the deceased Emperor's consort, Umako's niece, moved against Anahobe and Moriya, who had not been able to combine their strength. The destruction of Prince Anahobe was easily effected, but the work of dealing with the o-muraji taxed the resources of the Soga to the utmost. Moriya himself ascended a tree and by skill of archery held his assailants long at bay. Archery had been practised assiduously by the Yamato warrior from time immemorial, and arrows possessing remarkable power of penetration had been devised. There was an archery hall within the enclosure of the palace; whenever envoys or functionaries from foreign countries visited Yamato they were invited to shoot there; frequent trials of skill took place, and when oversea sovereigns applied for military aid, it was not unusual to send some bundles of arrows in lieu of soldiers.

Thus, the general of the Mononobe, perched among the branches of a tree, with an unlimited supply of shafts and with highly trained skill as a bowman, was a formidable adversary.

Moriya and his large following of born soldiers drove back the Soga forces three times. Success seemed to be in sight for the champion of the *Kami*. At this desperate stage Prince Shotoku – then a lad of sixteen – fastened to his helmet images of the "Four Guardian Kings of Heaven" and vowed to build a temple in their honour if victory was vouchsafed to his arms. At the same time, the *o-omi*, Umako, took oath to dedicate temples and propagate Buddhism. The combat had now assumed a distinctly religious character. Shotoku and Umako advanced again to the attack; Moriya was shot down; his family and followers fled, were put to the sword or sent into slavery, and all his property was confiscated.

An incident of this campaign illustrates the character of the Japanese soldier as revealed in the pages of subsequent history: a character whose prominent traits were dauntless courage and romantic sympathy. Yorozu, a dependent of the *o-muraji*, was reduced to the last straits after a desperate fight. The *Chronicles* say: "Then he took the sword which he wore, cut his bow into three pieces, and bending his sword, flung it into the river. With a dagger which he had besides, he stabbed himself in the throat and died. The governor of Kawachi having reported the circumstances of Yorozu's death to the Court, the latter gave an order that his body should be cut into eight pieces and distributed among the eight provinces." In accordance with this order the governor was about to dismember the corpse when thunder pealed and a great rain fell. "Now there was a white dog which had been kept by Yorozu. Looking up and looking down, it went round, howling beside the body, and at last, taking up the head in its mouth, it placed it on an ancient mound, lay down close by, and starved to death. When this was reported to the Court, the latter, moved by profound pity, issued an order that the dog's conduct should be handed down to after ages, and that the kindred of Yorozu should be allowed to construct a tomb and bury his remains." After order had been restored, Prince Shotoku fulfilled his vow by building in the province of Settsu a temple dedicated to the Four Guardian Kings of Heaven (*Shitenno-ji*), and by way of endowment there were handed over to it one-half of the servants of the *o-muraji*, together with his house and a quantity of other property.

The Thirty-Second Emperor Sushun

The deaths of Prince Anahobe and Moriya left the Government completely in the hands of Soga no Umako. There was no *o-muraji*; the *o-omi* was supreme. At his instance the crown was placed upon the head of his youngest nephew, Sushun. But Sushun entertained no friendship for Umako nor any feeling of gratitude for the latter's action in contriving his succession to the throne. Active, daring, and astute, he judged the *o-omi* to be swayed solely by personal ambition, and he placed no faith in the sincerity of the great official's Buddhist propaganda. Meanwhile, the fortunes of the new faith prospered. When the dying Emperor, Yomei, asked to be qualified for Nirvana, priests were summoned from Kudara. They came in 588, the first year of Sushun's reign (588–92), carrying relics (*sarira*), and they were accompanied by ascetics, temple-architects, metal-founders, potters, and a pictorial artist.

The Indian creed now began to present itself to the Japanese people, not merely as a vehicle for securing insensibility to suffering in this life and happiness in the next, but also as a great protagonist of refined progress, gorgeous in paraphernalia, impressive in rites, eminently practical in teachings, and substituting a vivid rainbow of positive hope for the negative pallor of Shinto. Men began to adopt the stole; women to take the veil, and people to visit the hills in search of timbers suited for the frames of massive temples. Soga no Umako, the ostensible leader of this great movement, grew more and more arrogant and arbitrary. The youthful Emperor confided in Prince Shotoku, avowing his aversion to the *o-omi* and his uncontrollable desire to be freed from the incubus of such a minister. Shotoku counselled patience, but Sushun was impetuous.

A Court lady betrayed his designs to the *o-omi*, and the latter decided that the Emperor must be destroyed. An assassin was found in the person of Koma, a naturalized Chinese, suzerain of the *Aya uji*, and, being introduced into the palace by the *o-omi* under pretence of offering textile fabrics from the eastern provinces, he killed the Emperor. So omnipotent was the Soga chief that his murderous envoy was not even questioned. He received open thanks from his employer and might have risen to high office had he not debauched a daughter of the *o-omi*. Then Umako caused him to be hung from a tree and made a target of his body, charging him with having taken the Emperor's life. The unfortunate Sushun was interred on the day of his murder, an extreme indignity, yet no one ventured to protest; and even Prince Shotoku, while predicting that the assassin would ultimately suffer retribution, justified the assassination on the ground that previous misdeeds had deserved it.

Sushun was doomed from the moment of his accession. His elder brother had perished at the hands of Umako's troops, and if he himself did not meet the same fate, absence of plausible pretext alone saved him. To suffer him to reign, harbouring, as he must have harboured, bitter resentment against his brother's slayer, would have been a weakness inconsistent with Umako's character. Sushun was placed on the throne as a concession to appearance, but, at the same time, he was surrounded with creatures of the *o-omi*, so that the latter had constant cognizance of the sovereign's every word and act.

The very indignity done to Sushun's remains testifies the thoroughness of the Soga plot. It has been shown that in early days the erection of a tomb for an Imperial personage was a heavy task, involving much time and labour. Pending the completion of the work, the corpse was put into a coffin and guarded day and night, for which purpose a separate palace was erected. When the sepulchre had been fully prepared, the remains were transferred thither with elaborate ceremonials, and the tomb was thenceforth under the care of guardians (*rioko*).

All these observances were dispensed with in the case of the Emperor Sushun. His remains did not receive even the measure of respect that would have been paid to the corpse of the commonest among his subjects. Nothing could indicate more vividly the omnipotence of the *o-omi*; everything had been prepared so that his partisans could bury the body almost before it was cold. Had Prince Shotoku protested, he would have been guilty of the futility described by a Chinese proverb as "spitting at the sky." Besides, Shotoku and Umako were allies otherwise. The Soga minister, in his struggle with the military party, had needed the assistance of Shotoku, and had secured it by community of allegiance to Buddhism. The prince, in his projected struggle against the *uji* system, needed the assistance of Buddhist disciples in general, and in his effort to reach the throne, needed the assistance of Umako in particular. In short, he was building the edifice of a great reform, and to have pitted himself, at the age of nineteen, against the mature strength of the *o-omi* would have been to perish on the threshold of his purpose.

The Thirty-Third Empress Suiko

By the contrivance of Umako, the consort of the Emperor Bidatsu was now placed on the throne (593–628), Prince Shotoku being nominated Prince Imperial and regent. The Soga-*uji* held absolute power in every department of State affairs.

One of the most remarkable documents in Japanese annals is the *Jushichi Kempo*, or *Seventeen-Article Constitution*, compiled by Shotoku Taishi in 604 CE. It is commonly spoken of as the first written law of Japan. But it is not a body of laws in the proper sense of the term. There are no penal provisions, nor is there any evidence of promulgation with Imperial sanction. The seventeen articles are simply moral maxims, based on the teachings of Buddhism and Confucianism, and appealing to the sanctions of conscience. Prince Shotoku, in his capacity of regent, compiled them and issued them to officials in the guise of "instructions."

I. Harmony is to be valued, and the avoidance of wanton opposition honoured. All men are swayed by class feeling and few are intelligent. Hence some disobey their lords and fathers or maintain feuds with neighbouring villages. But when the high are harmonious and the low friendly, and when there is concord in the discussion of affairs, right views spontaneously find acceptance. What is there that cannot be then accomplished?

II. Reverence sincerely the Three Treasures – Buddha, the Law, and the Priesthood – for these are the final refuge of the

Four Generated Beings (beings produced in transmigration by the four processes of being born from eggs, from a womb, from fermentation, or from metamorphosis) and the supreme objects of faith in all countries. What man in what age can fail to revere this law? Few are utterly bad: they may be taught to follow it. But if they turn not to the Three Treasures, wherewithal shall their crookedness be made straight?

III. When you receive the Imperial Commands fail not to obey scrupulously. The lord is Heaven; the vassal, Earth. Heaven overspreads; Earth upbears. When this is so, the four seasons follow their due course, and the powers of Nature develop their efficiency. If the Earth attempt to overspread, Heaven falls in ruin. Hence when the lord speaks, the vassal hearkens; when the superior acts, the inferior yields compliance. When, therefore, you receive an Imperial Command, fail not to carry it out scrupulously. If there be want or care in this respect, a catastrophe naturally ensues.

IV. Ministers and functionaries should make decorous behavior their guiding principle, for decorous behavior is the main factor in governing the people. If superiors do not behave with decorum, inferiors are disorderly; if inferiors are wanting in proper behaviour, offences are inevitable. Thus it is that when lord and vassal behave with propriety, the distinctions of rank are not confused; and when the people behave with propriety, the government of the State proceeds of itself.

V. Refraining from gluttony and abandoning covetous desires, deal impartially with the suits brought before you. Of complaints preferred by the people there are a thousand in one day: how many, then, will there be in a series of years? Should he that decides suits at law make gain his ordinary motive and hear causes with a view to receiving bribes, then will the suits of the rich man be like a stone flung into water, while the plaints of the poor will resemble water cast on a stone. In such circumstances, the poor man will not know whither to betake himself, and the duty of a minister will not be discharged.

VI. Chastise that which is evil and encourage that which is good. This was the excellent rule of antiquity. Conceal not, therefore, the good qualities of others, and fail not to correct that which is wrong when you see it. Flatterers and deceivers are a sharp weapon for the overthrow of the State, and a pointed sword for the destruction of the people. Sycophants are also fond, when they meet, of dilating to their superiors on the errors of their inferiors; to their inferiors, they censure the faults of their superiors. Men of this kind are all wanting in fidelity to their lord, and in benevolence towards the people. From such an origin great civil disturbances arise.

VII. Let every man have his own charge, and let not the spheres of duty be confused. When wise men are entrusted with office, the sound of praise arises. If unprincipled men hold office, disasters and tumults are multiplied. In this world, few are born with knowledge: wisdom is the product of earnest meditation. In all things, whether great or small, find the right man, and they will surely be well managed: on all occasions, be they urgent or the reverse, meet with but a wise man and they will of themselves be amenable. In this way will the State be eternal and the Temples of the Earth and of Grain [the Imperial House] will be free from danger. Therefore did the wise sovereigns of antiquity seek the man to fill the office, and not the office for the sake of the man.

VIII. Let the ministers and functionaries attend the Court early in the morning, and retire late. The business of the State does not admit of remissness, and the whole day is hardly enough for its accomplishment. If, therefore, the attendance at Court is late, emergencies cannot be met: if officials retire soon, the work cannot be completed.

IX. Good faith is the foundation of right. In everything let there be good faith, for in it there surely consists the good and the bad, success and failure. If the lord and the vassal observe good faith one with another, what is there which cannot be accomplished? If the lord and the vassal do not observe good faith towards one another, everything without exception ends in failure.

X. Let us cease from wrath, and refrain from angry looks. Nor let us be resentful when others differ from us. For all men have hearts, and each heart has its own leanings. Their right is our wrong, and our right is their wrong. We are not unquestionably sages nor are they unquestionably fools. Both of us are simply ordinary men. How can anyone lay down a rule by which to distinguish right from wrong? For we are all, one with another, wise and foolish like a ring which has no end. Therefore, although others give way to anger, let us, on the contrary, dread our own faults, and though we alone may be in the right, let us follow the multitude and act like them.

XI. Give clear appreciation to merit and demerit, and deal out to each its sure reward or punishment. In these days, reward does not attend upon merit, nor punishment upon crime. Ye high functionaries who have charge of public affairs, let it be your task to make clear rewards and punishments.

XII. Let not the provincial authorities or the *kuni no miyatsuko* levy exactions on the people. In a country there are not two lords; the people have not two masters. The sovereign is the master of the people of the whole country. The officials to whom he gives charge are all his vassals. How can they, as well as the Government, presume to levy taxes on the people?

XIII. Let all persons entrusted with office attend equally to their functions. Owing to illness or despatch on missions their work may sometimes be neglected. But whenever they are able to attend to business, let them be as accommodating as though they had cognizance of it from before, and let them not hinder public affairs on the score of not having had to do with them.

XIV. Ministers and functionaries, be not envious. If we envy others, they, in turn, will envy us. The evils of envy know no limit. If others excel us in intelligence, it gives us no pleasure; if they surpass us in ability, we are envious. Therefore it is not until after the lapse of five hundred years that we at last meet with a wise man, and even in a thousand years we hardly obtain one sage. But if wise men and sages be not found, how shall the country be governed?

XV. To turn away from that which is private and to set one's face towards that which is public this is the path of a minister. If a man is influenced by private motives, he will assuredly feel resentment; if he is influenced by resentment, he will assuredly fail to act harmoniously with others; if he fails to act harmoniously with others, he will assuredly sacrifice the public interest to his private feelings. When resentment arises, it interferes with order and is subversive of law. Therefore, in the first clause it was said that superiors and inferiors should agree together. The purport is the same as this.

XVI. Let the employment of the people in forced labour be at seasonable times. This is an ancient and excellent rule. Let them be employed, therefore, in the winter months when they have leisure. But from spring to autumn, when they are engaged in agriculture or with the mulberry trees, the people should not be employed. For if they do not attend to agriculture, what will they have to eat? If they do not attend to the mulberry trees, what will they do for clothing?

XVII. Decisions on important matters should not be rendered by one person alone: they should be discussed by many. But small matters being of less consequence, need not be consulted about by a number of people. It is only in the discussion of weighty affairs, when there is an apprehension of miscarriage, that matters should be arranged in concert with others so as to arrive at the right conclusion.

With the exception of the doctrine of expediency, enunciated at the close of the tenth article, the code of Shotoku might be taken for guide by any community in any age. The political purport of his code is more remarkable. In the whole seventeen articles there is nothing to inculcate worship of the *Kami* or observance of Shinto rites. Again, whereas, according to the Japanese creed, the sovereign power is derived from the Imperial ancestor, the latter is nowhere alluded to. The seventh article makes the eternity of the State and the security of the Imperial house depend upon wise administration by well-selected officials, but says nothing of hereditary rights. How is such a vital *omission* to be interpreted, except on the supposition that Shotoku, who had witnessed the worst abuses incidental to the hereditary system of the *uji*, intended by this code to enter a solemn protest against that system?

Further, the importance attached to the people is a very prominent feature of the code, amounting to a distinct condemnation of the *uji* system, under which the only people directly subject to the sovereign were those of the *minashiro*, and those who had been naturalized or otherwise specially assigned, all the rest being practically the property of the *uji*, and the only lands paying direct taxes to the Throne were the domains of the *miyake*.

Forty-two years later (646 CE), the abolition of private property in persons and lands was destined to become the policy of the State, but its foundations seem to have been laid in Shotoku's time. It would be an error to suppose that the neglect of Shinto suggested by the above code was by any means a distinct feature of the era, or even a practice of the prince himself. In fact, Shotoku, for all his enthusiasm in the cause of Buddhism, seems to have shrunk from anything like bigoted exclusiveness. He is quoted as saying: "The management of State affairs cannot be achieved unless it is based on knowledge, and the sources of knowledge are Confucianism, Buddhism, and Shinto."

Prince Shotoku died in the year 621. The *Records* do not relate anything of his illness: they say merely that he foresaw the day and hour of his own death. The last months of Shotoku's life were devoted to compiling, in concert with the *o-omi* Umako, "a history of the Emperors; a history of the country, and the original record of the *omi*, the *muraji*, the *tomo no miyatsuko*, the *kuni no miyatsuko*, the 180 *be*, and the free subjects." This, the first Japanese historical work, known as the *Kujihongi*, was completed in the year 620.

Shotoku's name is further connected with calendar making, though no particulars of his work in that line are on record. Japanese historians speak of him as the father of his country's civilization. They say that he breathed life into the nation; that he raised the status of the empire; that he laid the foundations of Japanese learning; that he fixed the laws of decorum; that he imparted a new character to foreign relations, and that he was an incarnation of the Buddha, specially sent to convert Japan.

THE SPREAD OF JAPANESE BUDDHISM

The roots of Japanese Buddhism were watered with blood, as have been the roots of so many religions in so many countries. From the day of the destruction of the military party under the *o-muraji* Moriya, the foreign faith flourished. Then – as has been shown – were built the first two great temples, and then, for the first time, a Buddhist place of worship was endowed with rich estates and an ample number of serfs to till them. Thenceforth the annals abound with references to the advent of Buddhist priests from Korea, bearing relics or images. The *omi* and the *muraji* vied with each other in erecting shrines, and in 605, we find the Empress Suiko commanding all high dignitaries of State to make 16-foot images of copper and of embroidery. Buddhist festivals were instituted in 606, and their magnificence, as compared with the extreme simplicity of the Shinto rites, must have deeply impressed the people.

In a few decades Buddhism became a great social power, and since its priests and nuns were outside the sphere of ordinary administration, the question of their control soon presented itself. It became pressing in 623 when a priest killed his grandfather with an axe. The Empress Suiko, who was then on the throne, would have subjected the whole body of priests and nuns to judicial examination, a terrible ordeal in those days of torture; but at the instance of a Korean priest, officials corresponding to bishops (*sojo*), high priests (*sozu*) and abbots (*hotto*) were appointed from the ranks of Buddhism, and the duty of prescribing law and order was entrusted to them. This involved registration of all the priesthood, and it was thus found (623) that the temples numbered 46; the priests 816, and the nuns 569.

Buddhism obtained a firm footing among the upper classes during the first century after its introduction but the mass of the people remained, for the most part, outside the pale. They continued to believe in the *Kami* and to worship them. Thus, when a terribly destructive earthquake occured in 599, it was to the *Kami* of earthquakes that prayers were offered at his seven shrines in the seven home provinces (Kinai), and not to the Merciful Buddha, though the saving grace of the latter had then been preached for nearly a cycle. The first appeal to the foreign deity in connexion with natural calamity was in the opening year (642) of the Empress Kogyoku's reign when, in the presence of a devastating drought, an imposing Buddhist service was held in the south court of the Great Temple. But there was no success; and not until the Empress herself had made a progress to the source of a river and worshipped towards the four quarters, did abundant rain fall.

The people at large adhered to their traditional cult and were easily swayed by superstitions. The first half of the seventh century was marked by abnormal occurrences well calculated to disturb men's minds. There were comets (twice); there was a meteor of large dimensions; there were eclipses of the sun and moon; there were occultations of Venus; there was snow in July and hail "as large as peaches" in May, and there was a famine

(621) when old people ate roots of herbs and died by the wayside, when infants at the breast perished with their mothers, and when thieves and robbers defied authority. It is not, perhaps, surprising in such circumstances, and when witches and wizards abounded, that people fell into strange moods, and were persuaded to regard a caterpillar as the "insect of the everlasting world," to worship it, and to throw away their valuables in the belief that riches and perpetual youth would be thus won.

INTERCOURSE WITH CHINA

The *Records* show that in the year 540 CE, during the reign of Kinmei, immigrants from Tsin and Han were assembled and registered, when their number was found to be 7053 households. It was in 552 CE, during the reign of this same Kinmei, that Buddhism may be said to have found a home in Japan. China was then under the sceptre of the Liang dynasty, whose first sovereign, Wu, had been such an enthusiastic Buddhist that he abandoned the throne for a monastery. Yet China took no direct part in introducing the Indian faith to Japan, nor does it appear that from the fourth century CE down to the days of Shotoku Taishi, Japan thought seriously of having recourse to China as the fountain-head of the arts, the crafts, the literature, and the moral codes which she borrowed during the period from Korea.

Something of this want of enterprise may have been attributable to the unsettled state of China's domestic politics; something to the well-nigh perpetual troubles between Japan and Korea – troubles which not only taxed Japan's resources but also blocked the sole route by which China was then accessible, namely, the route through Korea. But when the Sui dynasty (589–619 CE) came to the Chinese throne, its founder, the Emperor Wen, on the one hand, devoted himself to encouraging literature and commerce; and on the other, threw Korea and Japan into a ferment by invading the former country at the head of a huge army. This happened when Shotoku Taishi was in his sixteenth year, and though the great expedition proved abortive, it brought China into vivid prominence, and when news reached Japan of extensions of the Middle Kingdom's territories under Wen's successor, the Japanese Crown Prince determined to open direct intercourse with the Sui Court; not only for literary and religious purposes, but also to study the form of civilization which the whole Orient then revered. This resolve found practical expression in the year 607, when the *omi* Imoko was sent as envoy to the Sui Court, a Chinese of the Saddlers' Corporation, by name Fukuri, being attached to him in the capacity of interpreter. China received these men hospitably and sent an envoy of her own, with a suite of twelve persons, to the Yamato sovereign in the following year.

The annals contain an instructive description of the ceremony connected with the reception of this envoy in Japan. He was met in Tsukushi (Kyushu) by commissioners of welcome, and was conducted thence by sea to Naniwa (now Osaka), where, at the mouth of the river, thirty "gaily-decked" boats awaited him, and he and his suite were conducted to a residence newly built for the occasion. Six weeks later they entered the capital, after a message of welcome had been delivered to them by a *muraji*. Seventy-five fully caparisoned horses were placed at their disposal, and after a further rest of nine days, the envoy's official audience took place. He did not see the Empress' face.

Her Majesty was secluded in the hall of audience to which only the principal ministers were admitted. Hence the ceremony may be said to have taken place in the court-yard. There the gifts brought by the envoy were ranged, and the envoy himself, introduced by two high officials, advanced to the front of the court, made obeisance twice, and, kneeling, declared the purport of his mission. The despatch carried by him ran as follows:

"The Emperor greets the sovereign of Wa.[Japan] Your envoy and his suite have arrived and have given us full information. We, by the grace of heaven, rule over the universe. It is Our desire to diffuse abroad our civilizing influence so as to cover all living things, and Our sentiment of loving nurture knows no distinction of distance. Now We learn that Your Majesty, dwelling separately beyond the sea, bestows the blessings of peace on Your subjects; that there is tranquillity within Your borders, and that the customs and manners are mild. With the most profound loyalty You have sent Us tribute from afar, and We are delighted at this admirable token of Your sincerity. Our health is as usual, notwithstanding the increasing heat of the weather. Therefore We have sent Pei Shieh-ching, Official Entertainer of the Department charged with the Ceremonial for the Reception of Foreign Ambassadors, and his suite, to notify to you the preceding. We also transmit to you the products of which a list is given separately."

The haughty condescension of the Chinese despatch does not appear to have offended the Japanese – China's greatness seems to have been fully recognized. When, a month later, the envoy took his departure, the same Imoko was deputed to accompany him, bearing a despatch which answered China's grandiloquent prolixity with half a dozen brief lines.

RANKS AND HIERARCHY IN JAPAN

It will be recognized by considering the *uji* system that while many titles existed in Japan, there was practically no promotion. A man might be raised to *uji* rank. Several instances of that kind have been noted, especially in the case of foreign artists or artisans migrating to the island from Korea or China. But nothing higher was within reach, and for the hereditary *Kami* of an *uji* no reward offered except a gift of land, whatever services he might render to the State. Such a system could not but tend to perfunctoriness in the discharge of duty. Perception of this defect induced the regent, Shotoku, to import from China (603 CE) the method of official promotion in vogue under the Sui dynasty and to employ caps as insignia of rank. Twelve of such grades were instituted, and the terminology applied to them was based on the names of six moral qualities – virtue, benevolence, propriety, faith, justice, and knowledge – each comprising two degrees, "greater" and "lesser." The caps were made of sarcenet, a distinctive colour for each grade, the cap being gathered upon the crown in the shape of a bag with a border attached. The three highest ranks of all were not included in this category.

THE EMPEROR JOMEI AND THE EMPRESS KOGYOKU

In the year 626, the omnipotent Soga chief, the *o-omi* Umako, died. His office of *o-omi* was conferred on his son, Emishi, who behaved with even greater arrogance and arbitrariness than his father had shown. The Empress Suiko died in 628, and the question of the accession at once became acute. Two princes were eligible; Tamura, grandson of the Emperor Bidatsu, and Yamashiro, son of Shotoku Taishi. Prince Yamashiro was a calm, virtuous, and faithful man. He stated explicitly that the Empress, on the eve of her demise, had nominated him to be her successor. But Prince Tamura had the support of the *o-omi*, Emishi, whose daughter he admired. No one ventured to oppose the will of the Soga chieftain except Sakaibe no Marise, and he with his son were ruthlessly slain by the orders of the *o-omi*.

Prince Tamura then (629) ascended the throne – he is known in history as Jomei (629–41) – but Soga no Emishi virtually ruled the empire. Jomei died in 641, after a reign of twelve years, and by the contrivance of Emishi the sceptre was placed in the hands of an Empress, Kogyoku (642–45), a great-granddaughter of the Emperor Bidatsu, the claims of the son of Shotoku Taishi being again ignored. One of the first acts of the new sovereign was to raise Emishi to the rank held by his father, the rank of *o-omi*, and there then came into prominence Emishi's son, Iruka, who soon wielded power greater than even that possessed by his father. Iruka's administration, however, does not appear to have been altogether unwholesome. The *Chronicles* say that "thieves and robbers were in dread of him, and that things dropped on the highway were not picked up." But Emishi rendered himself conspicuous chiefly by aping Imperial state. He erected an ancestral temple; organized performances of a Chinese dance (*yatsura*) which was essentially an Imperial pageant; levied imposts on the people at large for the construction of tombs – one for himself, another for his son, Iruka – which were openly designated *misasagi* (Imperial sepulchres); called his private residence *mikado* (sacred gate); conferred on his children the title of *miko* (august child), and exacted forced labour from all the people of the Kamutsumiya estate, which belonged to the Shotoku family.

This last outrage provoked a remonstrance from Shotoku Taishi's daughter, and she was thenceforth reckoned among the enemies of the Soga. One year later (643), this feud ended in bloodshed. Emishi's usurpation of Imperial authority was carried so far that he did not hesitate to confer the rank of *o-omi* on his son, Iruka, and upon the latter's younger brother also. Iruka now conceived the design of placing upon the throne Prince Furubito, a son of the Emperor Jomei. It will be remembered that the Soga chief, Emishi, had lent his omnipotent influence to secure the sceptre for Jomei, because of the latter's affection for Emishi's daughter. This lady, having become one of Jomei's consorts, had borne to him Prince Furubito, who was consequently Iruka's uncle. Iruka determined that the prince should succeed the Empress Kogyoku. To that end it was necessary to remove the Shotoku family, against which, as shown above, the Soga had also a special grudge. Not even the form of devising a protest was observed. Orders were simply issued to a military force that the Shotoku house should be extirpated. Its representative was Prince Yamashiro, the same who had effaced himself so magnanimously at the time of Jomei's accession. He behaved with ever greater nobility on this occasion. Having by a ruse escaped from the Soga troops, he was urged by his followers to flee to the eastern provinces, and there raising an army, to march back to the attack of the Soga.

There is reason to think that this policy would have succeeded. But the prince replied: "I do not wish it to be said by after generations that, for my sake, anyone has mourned the loss of a father or a mother. Is it only when one has conquered in battle that one is to be called a hero? Is he not also a hero who has made firm his country at the expense of his own life?" He then returned to the temple at Ikaruga, which his father had built, and being presently besieged there by the Soga forces, he and the members of his family, twenty-three in all, committed suicide. This tragedy shocked even Emishi. He warned Iruka against the peril of such extreme measures.

There now appears a statesman destined to leave his name indelibly written on the pages of Japanese history, Kamatari, *muraji* of the *Nakatomi-uji*. The *Nakatomi*'s functions were specially connected with Shinto rites, and Kamatari must be supposed to have entertained little good-will towards the Soga, who were the leaders of the Buddhist faction, and whose feud with the military party sixty-seven years previously had involved the violent death of Katsumi, then (587) *muraji* of the *Nakatomi*. Moreover, Kamatari makes his first appearance in the annals as chief Shinto official. Nevertheless, it is not apparent that religious zeal or personal resentment was primarily responsible for Kamatari's determination to compass the ruin of the Soga. Essentially an upright man and a loyal subject, he seems to have been inspired by a frank resolve to protect the Throne against schemes of lawless ambitions, unconscious that his own family, the *Fuji*wara, were destined to repeat on a still larger scale the same abuses.

The succession may be said to have had three aspirants at that time: first, Prince Karu, younger brother of the Empress Kogyoku; secondly, Prince Naka, her son, and thirdly, Prince Furubito, uncle of Soga no Iruka. The last was, of course, excluded from Kamatari's calculations, and as between the first two he judged it wiser that Prince Karu should have precedence in the succession, Prince Naka not being old enough. The conspiracy that ensued presents no specially remarkable feature. Kamatari and Prince Naka became acquainted through an incident at the game of football, when the prince, having accidently kicked off his shoe, Kamatari picked it up and restored it to him on bended knee. The two men, in order to find secret opportunities for maturing their plans, became fellow students of the doctrines of Chow and Confucius under the priest Shoan, who had been among the eight students that accompanied the Sui envoy on his return to China in the year 608.

Intimate relations were cemented with a section of the Soga through Kurayamada, whose daughter Prince Naka married, and trustworthy followers having been attached to the prince, the conspirators watched for an occasion. It was not easy to find one. The Soga mansion, on the eastern slope of Mount Unebi, was a species of fortress, surrounded by a moat and provided with an armoury having ample supply of bows and arrows. Emishi, the *o-omi*, always had a guard of fifty soldiers when he went abroad, and Iruka, his son, wore a sword "day and night." Nothing offered except to convert the palace itself into a place of execution. On the twelfth day of the sixth month, 645, the Empress held a Court in the great hall of audience to receive memorials and tribute from the three kingdoms of Korea. All present, except her Majesty and Iruka, were privy to the plot. Iruka having been beguiled into laying aside his sword, the reading of the memorials was commenced by Kurayamada, and Prince Naka ordered the twelve gates to be closed simultaneously. At that signal, two swordsmen should have advanced and fallen upon Iruka; but they showed themselves so timorous that Prince Naka himself had to lead them to the attack. Iruka, severely wounded, struggled to the throne and implored for succour and justice; but when her Majesty in terror asked what was meant, Prince Naka charged Iruka with attempting to usurp the sovereignty. The Empress, seeing that her own son led the assassins, withdrew at once, and the work of slaughtering Iruka was completed, his corpse being thrown into the court-yard, where it lay covered with straw matting.

Prince Naka and Karaatari had not been so incautious as to take a wide circle of persons into their confidence. But they were immediately joined by practically all the nobility and high officials, and the *o-omi*'s troops having dispersed without striking a blow, Emishi and his people were all executed. The Empress Kogyoku at once abdicated in favour of her brother, Prince Kara, her son, Prince Naka, being nominated Prince Imperial. Her Majesty had worn the purple for only three years. All this was in accord with Kamatari's carefully devised plans. They were epoch making.

RELATIONS WITH KOREA

The story of Japan's relations with Korea throughout the period of over a century, from the accession of Kinmei (540) to the abdication of Kogyoku (645), is a series of monotonously similar chapters, the result for Japan being that she finally lost her position at Mimana. There was almost perpetual fighting between the petty kingdoms which struggled for mastery in the peninsula, and Kudara, always nominally friendly to Japan, never hesitated to seek the latter's assistance against Shiragi and

Koma. To these appeals the Yamato Court lent a not-unready ear, partly because they pleased the nation's vanity, but mainly because Kudara craftily suggested danger to Mimana unless Japan asserted herself with arms.

At all events, in answer to often iterated entreaties from Kudara, the Yamato Court did not make any practical response until the year 551, when it sent five thousand *koku* of barley-seed (?), followed, two years later, by two horses, two ships, fifty bows with arrows, and – a promise. Kudara was then ruled by a very enterprising prince (Yo-chang). Resolving to strike separately at his enemies, Koma and Shiragi, he threw himself with all his forces against Koma and gained a signal victory (553). Then, at length, Japan was induced to assist. An *omi* was despatched (554) to the peninsula with a thousand soldiers, as many horses and forty ships. Shiragi became at once the objective of the united forces of Kudara and Japan. A disastrous defeat resulted for the assailants. The Kudara army suffered almost complete extermination, losing nearly thirty thousand men, and history is silent as to the fate of the *omi*'s contingent. Nevertheless the fear of Japanese vengeance induced Shiragi to attempt to renew friendly relations with the Yamato Court by means of tribute-bearing envoys.

In the spring of the following year (562), Shiragi invaded Mimana, destroyed the Japanese station there and overran the whole region (ten provinces). No warning had reached Japan. Six months after his invasion of Mimana he renewed the despatch of envoys to Japan, and it was not until their arrival in Yamato that they learned Japan's mood. The Yamato Court did not wreak vengeance on these untimely envoys, but immediately afterwards an armed expedition was despatched to call Shiragi to account. The forces were divided into two corps, one being ordered to march under Ki no Omaro northwest from Mimana and effect a junction with Kudara; the other, under Kawabe no Nie, was to move eastward against Shiragi. This scheme became known to the Shiragi generals owing to the seizure of a despatch intended for Kudara. They attempted to intercept Omaro's corps, but were signally defeated.

Kawabe no Nie was an incompetent and pusillanimous captain. He and his men were all killed or taken prisoners, the only redeeming feature being the intrepidity of a Japanese officer, Tsugi no Ikina, who, with his wife and son, endured to be tortured and killed rather than utter an insult against their country.

Japan immediately despatched a strong army – from thirty to forty thousand men – but instead of directing it against Shiragi, sent it to the attack of Koma, under advice of the King of Kudara. Possibly the idea may have been to crush Koma, and having thus isolated Shiragi, to deal with the latter subsequently. If so, the plan never matured. Koma, indeed, suffered a signal defeat at the hands of the Japanese, but Shiragi remained unmolested.

Things remained thus for nine years. Tribute-bearing envoys arrived at intervals from Koma, but with Shiragi there was no communication. At last, in 571, an official was sent to demand from Shiragi an explanation of the reasons for the destruction of Mimana. The intention may have been to follow up this formality with the despatch of an effective force, but within a month the Emperor Kinmei died. On his death-bed he is said to have taken the Prince Imperial – Bidatsu – by the hand and said: "Thou must make war on Shiragi and establish Mimana as a feudal dependency, renewing a relationship like that of husband and wife, just as it was in former days. If this be done, in my grave I shall rest content."

Twelve years passed before Bidatsu took any step to comply with this dying injunction. During that long interval there were repeated envoys from Koma, now a comparatively feeble principality, and Shiragi made three unsuccessful overtures to renew amicable relations. At length, in 583, the Emperor announced his intention of carrying out the last testament of his predecessor. But, after consulting with a Japanese, Nichira, who had served for many years at the Kudara Court and was thoroughly familiar with the conditions existing in Korea, who counselled against taking up arms, the Emperor made no further attempt to resolve the Korean problem.

In the year 591, the ill-fated Emperor Sushun conceived the idea of sending a large army to re-establish his country's prestige in the peninsula, but his own assassination intervened, and for the space of nine years the subject was not publicly revived. Then, in 600, the Empress Suiko being on the throne, a unique opportunity presented itself. War broke out between Shiragi and Mimana. The Yamato Court at once despatched a force of ten thousand men to Mimana's aid, and Shiragi, having suffered a signal defeat, made act of abject submission, restoring to Mimana six of its original provinces and promising solemnly to abstain from future hostilities. The Japanese committed the error of crediting Shiragi's sincerity. They withdrew their forces, but no sooner had their ships passed below the horizon than Shiragi once more invaded Mimana. Japan must be said to have been the victim of special ill-fortune when an army of twenty-five thousand men, assembled in Tsukushi for the invasion of Shiragi, was twice prevented from sailing by unforeseeable causes, one being the death of Prince *Kume*, its commander-in-chief; the other, the death of the consort of his successor, Prince Taema.

These things happened in the year 603, and for the next five years all relations with Korea seem to have been severed. Then (608) the Yamato Court began to welcome immigrants from a country with which it was virtually at war. Two years later (610), Shiragi and Mimana, acting in concert, sent envoys who were received with all the pomp and ceremony prescribed by Shotoku Taishi's code of decorum. The Yamato Court had evidently now abandoned all idea of punishing Shiragi or restoring the station at Mimana. But Shiragi was nothing if not treacherous and was planning another invasion of the latter, which took place in 622. When the news reached Japan, the Empress Suiko would have sent an envoy against Shiragi, but it was deemed wiser to employ diplomacy in the first place.

Two plenipotentiaries were therefore sent from Japan. Their mission proved very simple. Shiragi acquiesced in all their proposals and pledged itself once for all to recognize Mimana as a dependency of Japan. But after the despatch of these plenipotentiaries, the war-party in Japan had gained the ascendancy, and a great flotilla carrying thousands of armed men was dispatched. Shiragi did not attempt to resist. The King tendered his submission and it was accepted without a blow having been struck. But there were no tangible results. Friendly, though not intimate, relations were still maintained with the three kingdoms of Korea, mainly because the peninsula long continued to be the avenue by which the literature, arts, and crafts of China under, the Tang dynasty found their way to Japan.

CHINESE INFLUENCE

Although Japan's military influence on the neighbouring continent waned perceptibly from the reign of Kinmei (540–571) onwards, a stream of Chinese civilization flowed steadily into the Island Empire from the west. Many of the propagandists of this civilization remained permanently in Japan, where they received a courteous welcome, being promoted to positions of trust and admitted to the ranks of the nobility. Thus a book (the *Seishi-roku*), published in 814, which has been aptly termed the "peerage of Japan," shows that, at that time, nearly one-third of the Japanese nobility traced their descent to Chinese or Korean ancestors in something like equal proportions.

After the advent of Buddhism (552), however, Chinese culture found new expansion eastward. In 554, there arrived a party of experts, including a man learned in the calendar, a professor of divination, a physician, two herbalists, and four musicians. The record says that these men, who, with the exception of the Chinese doctor of literature, were all Koreans, took the place of an equal number of their countrymen who had resided in Japan for some years. Thenceforth such incidents were frequent.

From the accession of the Empress Suiko (593), the influence of Shotoku Taishi made itself felt in every branch of learning, and thenceforth China and Japan may be said to have stood towards each other in the relation of teacher and pupil. Literature, the ideographic script, calendar compiling, astronomy, geography, divination, magic, painting, sculpture, architecture, tile-making, ceramics, the casting of metal, and other crafts were all cultivated assiduously under Chinese and

Korean instruction. In architecture, all substantial progress must be attributed to Buddhism, for it was by building temples and pagodas that Japanese ideas of dwelling-houses were finally raised above the semi-subterranean type, and to the same influence must be attributed signal and rapid progress in the art of interior decoration. The style of architecture adopted in temples was a mixture of the Chinese and the Indian.

None of the religious edifices then constructed has survived in its integrity to the present day. One, however – the Horyu-ji, at Nara – since all its restorations have been in strict accord with their originals, is believed to be a true representative of the most ancient type. It was founded by Shotoku Taishi and completed in 607. At the time of its construction, this Horyu-ji was the chief academy of Buddhist teaching, and it therefore received the name of Gakumon-ji (Temple of Learning). Among its treasures is an image of copper and gold which was cast by the Korean artist, Tori – commonly called Tori Busshi, or Tori the image-maker – to order of Shotoku; and there is mural decoration from the brush of a Korean priest, Doncho. This building shows that already in the seventh century an imposing type of wooden edifice had been elaborated – an edifice differing from those of later epochs in only a few features; as, slight inequality in the scantling of its massive pillars; comparatively gentle pitch of roof; abnormally overhanging eaves, and shortness of distance between each storey of the pagoda. These sacred buildings were roofed with tiles, and were therefore called *kawara-ya* (tiled house) by way of distinction, for all private dwellings, the Imperial palace not excepted, continued to have thatched roofs in the period now under consideration.

EVERYDAY LIFE

Considerable progress seems to have been made in matters relating to trade during this period. Markets were opened at several places in the interior, and coastwise commerce developed so much that, in 553 CE, it was found expedient to appoint an official for the purpose of numbering and registering the vessels thus employed. The Chinese settler, Wang Sin-i, who has already been spoken of as the only person able to decipher a Korean memorial, was given the office of *fune no osa* (chief of the shipping bureau) and granted the title of *fune no fubito* (registrar of vessels). There had not apparently been any officially recognized weights and measures in remote antiquity. The width of the hand (*ta* or *tsuka*) and the spread of the arms (*hiro*) were the only dimensions employed. By and by the Korean *shaku* (foot), which corresponds to 1.17 *shaku* of the present day, came into use. In Kenso's time (485–487) there is mention of a measure of rice being sold for a piece of silver, and the Emperor Kinmei (540–571) is recorded to have given 1000 *koku* of seed-barley to the King of Kudara.

Costume and Coiffure

Up to the time (603 CE) of the institution of caps as marks of rank, men were in the habit of dividing their hair in the centre and tying it above the ears in a style called *mizura*. But such a fashion did not accord with the wearing of caps which were gathered up on the crown in the shape of a bag. Hence men of rank took to binding the hair in a queue on the top of the head. The old style was continued, however, by men having no rank and by youths. A child's hair was looped on the temples in imitation of the flower of a gourd – hence called *hisago-bana* – and women wore their tresses hanging free. The institution of caps interfered also with the use of hairpins, which were often made of gold and very elaborate. These now came to be thrust, not directly into the hair, but through the cord employed to tie the cap above. It is recorded that, in the year 611, when the Empress Suiko and her Court went on a picnic, the colour of the ministers' garments agreed with that of their official caps, and that each wore hair-ornaments which, in the case of the two highest functionaries, were made of gold; in the case of the next two, of leopards' tails; and in the case of lower ranks, of birds' tails.

On a more ceremonious occasion, namely, the reception of the Chinese envoys from the Sui Court, the *Chronicles* state that Japanese princes and ministers "all wore gold hair-ornaments, and their garments were of brocade, purple, and embroidery, with thin silk stuffs of various colours and patterns." Costume had become thus gorgeous after the institution of Buddhism and the establishment of intercourse direct with the Sui, and, subsequently, the Tang dynasty. Even in the manner of folding the garments over the breast – not from right to left but from left to right – the imported fashion was followed. Wadded garments are incidently mentioned in the year 643 CE.

Music and Amusements

Music, indeed, may be said to have benefitted largely by the advent of Buddhism, for the services of the latter required a special kind of music. The first foreign teacher of the art was a Korean, Mimashi, who went to Japan in 612 CE, after having studied both music and dancing for some years in China. A dwelling was assigned to him at Sakurai (in Yamato) and he trained pupils. At the instance of Prince Shotoku and for the better performance of Buddhist services, various privileges were granted to the professors of the art. They were exempted from the discharge of official duties and their occupation became hereditary. Several ancient Japanese books contain reference to music and dancing, and in one work (the *Horyu-ji Shizai-cho*, 747 CE) illustrations are given of the wooden masks worn by dancers and the instruments used by musicians of the Wu (Chinese) school. These masks were introduced by Mimashi and are still preserved in the temple Horyu-ji.

In the matter of pastimes, a favourite practice, first mentioned in the reign of the Empress Suiko, was a species of picnic called "medicine hunting" (*kusuri-kari*). It took place on the fifth day of the fifth month. The Empress, her ladies, and the high functionaries, all donned gala costumes and went to hunt stags, for the purpose of procuring the young antlers, and to search for "deer-fungus" (*shika-take*), the horns and the vegetables being supposed to have medical properties. Football is spoken of as having inaugurated the afterwards epoch-making friendship between Prince Naka and Kamatari. It was not played in the Occidental manner, however. The game consisted in kicking a ball from player to player without letting it fall. This was apparently a Chinese innovation. Here, also, mention may be made of thermal springs. Their sanitary properties were recognized, and visits were paid to them by invalids. The most noted were those of Dogo, in Iyo, and Arima, in Settsu. The Emperor Jomei spent several months at each of these, and Prince Shotoku caused to be erected at Dogo a stone monument bearing an inscription to attest the curative virtues of the water.

THE DAIKA REFORMS

Over a short space of time the Daika Reforms – heavily influenced by the Confucianism of Tang China – irrevocably transformed Japanese society by reasserting imperial might after the defeat of the recalcitrant Soga clan. The Emperor's authority, as in China, was now made absolute, reinforced by the further centralization of the state and a complete administrative overhaul. Hereditary titles were also abolished to dissuade ambitious nobles from overstepping the mark, while sweeping criminal, administrative and land reforms ensured the renewed imperial loyalties of all subjects. This process also included the peasantry, whose allegiances were now owed to the Emperor rather than to regional overlords.

THE THIRTY-SIXTH SOVEREIGN, THE EMPEROR KOTOKU

After the fall of the Soga and the abdication of the Empress Kogyoku, her son, Prince Naka, would have been the natural successor, and such was her own expressed wish. But the prince's procedure was largely regulated by Kamatari, who, alike in the prelude and in the sequel of this crisis, proved himself one of the greatest statesmen Japan ever produced. He saw that the Soga influence, though broken, was not wholly shattered, and he understood that the great administrative reform which he contemplated might be imperilled were the throne immediately occupied by a prince on whose hands the blood of the Soga chief was still warm. Therefore he advised Prince Naka to stand aside in favour of his maternal uncle, Prince Karu, who could be trusted to co-operate loyally in the work of reform and whose connexion with the Soga overthrow had been less conspicuous. But to reach Prince Karu it was necessary to pass over the head of another prince, Furubito, Naka's half-brother, who had the full sympathy of the remnant of the Soga clan. The throne was therefore offered to him. But since the offer followed, instead of preceding the Empress' approval of Prince Karu, Furubito recognized the farce, and threw away his sword and declared his intention of entering religion.

Very soon the Buddhist monastery at Yoshino, where he received the tonsure, became a rallying point for the Soga partisans, and a war for the succession seemed imminent. Naka, however, now Prince Imperial, was not a man to dally with such obstacles. He promptly sent to Yoshino a force of soldiers who killed Furubito with his children and permitted his consorts to strangle themselves. Prince Naka's name must go down to all generations as that of a great reformer, but it is also associated with a terrible injustice.

Too readily crediting a slanderous charge brought against his father-in-law, Kurayamada, who had stood at his right hand in the great *coup d'état* of 645, he despatched a force to seize the alleged traitor. Kurayamada fled to a temple, and there, declaring that he would "leave the world, still cherishing fidelity in his bosom," he committed suicide, his wife and seven children sharing his fate. Subsequent examination of his effects established his innocence, and his daughter, consort of Prince Naka, died of grief.

THE DAIKA OR "GREAT CHANGE"

Not for these things, however, but for sweeping reforms in the administration of the empire is the reign of Kotoku (645–54) memorable. Prince Naka and Kamatari, during the long period of their intimate intercourse prior to the deed of blood in the great hall of audience, had fully matured their estimates of the Sui and Tang civilization as revealed in documents and information carried to Japan by priests, literati, and students, who, since the establishment of Buddhism, had paid many visits to China. They appreciated that the system prevailing in their own country from time immemorial had developed abuses which were sapping the strength of the nation, and in sweeping the Soga from the path to the throne, their ambition had been to gain an eminence from which the new civilization might be authoritatively proclaimed.

Speaking broadly, their main objects were to abolish the system of hereditary office-holders; to differentiate aristocratic titles from official ranks; to bring the whole mass of the people into direct subjection to the Throne, and to establish the Imperial right of ownership in all the land throughout the empire.

A coronation ceremony of unprecedented magnificence took place. High officials, girt with golden quivers, stood on either side of the dais forming the throne, and all the great functionaries – *omi*, *muraji*, and *miyatsuko* – together with representatives of the 180 hereditary corporations (*be*) filed past, making obeisance. The title of "Empress Dowager" was conferred for the first time on Kogyoku, who had abdicated; Prince Naka was made Prince Imperial; the head of the great *uji* of Abe was nominated minister of the Left (*sa-daijiri*); Kurayamada, of the Soga-*uji*, who had shared the dangers of the conspiracy against Emishi and Iruka, became minister of the Right (*u-daijiri*), and Kamatari himself received the post of minister of the Interior (*nai-daijin*), being invested with the right to be consulted on all matters whether of statecraft or of official personnel.

These designations, "minister of the Left", "minister of the Right," and "minister of the Interior," were new in Japan. Neither was required, in his new capacity, to take instructions from any save the Emperor, nor did any one of the three high dignitaries nominally represent this or that congeries of *uji*. A simultaneous innovation was the appointment of a Buddhist priest, Bin, and a literatus, Kuromaro, to be "national doctors." These men had spent some years at the Tang Court and were well versed in Chinese systems.

The next step taken was to assemble the ministers under a patriarchal tree, and, in the presence of the Emperor, the Empress Dowager, and the Prince Imperial, to pronounce, in the names of the *Kami* of heaven and the *Kami* of earth – the *Tenshin* and the *Chigi* – a solemn imprecation on rulers who attempted double-hearted methods of government, and on vassals guilty of treachery in the service of their sovereign. This amounted to a formal denunciation of the Soga as well as a pledge on the part of the new Emperor. The Chinese method of reckoning time by year-periods was then adopted, and the year 645 CE became the first of the Daika era.

Then the reformers commenced their work in earnest. Governors (*kokushi*) were appointed to all the eastern provinces and became an integral part of the administrative machinery. That meant that the government of the provinces, instead of being administered by hereditary officials, altogether irrespective of their competence, was entrusted for a fixed term to men chosen on account of special aptitude. The eastern provinces were selected for inaugurating this experiment, because their distance from the capital rendered the change less conspicuous. Moreover, the appointments were given, as far as possible, to the former *miyatsuko* or *mikotomochi*. An ordinance was now issued for placing a petition-box in the Court and hanging a bell near it. The box was intended to serve as a receptacle for complaints and representations. Anyone had a right to present such documents. They were to be collected and conveyed to the Emperor every morning, and if a reply was tardy, the bell was to be struck.

Precautions against any danger of disturbance were adopted by taking all weapons of war out of the hands of private individuals and storing them in arsenals specially constructed on waste lands. The whole nation was now divided into freemen (*ryomin*) and bondmen (*senmin*), and a law was enacted that, since among slaves no marriage tie was officially recognized, a child of mixed parentage must always be regarded as a bondman. On that basis a census was ordered to be taken, and in it were included not only the people of all classes, but also the area of cultivated and throughout the empire.

At the same time stringent regulations were enacted for the control and guidance of the provincial governors. They were to take counsel with the people in dividing the profits of agriculture. They were not to act as judges in criminal cases or to accept bribes from suitors in civil ones; their staff, when visiting the capital, was strictly limited, and the use of public-service horses as well as the consumption of State provisions was vetoed unless they were travelling on public business. Finally, they were enjoined to investigate carefully all claims to titles and all alleged rights of land tenure. The next step was the most drastic and far-reaching of all. Hereditary corporations were entirely abolished, alike those established to commemorate the name of a sovereign or a prince and those employed by the nobles to cultivate their estates. The estates themselves were escheated. Thus, at one stroke, the lands and titles of the hereditary aristocracy were annulled, just as was destined to be the case in the Meiji era, twelve centuries later.

Two kinds of taxes were thenceforth imposed, namely, ordinary taxes and commuted taxes. The ordinary consisted of twenty sheaves of rice per *cho* (equivalent to about eight sheaves per acre), and the commuted tax – in lieu of forced labour – was fixed at a piece of silk fabric forty feet in length by two and a half feet in breadth per *cho*, being approximately a length of sixteen feet per acre. The dimensions of the fabric were doubled in the case of coarse silk, and quadrupled in the case of cloth woven from hemp or from the fibre of the inner bark of the paper-mulberry. A commuted tax was levied on houses also, namely, a twelve-foot length of the above cloth per house. No currency existed in that age. All payments were made in kind. In every homestead there was an alderman who kept the register, directed agricultural operations, enforced taxes, and took measures to prevent crime as well as to judge it.

Thus it is seen that a regular system of national taxation was introduced and that the land throughout the whole empire was considered to be the property of the Crown. As for the nobles who were deprived of their estates, sustenance gifts were given to them, but there is no record of the bases upon which these gifts were assessed. With regard to the people's share in the land, the plan pursued was that for every male or female over five years of age two *tan* (about half an acre) should be given to the former and one-third less to the latter, these grants being made for a period of six years, at the end of which time a general restoration was to be effected. A very striking evidence of the people's condition is that every adult male had to contribute a sword, armour, a bow and arrows, and a drum. This impost may well have outweighed all the others.

Another important reform regulated the dimensions of burial mounds. The construction of these on the grand scale adopted for many sovereigns, princes, and nobles had long harrassed the people, who were compelled to give their toil gratis for such a purpose. Kotoku did not undertake to limit the size of Imperial tombs. The rescript dealt only with those from princes downwards. Of these, the greatest tumulus permitted was a square mound with a side of forty-five feet at the base and a height of twenty-five feet, measured along the slope, a further restriction being that the work must not occupy more than one thousand men for seven days. The maximum dimensions were similarly prescribed in every case, down to a minor official, whose grave must not give employment to more than fifty men for one day. When ordinary people died, it was directed that they should be buried in the ground without a day's delay. Cemeteries were ordered to be constructed for the first time, and peremptory injunctions were issued against self-destruction to accompany the dead; against strangling men or women by way of sacrifice; against killing the deceased's horse, and against cutting the hair or stabbing the thighs by way of showing grief. It must be assumed that all these customs existed.

Other evil practices are incidentally referred to in the context of the Daika reforms. Thus it appears that slaves occasionally left their lawful owners owing to the latter's poverty and entered the service of rich men, who thereafter refused to give them up; that when a divorced wife or concubine married into another family, her former husband, after the lapse of years, often preferred claims against her new husband's property; that men, relying on their power, demanded people's daughters in marriage, and in the event of the girl entering another house, levied heavy toll on both families; that when a widow, of ten or twenty years' standing, married again, or when a girl entered into wedlock, the people of the vicinity insisted on the newly wedded couple performing the Shinto rite of *harai* (purgation), which was perverted into a device for compelling offerings of goods and wine; that the compulsory performance of this ceremony had become so onerous as to make poor men shrink from giving burial to even their own brothers who had died at a distance from home, or hesitate to extend aid to them in mortal peril, and that when a forced labourer cooked his food by the roadside or borrowed a pot to boil his rice, he was often obliged to perform expensive purgation.

OFFICIAL ORGANIZATION

At the head of all officials were the *sa-daijin* (minister of the Left), the *u-daijin* (minister of the Right) and the *nai-daijin* (minister of the Interior), and after them came the heads of departments, of which eight were established, after the model of the Tang Court in China. They were the Central Department (*Nakatsukasa-sho*); the Department of Ceremonies (*Shikibu-sho*); the Department of Civil Government (*Jibu-sho*); the Department of Civil Affairs (*Mimbu-sho*); the Department of War (*Hyobu-sho*); the Department of Justice (*Gyobu-sho*); the Treasury (*Okura-sho*), and the Household Department (*Kunai-sho*).

In a province the senior official was the governor, and under him were heads of districts, aldermen of homesteads (fifty houses), elders of five households – all the houses being divided into groups of five for purposes of protection – and market commissioners who superintended the currency (in kind), commerce, the genuineness of wares, the justness of weights and measures, the prices of commodities, and the observance of prohibitions. Since to all official posts men of merit were appointed without regard to lineage, the cap-ranks inaugurated by Prince Shotoku were abolished, and replaced by new cap-grades, nineteen in all, which were distinguished partly by their borders, partly by their colours, and partly by their materials and embroidery. Hair-ornaments were also a mark of rank. They were cicada-shaped, of gold and silver for the highest grades, of silver for the medium grades, and of copper for the low grades. The caps indicated official status without any reference to hereditary titles.

The main features of the political developments of the Dakia era was that the entire nation became the public people of the realm and the whole of the land became the property of the Crown, the hereditary nobles being relegated to the rank of State pensioners. This metamorphosis entailed taking an accurate census of the population; making a survey of the land; fixing the boundaries of provinces, districts, and villages; appointing officials to administer the affairs of these local divisions, and organizing the central government with boards and bureaux. The system of taxation also had to be changed, and the land had to be apportioned to the people.

There was, indeed, one defect in the theory of the new system. From time immemorial the polity of the empire had been based on the family relation. The sovereign reigned in virtue of his lineage, and the hereditary nobles owed their high positions and administrative competence equally to descent. To discredit the title of the nobles was to disturb the foundation of the Throne itself, and to affirm that want of virtue constituted a valid reason for depriving the scions of the gods of their inherited functions. Nothing could be at greater variance with the cardinal tenet of the Japanese polity, which holds that "the King can do no wrong" and that the Imperial line must remain unbroken to all eternity.

THE THIRTY-SEVENTH SOVEREIGN, THE EMPRESS SAIMEI

On the demise of Kotoku, in 654, his natural successor would have been Prince Naka, who, ten years previously, had chosen to reform the empire rather than to rule it. The Empress Kogyoku was again raised to the throne under the name of Saimei (655–61) – the first instance of a second accession in Japanese history. She reigned nearly seven years, and the era is remarkable chiefly for expeditions against the Yemishi and for complications with Korea.

RELATIONS WITH KOREA

It has been shown how, in 562 CE, the Japanese settlement in Mimana was exterminated; how the Emperor Kinmei's dying behest to his successor was that this disgrace must be removed; how subsequent attempts to carry out his testament ended in failure, owing largely to Japan's weak habit of trusting the promises of Shiragi, and how, in 618, the Sui Emperor, Yang, at the head of a great army, failed to make any impression on Korea.

Thereafter, intercourse between Japan and the peninsula was of a fitful character unmarked by any noteworthy event until, in the second year (651) of the "White Pheasant" era, the Yamato Court essayed to assert itself in a futile fashion by refusing to give audience to Shiragi envoys because they wore costumes after the Tang fashion without offering any excuse for such a caprice. Kotoku was then upon the Japanese throne, and Japan was busily occupied importing and assimilating Tang institutions. That she should have taken umbrage at similar imitation on Shiragi's part seems capricious. Shiragi sent no more envoys, and presently (655), now saw and seized an opportunity offered by the debauchery and misrule of the King of Kudara, attacking its neighbour and once more supplicated Tang's aid in 660. The second appeal produced a powerful response. Kao-sung, then the Tang Emperor, despatched a general, Su Ting-fang, at the head of an army of two hundred thousand men. Kudara was crushed. It lost ten thousand men, and all its prominent personages, from the debauched King downwards, were sent as prisoners to Tang. But one great captain, Pok-sin, saved the situation. Collecting the fugitive troops of Kudara he fell suddenly on Shiragi and drove her back, thereafter appealing for Japanese aid.

At the Yamato Court Shiragi was now regarded as a traditional enemy and the Empress Saimei decided that Kudara must be helped. Living in Japan at that time was Phung-chang, a younger brother of the deposed King of Kudara. It was resolved that he should be sent to the peninsula accompanied by a sufficient force to place him on the throne. But Saimei died before the necessary preparations were completed, and the task of carrying out a design which had already received his endorsement devolved upon Prince Naka, the great reformer. A fleet of 170 ships carrying an army of thirty-seven thousand men escorted Phung-chang from Tsukushi, and the kingdom of Kudara was restored. But at the conclusive battle at Paik-chhon-ku (Ung-jin) in 662, the Japanese experience a crushing defeat. Only a remnant found its way back to Tsukushi. Kudara and Koma fell, and Japan lost its last footing in the region.

From Kudara, after its overthrow by China, there migrated almost continuously for some time a number of inhabitants who became naturalized in Japan. Japan extended its hospitality to the men whose independence it had not been able to assert and relations with the Japanese neighbour ended humanely though not gloriously. They had cost Japan heavily in life and treasure, but it had been repaid fully with the civilization which Korea helped her to import.

THE THIRTY-EIGHTH SOVEREIGN, THE EMPEROR TENCHI

After the death of the Empress Saimei in the year 661, there was an interregnum of seven years. The explanation is that the Crown Prince, Naka, while taking the sceptre, did not actually wield it. He entrusted the administrative functions to his younger brother, Oama, and continued to devote himself to the great work of reform. In the year 668, judging that his reforms had been sufficiently assimilated to warrant confidence, he formally ascended the throne and is known in history as Tenchi (Heavenly Intelligence). He ruled until 671.

Only four years of life remained to him, and almost immediately after his accession he lost his great coadjutor, Kamatari. It is related that in the days when the prince and Kamatari planned the outlines of their great scheme, they were accustomed to meet for purposes of conference in a remote valley on the east of the capital, where an aged wistaria happened to be in bloom at the most critical of their consultations. Kamatari therefore desired to change his *uji* name from *Nakatomi* to Fujiwara (wisteria), and the prince, on ascending the throne, gave effect to this request. There thus came into existence a family, the most famous in Japanese history. The secluded valley where the momentous meetings took place received the name of Tamu no Mine, and a shrine stands there now in memory of Kamatari. The Emperor conferred on the deceased statesman posthumous official rank, the first instance of a practice destined to became habitual in Japan.

During the reign of Tenchi there was enacted a body of twenty-two laws called the *Omi Ritsu-ryo* (the Omi Statutes), Omi, on the shore of Lake Biwa, being then the seat of the Imperial Court. Unfortunately this valuable document did not survive. Our knowledge of it is confined to a statement in the *Memoirs of Kamatari* that it was compiled in the year 667. Two years later – that is to say, in the year after Tenchi's actual accession – the census register, which had formed an important feature of the Daika reforms, became an accomplished fact.

THE THIRTY-NINTH SOVEREIGN, THE EMPEROR KOBUN

Among four "palace ladies" (*uneme*) upon whom the Emperor Tenchi looked with favour, one, Yaka of Iga province, bore him a son known in his boyhood days as Prince Iga but afterwards called Prince Otomo. The dignity of Crown Prince was bestowed on Tenchi's younger brother, Oama. But during these seven years of nominal interregnum, the fame of Tenchi's son, Prince Otomo, also grew upon men's lips. An ancient book speaks of him as "wise and intelligent; an able administrator alike of civil and of military affairs; commanding respect and esteem; sage of speech, and rich in learning." When the Emperor actually ascended the throne, Otomo had reached his twentieth year, and four years later (671) the sovereign appointed him prime minister (*dajo daijin*), an office then created for the first time.

Thenceforth the question of Tenchi's successor began to be disquieting. The technical right was on Oama's side, but the paternal sympathy was with Otomo. When, within a few months of Otomo's appointment as *dajo daijin*, the sovereign found himself mortally sick, he summoned Oama and named him to succeed But Oama, having been warned of a powerful conspiracy to place Otomo on the throne, and not unsuspicious that it had the Emperor's sympathy, declined the honour and announced his intention of entering religion, which he did by retiring to the monastery at Yoshino. The conspirators, at whose head were the minister of the Left, Soga no Akae, and the minister of the Right, *Nakatomi* no Kane, aimed at reverting to the times when, by placing on the throne a prince of their own choice, one or two great *uji* had grasped the whole political power. The prime mover was Kane, *muraji* of the *Nakatomi*.

Immediately after Tenchi's death, which took place at the close of 671, and after the accession of Prince Otomo – known in history as the Emperor Kobun (672) – the conspirators began to concert measures for the destruction of Prince Oama, whom they regarded as a fatal obstacle to the achievement of their purpose. Oama fled precipitately. He did not even wait for a palanquin or a horse. His course was shaped eastward, for two reasons: the first, that his domains as Prince Imperial had been in Ise and Mino; the second, that since in the eastern provinces the Daika reforms had been first put into operation, in the eastern provinces, also, conservatism might be expected to rebel with least reluctance.

The struggle that ensued was the fiercest Japan had witnessed since the foundation of the empire. For twenty days there was almost continuous fighting. Thousands flocked to Prince

Oama's standard; the nation evidently regarded Prince Oama as the champion of the old against the new. The crowning contest took place at the Long Bridge of Seta, which spans the waters of Lake Biwa at the place where they narrow to form the Seta River. Deserted by men who had sworn to support him, his army shattered, and he himself a fugitive, the Emperor fled to Yamazaki and there committed suicide. Not because of its magnitude alone but because its sequel was the dethronement and suicide of a legitimate Emperor, this struggle presents a shocking aspect to Japanese eyes. It is known in history as the "Jinshin disturbance," so called after the cyclical designation of the year (672) when it occurred.

THE FORTIETH SOVEREIGN, THE EMPEROR TEMMU

Prince Oama succeeded to the throne and is known in history as the fortieth Sovereign, Temmu (673–86). During the fourteen years of his reign he completed the administrative systems of the Daika era, and asserted the dignity and authority of the Court to an unprecedented degree. The Daika reformers had invariably contrived that conciliation should march hand in hand with innovation. Temmu administered State affairs with little recourse to ministerial aid but always with military assistance in the background. He was especially careful not to sow the seeds of the abuses which his immediate predecessors had worked to eradicate. Thus, while he did not fail to recognize the services of those that had stood by him in the Jinshin tumult, he studiously refrained from rewarding them with official posts, and confined himself to bestowing titles of a purely personal character together with posthumous rank in special cases.

A law, comprising no less than ninety-two articles, was enacted for guidance in Court ceremonials, the demeanour and salutation of each grade of officials being explicitly set forth. It is worthy of note that a veto was imposed on the former custom of kneeling to make obeisance and advancing or retreating in the presence of a superior on the knees and hands; all salutations were ordered to be made standing.

Temmu did not neglect appeals to religion and devices to win popularity. He is seen endowing shrines, erecting temples, and organizing religious fetes on a sumptuous scale. If, again, all persons in official position were required to support armed men; if the provincials were ordered to practise military exercises, and if arms were distributed to the people in the home provinces (Kinai), at the same time taxes were freely remitted, and amnesties were readily granted. Further, if much attention was paid to archery, and if drastic measures were adopted to crush the partisans of the Omi Court who still occasionally raised the standard of revolt, the sovereign devoted not less care to the discharge of the administrative functions.

Temmu never appointed to posts in the Government men who did not give promise of competence. All those who possessed a claim on his gratitude were nominated chamberlains (*toneri*), and having been thus brought under observation, were subsequently entrusted with official functions commensurate with their proved ability. The same plan was pursued in the case of females. New titles were designed to replace the old-time *kabane* (or *sei*), in that whereas the kabane had always been hereditary, and was generally associated with an office, the new sei was obtained by special grant, and, though it thereafter became hereditary, it was never an indication of office bearing. Eight of these new titles were instituted by Temmu, namely, *mahito, asomi, sukune, imiki, michi-no-shi, omi, muraji,* and *inagi,* and their nearest English equivalents are, perhaps, duke, marquis, count, lord, viscount, baron, and baronet. The new peerage was, in fact, designed not only to supplant, but also to discredit, the old.

Thus, in the first place, the system was abolished under which all *uji* having the title of *omi* were controlled by the *o-omi,* and all having the title of *muraji* by the *o-muraji*; and in the second, though the above eight *sei* were established, not every *uji* was necessarily granted a title. Only the most important received that distinction, and even these found themselves relegated to a comparatively low place on the list. No change was made in the traditional custom of entrusting the management of each *uji*'s affairs to its own *Kami.* But, in order to guard against the abuses of the hereditary right, an *uji no Kami* ceased in certain cases to succeed by birthright and became elective, the election requiring Imperial endorsement.

The effect of these measures was almost revolutionary. They changed the whole fabric of the Japanese polity. But success was menaced by a factor which could scarcely have been controlled. The arable lands in the home provinces at that time probably did not exceed 130,000 acres, and the food stuffs produced cannot have sufficed for more than a million persons. Gradually, as families multiplied, the conditions of life became too straitened in such circumstances, and relief began to be sought in provincial appointments, which furnished opportunities for getting possession of land. It was in this way that local magnates had their origin and the seeds of genuine feudalism were sown. Another direction in which success fell short of purpose was in the matter of the hereditary guilds (*be*). The Daika reforms had aimed at converting everyone in the empire into a veritable unit of the nation, not a mere member of an *uji* or a *tomobe*. But it proved impossible to carry out this system in the case of the *tomobe* (called also *kakibe*), or labouring element of the *uji*, and the *yakabe*, or domestic servants of a family. To these their old status had to be left.

THE FORTY-FIRST SOVEREIGN, THE EMPRESS JITO

The **Emperor Temmu** died in 686, and the throne remained nominally unoccupied until 690. Temmu desired that the additions made by him to the Daika system should be consolidated by the genius of his wife before the sceptre passed finally into the hands of his son. Jito had stood by her husband's side when, as Prince Oama, he had barely escaped the menaces of the Omi Court, and there is reason to think that she had subsequently shared his administrative confidence as she had assisted at his military councils. The heir to the throne, Prince Kusakabe, was then in his twenty-fifth year, but he quietly endorsed the paternal behest that his mother should direct State affairs. The arrangement was doubtless intended to be temporary, but Kusakabe died three years later, and yielding to the solicitations of her ministers, Jito then finally ascended the throne (690–97).

However, the Emperor Temmu had left several sons by secondary consorts, and the eldest survivor of these, Prince

Otsu, listening to the counsels of the Omi Court's partisans and prompted by his own well-deserved popularity and military prowess, intrigued to seize the throne. He was executed in his house, all his followers, over thirty in number, were pardoned – rare clemency in those days.

The most important legislation of the Empress Jito's reign related to slaves. In the year of her accession (690), she issued an edict ordering that interest on all debts contracted prior to, or during the year (685) prior to Temmu's death should be cancelled. Temmu himself had created the precedent for this. Jito's edict provided that anyone already in servitude on account of a debt should be relieved from serving any longer on account of the interest. Thus it is seen that the practice of pledging the service of one's body in discharge of debt was in vogue at that epoch, and that it received official recognition with the proviso that the obligation must not extend to interest. Debts, therefore, had become instruments for swelling the ranks of the slave class. It has been shown already that degradation to slavery was a common punishment or expiation of a crime, and the annals of the period under consideration indicate that men and women of the slave class were bought and sold like any other chattels.

The usual price of an able-bodied slave was one thousand bundles of rice. It is not to be inferred, however, that the sale of freemen into slavery was sanctioned by law. During the reign of the Emperor Temmu, a farmer of Shimotsuke province wished to sell his child on account of a bad harvest, but his application for permission was refused, though forwarded by the provincial governor. In fact, sales or purchases of the junior members of a family by the seniors were not publicly permitted, although such transactions evidently took place. Even the manumission of a slave required official sanction. Another rule enacted in Jito's time was that the slaves of an *uji*, when once manumitted, could not be again placed on the slaves' register at the request of a subsequent *uji no Kami*. Finally this same sovereign enacted that yellow-coloured garments should be worn by freemen and black by slaves. History shows that the sale and purchase of human beings in Japan, subject to the above limitations, was not finally forbidden until the year 1699.

Compulsory military service was inaugurated until the reign of the Empress Jito, when (689) her Majesty instructed the local governors that one-fourth of the able-bodied men in each province should be trained every year in warlike exercises. This was the beginning of the conscription system in Japan.

THE ORDER OF SUCCESSION

There had been a departure from the rule of primogeniture when it came to the imperial succession in Japan, and since the time of Nintoku the eligibility of brothers also had been acknowledged in practice. During Jito's reign, the deaths of two Crown Princes in succession brought up the dangerous problem again for solution. The princes were Kusakabe and Takaichi. The former had been nominated by his father, Temmu, but was instructed to leave the reins of power in the hands of his mother, Jito, for a time. He died in the year 689, while Jito was still regent, and Takaichi, another of Temmu's sons, who had distinguished himself as commander of a division of troops in the Jinshin campaign, was made Prince Imperial. But he too died in 696, and it thus fell out that the only surviving and legitimate offspring of an Emperor who had actually reigned was Prince Kuzuno, son of Kobun.

To his accession, however, there was this great objection that his father, though wielding the sceptre for a few months, had borne arms in the Jinshin disturbance against Temmu and Jito, and was held to have forfeited his title by defeat and suicide. The Empress convened a State council, Prince Kuzuno also being present, and submitted the question for their decision. But none replied until Kuzuno himself, coming forward, declared that unless the principle of primogeniture were strictly followed, endless complications would be inevitable. This involved the sacrifice of his own claim and the recognition of Karu, eldest son of the late Kusakabe. The 14th of March, 696, when this patriotic declaration was made, is memorable in Japanese history as the date when the principle of primogeniture first received official approval. Six months afterwards, the Empress abdicated in favour of Prince Karu, known in history as forty-second sovereign, Mommu (697–707).

The Emperor Mommu took for consort a daughter of Fuhito, representative of the Fujiwara family and son of the great Kamatari. This union proved the first step towards a practice which soon became habitual and which produced a marked effect on the history of Japan, the practice of supplying Imperial consorts from the Fujiwara family.

THE DAIHO LEGISLATION OF EMPEROR MOMMU

Mommu's reign is a period memorable for legislative activity. The statutes of the "Code and Penal Law of Omi," were revised by the Emperor Mommu, who commenced the task in 681 and that, eleven years later, when the Empress Jito occupied the throne, this revised code was promulgated.

A second revision took place in the years 700 and 701 under instructions from the Emperor Mommu, the revisers being a committee of ten, headed by Fuhito of the Fujiwara family, and by Mahito (Duke) Awada. Seventeen years later (718), by order of the Empress Gensho, further revision was carried out by another committee headed by the same Fujiwara Fuhito, now prime minister, and the amended volumes, ten of the Code and ten of the Law, were known thenceforth as the "New Statutes," or the "Code and Law of the Yoro Period."

The code covered a vast range of issues: from the administration of the Royal Household and the duties of its offers to family law, taxation, official ranks and titles, army and frontier defences, ceremonies, public works, ranks and titles, storage of rice and other staples, and criminal justice. This "Code and the Penal Law" accompanying it went into full operation from the Daiho era and remained in force thereafter, subject to the revisions above indicated. It will be observed that just as this remarkable body of enactments owed its inception in Japan to Kamatari, the great founder of the Fujiwara family, so every subsequent revision was presided over by one of his descendants.

It may be broadly stated that the Daika reformation, which formed the basis of this legislation, was a transition from the

Japanese system of heredity to the Chinese system of morality. The penal law (*ritsu*) was undoubtedly copied from the work of the Tang legislators, the only modification being in degrees of punishment.

The basic principle of the Daiho code was that the people at large, without regard to rank or pedigree, owed equal duty to the State; that only those having special claims on public benevolence were entitled to fixed exemptions, and that not noble birth but intellectual capacity and attainments constituted a qualification for office. Nevertheless Japanese legislators did not find it possible to apply fully these excellent principles. Habits of a millennium's growth could not be so lightly eradicated. For example, while declaring erudition and intelligence to be the unique qualifications for office, no adequate steps were taken to establish schools for imparting the former or developing the latter. In short, the nobles still retained a large part of their old power, and the *senmin* (slave) class still continued to labour under various disabilities.

The potency of the Daiho code varied in the direct ratio of the centralization of administrative authority. Whenever feudalism prevailed, the code lost its binding force. In the realm of criminal law it is only consistent with the teaching of all experience to find that mitigation of penalties was provided according to the rank of the culprit. There were eight major crimes (*hachi-gyaku*), all in the nature of offences against the State, the Court, and the family, and the order of their gravity was: (1) high treason (against the State); (2) high treason (against the Crown); (3) treason; (4) parricide, fratricide, etc.; (5) offences against humanity; (6) lèse majesté; (7) unfilial conduct, and (8) crimes against society. But there were also six mitigations (*roku-gi*), all enacted with the object of lightening punishments according to the rank, official position, or public services of an offender. As for slaves, being merely a part of their proprietor's property like any other goods and chattels, the law took no cognizance of them.

Under the Daiho code a more elaborate system of administrative organization was effected than that conceived by the Daika reformers. In the Central Government there were two boards, eight departments, and one office.

The *Jingi-kwan*, or Board of Religion (Shinto) stood at the head of all, in recognition of the divine origin of the Imperial family. Thus, though the models for the Daiho system were taken from China, they were adapted to Japanese customs and traditions, as is proved by the premier place given to the *Jingi-kwan*. Worship and religious ceremonial have always taken precedence of secular business in the Court of Japan. Not only at the central seat of government did the year commence with worship, but in the provinces, also, the first thing recorded by a newly appointed governor was his visit to the Shinto shrines, and on the opening day of each month he repaired thither to offer the gohei (angular bunches of white paper stripes, representing the cloth offerings originally tied to branches of the sacred cleyera tree at festival time). Religious rites, in short, were the prime function of government, and therefore, whereas the office charged with these duties ranked low in the Tang system, it was placed at the head of all in Japan.

Other offices were ranked below the *Jingi-kwan*, in descending order of importance: the *Daijo-kwan* (Privy Council); the

Nakatsukasa-sho, or Central Department of State; the *Shikibu-sho*, or Department of Ceremonies; the *Jibu-sho*, or Department of Civil Government; the *Mimbu-sho*, or Department of Civil Affairs. Other Government Departments were next in rank – Justice, Finance, Household, War, Censorship.

For administrative purposes the capital was divided into two sections, the Eastern and the Western, which were controlled by a Left Metropolitan Office and a Right Metropolitan Office, respectively. The *Dazai-fu* (Great Administrative Office) in Naniwa (Osaka), owing to its distance from the capital, came to be regarded as a place of exile for high officials who had fallen out of Imperial favour.

The empire was divided into provinces (*kuni*) of four classes – great, superior, medium, and inferior – and each province was subdivided into districts (*kori*) of five classes – great, superior, medium, inferior, and small. Each *kuni* was placed under a governor (*kokushi*), chosen on account of competence and appointed for a term of four years; each district (*kori*) was administered by a *cho* (chief).

THE MILITARY

The divisions into "left" and "right," and the precedence given to the left, were derived from China, but it has to be observed in Japan's case that the metropolis itself was similarly divided into left and right quarters, and the military guards were divided into Left and Right watches. Outside the capital each province had an army corps (*gundan*), and one-third of all the able-bodied men (*seitei*), from the age of twenty to that of sixty, were required to serve with the colours of an army corps for a fixed period each year. From these provincial troops drafts were taken every year for a twelve-month's duty as palace guards (*eji*) in the metropolis, and others were detached for three-years' service as frontier guards (*saki-mori*) in the provinces lying along the western sea board.

The army corps differed numerically according to the extent of the province where they had their headquarters, but for each thousand men there were one colonel (*taiki*) and two lieutenant-colonels (*shoki*); for every five hundred men, one major (*gunki*); for every two hundred, one captain (*koi*); for every one hundred, a lieutenant (*ryosui*), and for every fifty, a sergeant-major (*taisei*). As for the privates, they were organized in groups of five (*go*); ten (*kwa*); and fifty (*tai*). Those who could draw a bow and manage a horse were enrolled in the cavalry, the rest being infantry. From each *tai* two specially robust men were selected as archers, and for each *kwa* there were six pack-horses. The equipment of a soldier on campaign included a large sword (*tachi*) and a small sword (*katana* or *sashi-zoe*) together with a quiver (*yanagui* or *ebira*); but in time of peace these were kept in store, the daily exercises being confined to the use of the spear, the catapult (*ishi-yumi*) and the bow, and to the practice of horsemanship. When several army corps were massed to the number of ten thousand or more, their staff consisted of a general (*shogun*), two lieutenant-generals (*fuku-shogun*), two army-inspectors (*gunkan*), four secretaries (*rokuji*), and four sergeants (*gunso*). If more than one such force took the field, the whole was commanded by a general-in-chief.

APPOINTMENT AND PROMOTION

The law provided that appointment to office and promotion should depend, not upon rank, but upon knowledge and capacity. Youths who had graduated at the university were divided into three categories: namely, those of eminent talent (*shusai*); those having extensive knowledge of the Chinese classics (*meikei*), and those advanced in knowledge (*shinshi*). Official vacancies were filled from these three classes in the order here set down, and promotion subsequently depended on proficiency. But admission to the portals of the university was barred to all except nobles or the sons and grandsons of literati. Scions of noble families down to the fifth rank had the right of entry, and scions of nobles of the sixth, seventh, and eighth ranks were admitted by nomination.

THE PEOPLE

According to the Daiho laws one family constituted a household. But the number of a family was not limited: it included brothers and their wives and children, as well as male and female servants, so that it might comprise as many as one hundred persons. The eldest legitimate son was the head of the household, and its representative in the eyes of the law. A very minute census was kept, which was revised every six years, two copies of the revised document being sent to the privy council (*Daijo-kwan*) and one kept in the district concerned.

To facilitate the preservation of good order and morality, each group of five households was formed into an "association of five" (*goho* or *gonin-gumi*) with a recognized head (*hocho*); and fifty households constituted a village (*sato* or *mura*), which was the smallest administrative unit. The village had a mayor (*richo*), whose functions were to keep a record of the number of persons in each household; to encourage diligence in agriculture and sericulture; to reprove, and, if necessary, to report all evil conduct, and to stimulate the discharge of public service. Thus the district chief (*guncho* or *gunryo*) had practically little to do beyond superintending the *richo*.

LAND AND TAXATION

The land laws of the Daiho era were based on the hypothesis that all land throughout the country was the property of the Crown, and that upon the latter devolved the responsibility of equitable distribution among the people. The law enacted that all persons, on attaining the age of five, became entitled to two *tan* of "rice land" (irrigated fields), females receiving two-thirds of that amount.

The theory of distribution was that the produce of one *tan* served for food, while with the produce of the second *tan* the cost of clothes and so forth was defrayed. The Daiho legislators alike laid down the principle that rice-fields thus allotted should be held for a period of six years only, after which they were to revert to the Crown for redistribution, but this provision proved quite unpracticable.

A different method was pursued, however, in the case of uplands (as distinguished from wet fields). These – called *onchi* – were parcelled out among the families residing in a district, without distinction of age or sex, and were held in perpetuity, never reverting to the Crown unless a family became extinct. The tenure of such land was conditional upon planting from one hundred to three hundred mulberry trees (for purposes of sericulture) and from forty to one hundred lacquer trees, according to the grade of the tenant family. Ownership of building-land (*takuchi*) was equally in perpetuity. Considerable tracts of land were reserved for special purposes – Court land or "official fields', which were under the direct control of the Imperial Household Department.

There were also three other kinds of special estates, namely, *iden*, or lands granted to mark official ranks (which ranged from 100–200 acres); *shokubunden*, or lands given as salary to office-holders (50–75 acres); and *koden*, or lands bestowed in recognition of merit (1.5–25 acres). Grants of land were given according to merit, with "great merit" ensuring the grant was given in perpetuity and, at the other end of the scale "inferior merit" only granting the land for the current generation.

There were three kinds of imposts; namely, tax (*so*), forced service (*yo* or *kayaku*) and tribute (*cho*). The tax was three per cent, of the gross produce of the land. The tribute was much more important, for it meant that every able-bodied male had to pay a fixed quantity of silk-fabric, pongee, raw-silk, raw-cotton, indigo, rouge, copper , and, if in an Imperial domain, an additional piece of cotton cloth, thirteen feet long. Finally, the forced service meant thirty days' labour annually for each able-bodied male and fifteen days for a minor. Exemption from forced labour was granted to persons of official rank, and the terms of exemption were strictly calibrated according to rank.

Forced labourers were allowed to rest from noon to 4 p.m. in July and August. They were not required to work at night. If they fell sick so as to be unable to labour out of doors, they were allowed only half rations. If they were taken ill on their way to their place of work, they were left to the care of the local authorities and fed at public charge. If they died, a coffin was furnished out of the public funds, and the corpse, unless claimed, was cremated, the ashes being buried by the wayside and a mark set up. Precise rules as to inheritance were laid down. A mother and a step-mother ranked equally with the eldest son for that purpose, each receiving two parts; younger sons received one part, and concubines and female children received one-half of a part. There were also strict rules as to the measure of relief from taxation granted in the event of crop-failure.

THE NARA EPOCH

This epoch, so-called because it saw the move of the official capital to Nara, was marked by the widespread acceptance of Buddhism which pervaded all levels of society. Magnificent temples were constructed in the Buddha's honour and the new faith began to leave an indelible mark on Japan's architecture, art, funeral rites and much more. Literature also flourished as written Japanese developed, with poetry in particular becoming a pursuit of the highest refinement. Politically, however, the rise of the Fujiwara clan, other aristocratic families and the outbreak of the Yemeshi revolt in the east signified a reversion back to the old ways and the undermining of the Daika Reforms.

THE FORTY-THIRD SOVEREIGN, THE EMPRESS GEMMYO

The Empress Gemmyo (708–15), fourth daughter of the Emperor Tenchi and consort of Prince Kusakabe, was the mother of the Emperor Mommu, whose accession had been the occasion of the first formal declaration of the right of primogeniture. Mommu, dying, willed that the throne should be occupied by his mother in trust for his infant son – afterwards Emperor Shomu.

In ancient times it was customary to change the locality of the Imperial capital with each change of sovereign. This custom, dictated by the Shinto conception of impurity attaching to sickness and death, exercised a baleful influence on architectural development, and constituted a heavy burden upon the people, whose forced labour was largely requisitioned for the building of the new palace. Kotoku, when he promulgated his system of centralized administration, conceived the idea of a fixed capital and selected Naniwa. But the Emperor Tenchi moved to Omi, Temmu to Asuka (in Yamato) and the Empress Jito to Fujiwara (in Yamato). Mommu remained at the latter place until the closing year (707) of his reign, when, finding the site inconvenient, he gave orders for the selection of another.

In the second year of the Empress Gemmyo's reign the Court finally removed to Nara, where it remained for seventy-five years, throughout the reigns of seven sovereigns. Nara, in the province of Yamato, lies nearly due south of Kyoto at a distance of twenty-six miles from the latter. To-day it is celebrated for scenic beauties – a spacious park with noble trees and softly contoured hills, sloping down to a fair expanse of lake, and enshrining in their dales ancient temples, wherein are preserved many fine specimens of Japanese art, glyptic and pictorial, of the seventh and eighth centuries. Nothing remains of the palace where the Court reside, but one building, a storehouse called *Shoso-in*, survives in its primitive form and constitutes a landmark in the annals of Japanese civilization, for it contains specimens of all the articles that were in daily use by the sovereigns of the Nara epoch.

JAPANESE COINS

There is obscurity about the production of the precious metals in old Japan. That gold, silver, and copper were known and used is certain, but during the first seven centuries of the Christian era, Japan relied on Korea mainly, and on China partially, for its supply of the precious metals.

Coined money had already been a feature of Chinese civilization since the fourth century before Christ, and when Japan began to take models from its great neighbour during the Sui and Tang dynasties, it cannot have failed to appreciate the advantages of artificial media of exchange. The annals allege that in 677 CE the first mint was established, and that in 683 an ordinance prescribed that the silver coins struck there should be superseded by copper. But this rule did not remain long in force, nor have any coins survived. It was in the year of the Empress Gemmyo's accession (708) that deposits of copper were found in the Chichibu district of Musashi province. Thenceforth, coins of copper – or more correctly, bronze – were regularly minted and gradually took the place of rice or cotton cloth as units of value.

From the close of the seventh century, a wave of mining industry swept over Japan. Silver was procured from the provinces of Iyo and Kii; copper from Inaba and Suo, and tin from Ise, Tamba, and Iyo. All this happened between the years 690 and 708, but the discovery of copper in the latter year in Chichibu was on comparatively the largest scale, and may be said to have given the first really substantial impetus to coining. For some unrecorded reason silver pieces were struck first and were followed by copper a few months later. Both were of precisely the same form – round with a square hole in the middle to facilitate threading on a string – both were of the same denomination (one *won*), and both bore the same superscription (*Wado Kaiho*, or "opening treasure of refined copper"), the shape, the denomination, and the legend being taken from a coin of the Tang dynasty struck eighty-eight years previously.

It was ordered that in using these pieces silver should be paid in the case of sums of or above four *mon*, and copper in the case of sums of or below three *won*, the value of the silver coin being four times that of the copper. But the silver tokens soon ceased to be current and copper mainly occupied the field, a position which it held for 250 years, from 708 to 958. The quality of the coins deteriorated steadily over this period, owing to growing scarcity of the supply of copper; and, partly to compensate for the increased cost of the metal, partly to minister to official greed, the new issues were declared, on several occasions, to have a value ten times as great as their immediate predecessors.

Much difficulty was experienced in weaning the people from their old custom of barter and inducing them to use coins. The Government seems to have recognized that there could not be any effective spirit of economy so long as perishable goods represented the standard of value, and in order to popularize the use of the new tokens as well as to encourage thrift, it was decreed that grades of rank would be bestowed upon men who had saved certain sums in coin. At that time (711), official salaries had already been fixed in terms of the *Wado sen*, with *mon* representing a lower-value unit of currency. The highest officials received thirty pieces of cloth, one hundred hanks of silk and two thousand *mon*, while in the case of an eighth-class official the corresponding figures were one piece of cloth and twenty *mon*.

Observing that the fundamental principle of a sound token of exchange was wholly disregarded in these *Wado sen*, since their intrinsic value bore no appreciable ratio to their purchasing power, and considering also the crudeness of their manufacture, it is not surprising to find that within a few months of their appearance they were extensively forged. The practice, pursued almost invariably, of multiplying by ten the purchasing power of each new issue of *sen*, proved, of course, enormously profitable to the issuers, but could not fail to distress the people and to render unpopular such arbitrarily varying tokens.

The Government spared no effort to correct the latter result, and some of the devices employed were genuinely progressive. No district governor (*gunryo*), however competent, was counted eligible for promotion unless he had saved six thousand *sen*, and it was enacted that all taxes might be paid in copper coin. In spite of all this, however, the use of metallic media was limited for a long time to the upper classes and to the inhabitants of the five home provinces. Elsewhere the old habit of barter continued.

THE FORTY-FOURTH SOVEREIGN, THE EMPRESS GENSHO

In the year 715, the Empress Gemmyo, after a reign of seven years, abdicated in favour of her daughter, Gensho (715–23). This is the only instance in Japanese history of an Empress succeeding an Empress. The reigns of these two Empresses are memorable for the compilation of the two oldest Japanese histories which have been handed down to the present epoch, the *Kojiki* and the *Nihongi*. The writing of history became thenceforth an imperially patronized occupation. Six works, covering the period from 697 to 887, appeared in succession and were known through all ages as the Six National Histories. It is noticeable that in the compilation of all these a leading part was taken by one or another of the great Fujiwara ministers, and that the fifth numbered among its authors the illustrious Sugawara Michizane.

THE FORTY-FIFTH SOVEREIGN, THE EMPEROR SHOMU

When the Emperor Mommu died (707), his son, the Prince Imperial, was too young to succeed. Therefore the sceptre came into the hands of Mommu's mother, who, after a reign of seven years, abdicated in favour of her daughter, the Empress Gensho, and, eight years later, the latter in turn abdicated in favour of her nephew, Shomu, who had now reached man's estate. Shomu's mother, Higami, was a daughter of Fujiwara Fuhito, and as the Fujiwara family did not belong to the *Kwobetsu* class, she had not attained the rank of Empress, but had remained simply Mommu's consort (*fujiri*). Her son, the Emperor Shomu, married another daughter of the same Fujiwara Fuhito by a different mother; that is to say, he took for consort his own mother's half-sister, Asuka. This lady, Asuka, laboured under the same disadvantage of lineage and could not properly be recognized as Empress. It is necessary to note these details for they constitute the preface to a remarkable page of Japanese history. Of Fujiwara Fuhito's two daughters, one,

Higami, was the mother of the reigning Emperor, Shomu, and the other, Asuka, was his consort. The blood relationship of the Fujiwara family to the Court could scarcely have been more marked, but its public recognition was impeded by the defect in the family's lineage.

Immediately after Shomu's accession (724–48), his mother, Higami, received the title of *Kwo-taifujin* (Imperial Great Lady). But the ambition of her family was to have her named *Kwo-taiko* (Empress Dowager). The Emperor also desired to raise his consort, Asuka, to the position of Empress. Consulting his ministers on the subject, he encountered opposition from Prince Nagaya, minister of the Left. This prince, a great-grandson of the Emperor Temmu, enjoyed high reputation as a scholar, was looked up to as a statesman of great wisdom, and possessed much influence owing to his exalted official position. He urged that neither precedent nor law sanctioned nomination of a lady of the *Shimbetsu* class to the rank of Empress. The Daiho code was indeed very explicit on the subject. The Japanese legislators had clearly enacted that an Empress must be taken from among Imperial princesses.

The lady Asuka bore a son to the Emperor three years after his accession. His Majesty was profoundly pleased. He caused a general amnesty to be proclaimed, presented gratuities to officials, and granted gifts to all children born on the same day. When only two months old, the child was created Prince Imperial, but in his eleventh month he fell ill. Buddhist images were cast; Buddhist Sutras were copied; offerings were made to the *Kami*, and an amnesty was proclaimed. Nothing availed. The child died, and the Emperor was distraught with grief. In this incident the partisans of the Fujiwara saw their opportunity. They caused it to be laid to Prince Nagaya's charge that he had compassed the death of the infant prince by charms and incantations. Two of the Fujiwara nobles were appointed to investigate the accusation, and they condemned the prince to die by his own hand. He committed suicide, and his wife and children died with him. Six months later, the lady Asuka was formally proclaimed Empress.

Thenceforth the Fujiwara family wielded the power of the State through the agency of their daughters. They furnished Empresses and consorts to the reigning sovereigns, and took their own wives from the Minamoto family, itself of Imperial lineage. To such an extent was the former practice followed that on two occasions three Fujiwara ladies served simultaneously in the palace. The elevation of the lady Asuka to be Empress Komyo marks an epoch in Japanese history.

The great Confucianist, Makibi, and the Buddhist prelate, Gembo, met with misfortune and became the victims of an unjust accusation because they attempted to assert the Imperial authority as superior to the growing influence of the Fujiwara. Makibi held the post of chamberlain of the Empress' household, and Gembo officiated at the "Interior monastery" (Nai-dojo) where the members of the Imperial family worshipped Buddha. The Emperor's mother, Higami, fell into a state of melancholia and invited Gembo to prescribe for her, which he did successfully. Thus, his influence in the palace became very great, and was augmented by the piety of the Empress, who frequently listened to discourses by the learned prelate. Fujiwara Hirotsugu was then governor of Yamato. Witnessing this state of affairs with uneasiness, he impeached Gembo. But the Emperor credited the priest's assertions, and removed

Hirotsugu to the remote post of *Dazai-fu* in Chikuzen. There he raised the standard of revolt and was with some difficulty captured and executed. The Fujiwara did not tamely endure this check. They exerted their influence to procure the removal of Makibi and Gembo from the capital, both being sent to Tsukushi (Kyushu), Makibi in the capacity of governor, and Gembo to build the temple Kwannon-ji. Gembo died a year later. There can be little doubt that the two illustrious scholars suffered for their fame rather than for their faults, and that their chief offences were overshadowing renown and independence of Fujiwara patronage.

COMMUNICATIONS WITH CHINA

In spite of the length and perils of a voyage from Japan to China in the seventh and eighth centuries – one embassy which sailed from Naniwa in the late summer of 659 did not reach China for 107 days – the journey was frequently made by Japanese students of religion and literature, just as the Chinese, on their side, travelled often to India in search of Buddhist enlightenment. This access to the refinement and civilization of the Tang Court contributed largely to Japan's progress, both material and moral.

In the year 716, Nakamaro, a member of the great Abe family, accompanied the Japanese ambassador to Tang and remained in China until his death in 770. He was known in China as Chao Heng, and the great poet, Li Pai, composed a poem in his memory, while the Tang sovereign conferred on him the posthumous title of "viceroy of Luchou." Not less celebrated was Makibi, who went to China at the same time as Nakamaro, and after twenty years' close study of Confucius, returned in 735, having earned such a reputation for profound knowledge of history, the five classics, jurisprudence, mathematics, philosophy, calendar making, and other sciences that the Chinese parted with him reluctantly. In Japan he was raised to the high rank of *asomi*, and ultimately became minister of the Right during the reign of Shotoku.

Such incidents speak eloquently of the respect paid in Japan to mental attainments and of the enlightened hospitality of China. In the realm of Buddhism perhaps even more than in that of secular science, this close intercourse made its influence felt. Priests went from Japan to study in China, and priests came from China to preach in Japan. For example, a Chinese missionary named Kanshi went to Japan accompanied by fourteen priests, three nuns, and twenty-four laymen, and the mission carried with it many Buddhist relics, images, and Sutras. Summoned to Nara in 754, he was treated with profound reverence, and on a platform specially erected before the temple Todai-ji, where stood the colossal image of Buddha – to be presently spoken of – the sovereign and many illustrious personages performed the most solemn rite of Buddhism under the ministration of Kanshin. He established a further claim on the gratitude of the Empress by curing her of an obstinate malady, and her Majesty would fain have raised him to the highest rank (*dai-sojo*) of the Buddhist priesthood. But he declined the honour. Subsequently, the former palace of Prince Nittabe was given to him as a residence and he built there the temple of Shodai-ji, which still exists.

BUDDHISM IN THE NARA EPOCH

Emperor Shomu was an earnest disciple of Buddhism. The most memorable event of his reign his abdication of the throne in order to enter religion, thus inaugurating a practice which was followed by several subsequent sovereigns and which materially helped the Fujiwara family to usurp the reality of administrative power. Shomu, on receiving the tonsure, changed his name to Shoman, and thenceforth took no part in secular affairs.

Emperor after Emperor worshipped the Buddha. Even Tenchi, who profoundly admired the Confucian philosophy and whose experience of the Soga nobles' treason might well have prejudiced him against the faith they championed; and even Temmu, whose ideals took the forms of frugality and militarism, were lavish in their offerings at Buddhist ceremonials. The Emperor Mommu enacted a law for the better control of priests and nuns, yet he erected the temple Kwannon-ji. The great Fujiwara statesmen, as Kamatari, Fuhito, and the rest, though they belonged to a family (the *Nakatomi*) closely associated with Shinto worship, were reverent followers of the Indian faith.

In spite, however, of all this zeal for Buddhism, the nation did not entirely abandon its traditional faith. The original cult had been ancestor worship. Each great family had its *uji no Kami*, to whom it made offerings and presented supplications. These deities were now supplemented, not supplanted. They were grafted upon a Buddhist stem, and shrines of the *uji no Kami* became *uji-tera*, or "*uji* temples." Thenceforth the temple (*tera*) took precedence of the shrine (*yashiro*). When spoken of together they became *ji-sha*. This was the beginning of Ryobu

Shinto, or mixed Shinto, which found full expression when Buddhist teachers, obedient to a spirit of toleration born of their belief in the doctrines of metempsychosis (reincarnation) and universal perfectibility, asserted the creed that the Shinto *Kami* were avatars (incarnations) of the numerous Buddhas.

The Nara epoch has not bequeathed to posterity many relics of the great religious edifices that came into existence under Imperial patronage during its seventy-five years. Built almost wholly of wood, these temples were gradually destroyed by fire. One object, however, defied the agent of destruction. It is a bronze Buddha of huge proportions, known now to all the world as the "Nara Daibutsu." On 7th November, 743 the Emperor Shomu proclaimed his intention of undertaking this work. The announcement promises that every contributor to the work shall be welcome, even actual work of casting began in 747 and was completed in three years, after seven failures. The image was not cast in its entirety; it was built up with bronze plates soldered together. A sitting depiction of the Buddha, it had a height of fifty-three and a half feet and the face was sixteen feet long, while on either side was an attendant bosatsu standing thirty feet high. For the image, 986,030,000 lbs. of copper were needed, and on the gilding of its surface 870 lbs. of refined gold were used.

Fortunately in the year 749 gold was found in the province of Mutsu, and people regarded the timely discovery as a special dispensation of Buddha. The great hall in which the image stood had a height of 120 feet and a width of 290 feet from east to west, and beside it two pagodas rose to a height of 230 feet each. Throughout the ten years occupied in the task of collecting materials and casting this *Daibutsu*, the Emperor solemnly worshipped Rushana Buddha three times daily, and on its completion he took the tonsure. It was not until the year 752, however, that the final ceremony of unveiling took place, and in the following year the temple – Todai-ji – was endowed with the taxes of five thousand households and the revenue from twenty-five thousand acres of rice-fields.

While all this religious fervour was finding costly expression among the aristocrats in Nara, the propagandists and patrons of Buddhism did not neglect the masses. In the year 741, provincial temples were officially declared essential to the State's well-being. These edifices had their origin at an earlier date. During the reign of Temmu (673–686) an Imperial decree ordered that throughout the whole country every household should provide itself with a Buddhist shrine and place therein a sacred image.

During Mommu's time (697–707), Buddhist hierarchs (*kokushi*) were appointed to the provinces. Their chief functions were to expound the Sutra and to offer prayers. The devout Shomu issued a command that each province must provide itself with a pagoda seven storeys high. By this order the provincial temples (*kokubun-ji*) were called into official existence, and presently their number was increased to two in each province, one for priests and one for nuns. The *kokushi* attached to these temples laboured in the cause of propagandism and religious education side by side with the provincial pundits (*kunihakase*), whose duty was to instruct the people in law and literature.

It is said to have been mainly at the instance of the Empress Komyo that the great image of Todai-ji was constructed and the provincial temples were established. But undoubtedly the original impulse came from a priest, Gyogi. Said to have been of Korean extraction, he was amply gifted with the personal magnetism which has always distinguished notably successful propagandists of religion. Wherever he preached and prayed, thousands of priests and laymen flocked to hear him, and so supreme was his influence that under his direction. By order of the Empress Gensho, Gyogi was thrown into prison for a time, such a disturbing effect did his propagandism produce on men's pursuit of ordinary bread winning; but he soon emerged and was taken into the Emperor Shomu's favour.

Gyogi's speech and presence exercised more influence than a hundred Imperial edicts. It is recorded that, by way of corollary to the task of reconciling the nation to the Nara Court's pious extravagance, perhaps the most memorable event in his career was the part he took in reconciling the indigenous faith and the imported. However fervent Shomu's belief in Buddhism, the country he ruled was the country of the *Kami*, and on descent from the *Kami* his own title to the throne rested. Thus, qualms of conscience may well have visited him when he remembered the comparatively neglected shrine of the Sun goddess at Ise. Gyogi undertook to consult the will of the goddess, and carried back a revelation which he interpreted in the sense that Amaterasu should be regarded as an incarnation of the Buddha. Thus was originated a theory which enabled Buddhism and Shinto to walk hand in hand for a thousand years, the theory that the Shinto *Kami* are avatars of the Buddha.

Side by side with the vigorous Buddhism of the Nara epoch, strange superstitions obtained currency and credence. Two may be mentioned as illustrating the mood of the age. One related to an ascetic, En no Ubasoku, who was worshipped by the people of Kinai under the name of En no Gyoja (En the anchorite). He lived in a cave on Katsuragi Mount for forty years, wore garments made of wisteria bark, and ate only pine leaves steeped in spring water. During the night he compelled demons to draw water and gather firewood, and during the day he rode upon clouds of five colours. Accused of treasonable designs, the Emperor Mommu sent soldiers to arrest him. But as he was able to evade them by recourse to his art of flying, they apprehended his mother in his stead, whereupon he at once gave himself up. In consideration of his filial piety his punishment was commuted to exile on an island off the Izu coast, and in deference to the Imperial orders he remained there quietly throughout the day, but devoted the night to flying to the summit of Mount Fuji or gliding over the sea. This En no Gyoja was the founder of a sect of priests calling themselves *Yamabushi*.

The second superstition relates to one of the genii named *Kume*. By the practice of asceticism he obtained supernatural power, and while riding one day upon a cloud, he passed above a beautiful girl washing clothes in a river, and became so enamoured of her that he lost his superhuman capacities and fell at her feet. She became his wife. Years afterwards it chanced that he was called out for forced labour, and, being taunted by the officials as a pseudo-genius, he fasted and prayed for seven days and seven nights. On the eighth morning a thunder-storm visited the scene, and after it, a quantity of heavy timber was found to have been moved, without any human effort, from the forest to the site of the projected building. The Emperor, hearing of this, granted him forty-five acres, on which he built the temple of *Kume*-dera.

Such tales found credence in the Nara epoch, and indeed all through the annals of early Japan there runs a well-marked thread of superstition which owed something of its obtrusiveness to intercourse with Korea and China, whence came professors of the arts of invisibility and magic. In the reign of the Empress Kogyoku, witches and wizards betray the people into all sorts of extravagances; and a Korean acolyte has for friend a tiger which teaches him all manner of wonderful arts, among others that of healing any disease with a magic needle. Later on, these and cognate creations of credulity take their appropriate places in the realm of folk-lore, but they rank with sober history in the ancient annals. In this respect Japan did not differ from other early peoples.

THE FORTY-SIXTH SOVEREIGN, THE EMPRESS KOKEN

In July, 749, the Emperor Shomu abdicated in favour of his daughter, Princess Abe, known in history as Koken (749–58). Her mother was the celebrated Princess Asuka, who, in spite of the *Shimbetsu* lineage of her Fujiwara family, had been made Shomu's Empress, and whose name had been changed to Komyo (Refulgence) in token of her illustrious piety. The daughter inherited all the mother's romance, but in her case it often degenerated into a passion more elementary than religious ecstasy. Shomu, having no son, made his daughter heir to the throne. Japanese history furnished no precedent for such a step. The custom had always been that a reign ceased on the death of a sovereign unless the Crown Prince had not yet reached maturity, in which event his mother, or some other nearly related princess, occupied the throne until he came of age and then surrendered the reins of government to his hands. Such had been the practice in the case of the Empresses Jito,

Gemmyo, and Gensho. Shomu, however, not only bequeathed the throne to a princess, but while himself still in the prime of life, abdicated in her favour.

Thereafter, at the recognized instance of the all-powerful Fujiwara family, Emperors often surrendered the sceptre to their heirs, themselves retiring into religious life with the secular title of *Da-joko* (Great ex-Emperor) and the ecclesiastical designation of *Ho-o* (pontiff). Shomu was the originator of this practice, but the annals are silent as to the motive that inspired him. It will be presently seen that under the skilful manipulation of the Fujiwara nobles, this device of abdication became a potent aid to their usurpation of administrative power, and from that point of view the obvious inference is that Shomu's unprecedented step was taken at their suggestion.

The fanaticism of the Emperor Shomu and his consort, Komyo, bore fruit during the reign of Koken. In the third year after Shomu's abdication, a decree was issued prohibiting the taking of life in any form. At the ceremony of opening the public worship of the great image of Buddha, the Empress in person led the vast procession of military, civil, and religious dignitaries to the temple Todai-ji. It was a fete of unparalleled dimensions. All officials of the fifth grade and upwards wore full uniform, and all of lesser grades wore robes of the colour appropriate to their rank. Ten thousand Buddhist priests officiated, and the Imperial musicians were re-enforced by those from all the temples throughout the home provinces. Buddhism in Japan had never previously received such splendid homage.

In the evening, the Empress visited the residence of the grand councillor, Fujiwara no Nakamaro, a grandson of the great Kamatari, who held the rank of *dainagon* and was at once a learned man and an able administrator. From the time of that visit to the *Tamura-no-tei* (Tamura mansion), as his residence was called, the Empress repaired thither frequently, and finally made it a detached palace under the name of *Tamura-no-miya*. Those that tried to put an end to the liaison were themselves driven from office, and Nakamaro's influence became daily stronger.

THE FORTY-SEVENTH SOVEREIGN, THE EMPEROR JUNNIN

In August, 758, the Empress, after a reign of four years, nominally abdicated in favour of the Crown Prince, Junnin (758–64), but continued to discharge all the functions of government herself. Her infatuation for Nakamaro seemed to increase daily. She bestowed on him in perpetuity the revenue from 3000 households and 250 acres of land. But then Koken's caprice took a new turn; she became a nun and transferred her affection to a priest, Yuge no Dokyo. Nakamaro did not tamely endure being discarded. He raised the standard of revolt and found that the nun could be as relentless as the Empress had been gracious. The rebellion – known as that of Oshikatsu (the Conqueror), a name that had been bestowed on him by Koken – proved a brief struggle. Nakamaro fell in battle and his head, together with those of his wife, his children, and his devoted followers to the number of thirty-four, was despatched to Nara.

The tumult had a more serious sequel. The Dowager Empress – so Koken had called herself – did not hesitate a moment. In the very month following Nakamaro's destruction, she charged that the Emperor was in collusion with the rebel; despatched a force of troops to surround the palace; dethroned Junnin; degraded him to the rank of a prince, and sent him and his mother into exile, where the conditions of confinement were made so intolerable that the ex-Emperor attempted to escape, was captured and killed.

THE FORTY-EIGHTH SOVEREIGN, THE EMPRESS SHOTOKU

The nun Koken now abandoned the veil and re-ascended the throne under the name of Shotoku (765–70). She now bestowed on Dokyo, her lover, a rank equal to that of the prime minister. All the civil and military magnates had to pay homage to him at the festival of the New Year in his exalted capacity. In the year after her second ascent of the throne she named him Ho-o (pontiff), a title never previously borne by any save her father, the ex-Emperor Shomu. Dokyo rose fully to the level of the occasion. He modelled his life in every respect on that of a sovereign and assumed complete control of the administration of the empire. He not only fared sumptuously but also built many temples, and as the Empress was not less extravagant, the burden of taxation became painfully heavy. But the priestly favourite, who seems to have had the ambition of ascending the throne, did not restrain his expenditure. Whether at his instigation or because his favour had become of paramount importance to all men of ambition, Asomaro, governor of the *Dazai-fu*, informed the Empress that, according to an oracle delivered by the god of War (Hachiman) at Usa, the nation would enjoy tranquillity and prosperity if Dokyo were its ruler.

The Empress had profound reverence for Hachiman, a fact that was well known to Asomaro and to Dokyo. Yet she hesitated to take this extreme step without fuller assurance. She ordered Wake no Kiyomaro to proceed to Usa and consult the deity once more. Kiyomaro was a fearless patriot and the answer carried back by him from the Usa shrine was explicitly fatal to Dokyo's hope. "The successor of the throne must be of the Imperial family and a usurper is to be rejected." Dokyo's wrath was extreme and Kiyomaro's was banished him to Osumi in the extreme south of Kyushu. Shortly afterwards, the Empress died. Dokyo and Asomaro were banished, and Kiyomaro was recalled from exile.

THE STATE OF THE PROVINCES

In the days of Shomu and Koken administrative abuses were not limited to the capital, they extended to the provinces also. Among the Daika and Daiho laws, the first that proved to be a failure was that relating to provincial governors. At the outset men of ability were chosen for these important posts, and their term of service was limited to four years. Soon, however, under Empress Koken the period of office was extended to six years. Moreover, whereas at first a newly appointed governor was supposed to live in the official residence of his predecessor, it quickly became the custom to build a new mansion for the incoming dignitary and leave the outgoing undisturbed. All such edifices were constructed by forced labour.

The provincial governors exercised the power of appointing and dismissing the district governors (*gunshi*) in their provinces, although this evil system had been prohibited in the time of Gemmyo. In connexion, too, with the rice collected for public purposes, there were abuses. This rice, so long as it lay in the official storehouses, represented so much idle capital. The provincial governors utilized it by lending the grain to the farmers in the spring, partly for seed purposes and partly for food, on condition that it should be paid back in the autumn with fifty per cent, increment. Subsequently this exorbitant figure was reduced to thirty per cent. But the result was ruin for many farmers. They had to hand over their fields and houses or sell themselves into bondage.

Thus, outlaws, living by plunder, became a common feature of the time, and there arose a need for guards more capable than those supplied by the system of partial conscription. Hence, in the reign of Shomu, the sons and brothers of district governors (*gunshi*) proficient in archery and equestrianism were summoned from Omi, Ise, Mino, and Echizen, and to them was assigned the duty of guarding the public storehouses in the provinces. At the same time many men of prominence and influence began to organize guards for their private protection. The ultimate supremacy of the military class had its origin in these circumstances.

In the Nara epoch, the Government spent fully one-half of its total income on works of piety. No country except in time of war ever devoted so much to unproductive expenditures. The enormous quantities of copper used for casting images not only exhausted the produce of the mines but also made large inroads upon the currency, hundreds of thousands of cash being thrown into the melting-pot. In 760 the Government struck a new coin – the *mannen tsuho* – which, while not differing appreciably from the old cash in intrinsic value, was arbitrarily invested with ten times the latter's purchasing power. The profit to the treasury was enormous; the disturbance of values and the dislocation of trade were proportionately great. Twelve years later (772), another rescript ordered that the new coin should circulate at par with the old. Such unstable legislation implies a very crude conception of financial requirements.

Land Reforms

It has been shown that the Daika reforms regarded all "wet fields" as the property of the Crown, while imposing no restriction on the ownership of uplands, these being counted as belonging to their reclaimers. Thus, large estates began to fall into private possession; conspicuously in the case of provincial and district governors, who were in a position to employ forced labour. These abuses became so flagrant that, in 767, reclamation was declared to constitute thereafter no title of ownership. Apparently, however, this veto proved unpractical, for five years later (772), it was rescinded, the only condition now attached being that the farmers must not be distressed. Yet again, in 784, another change of policy has to be recorded. A decree declared that governors must confine their agricultural enterprise to public lands, on penalty of being punished criminally. Finally, in 806, the pursuit of productive enterprise by governors in the provinces was once more sanctioned.

Thus, between 650 and 806, no less than five radical changes of policy are recorded. Great landed estates (*shoen*) accumulated in private hands throughout the empire, some owned by nobles, some by temples; and in order to protect their titles against the interference of the Central Government, the holders of these estates formed alliances with the great Court nobles in the capital, so that, in the course of time, a large part of the land throughout the provinces fell under the control of a few dominant families.

In the capital (Nara), on the other hand, the enormous sums squandered upon the building of temples, the casting or carving of images, and the performance of costly religious ceremonials gradually produced such a state of impecuniosity that, in 775, a decree was issued ordering that twenty-five per cent of the revenues of the public lands (*kugaideri*) should be appropriated to increase the emoluments of the metropolitan officials. When the Daika reforms were undertaken, the metropolitan magnates looked down upon their provincial brethren as an inferior order of beings, but in the closing days of the Nara epoch the situations were reversed, and the ultimate transfer of administrative power from the Court to the provincials began to be foreshadowed.

THE FUJIWARA FAMILY

The religious fanaticism of the Emperor Shomu and his consort, Komyo, brought disorder into the affairs of the Imperial Court, and gave rise to an abuse not previously recorded, namely, favouritism with its natural outcome, treasonable ambition. It began to be feared that the personal administration of the sovereign might be dangerous to the State. Thus, patriotic politicians conceived a desire not to transfer the sceptre to outside hands but to find among the scions of the Imperial family some one competent to save the situation, even though the selection involved violation of the principle of primogeniture. The death of the Empress Shotoku without issue and the consequent extinction of the Emperor Temmu's line furnished an opportunity to these loyal statesmen, and they availed themselves of it to set Konin upon the throne, as will be presently described.

In this crisis of the empire's fortunes, the Fujiwara family acted a leading part. Fuhito, son of the illustrious Kamatari, having assisted in the compilation of the Daika code and laws, and having served throughout four reigns – Jito, Mommu, Gemmyo, and Gensho – died at sixty-two in the post of minister of the Right, and left four sons, Muchimaro, Fusazaki, Umakai, and Maro. These, establishing themselves independently, founded the "four houses" of the Fujiwara. Muchimaro's home, being in the south (*nan*) of the capital, was called Nan-ke; Fusazaki's, being in the north (*hoku*), was termed Hoku-ke; Umakai's was spoken of as Shiki-ke, since he presided over the Department of Ceremonies (*Shiki*), and Maro's went by the name of Kyo-ke, this term also having reference to his office.

The Forty-ninth Sovereign, the Emperor Konin

When the Empress Shotoku died, no successor had been designated, and it seemed not unlikely that the country would be thrown into a state of civil war. The ablest among the princes of the blood was Shirakabe, grandson of the Emperor Tenchi. He was in his sixty-second year, had held the post of *nagon*, and unquestionably possessed erudition and administrative competence. Fujiwara Momokawa warmly espoused his cause, but this was opposed by Kibi no Makibi, minister of the Right, and his allies. By their united efforts Prince Shirakabe was proclaimed and became the Emperor Konin (770–81), his youngest son, Osabe, being appointed Prince Imperial.

Konin justified the zeal of his supporters, but his benevolent and upright reign has been sullied by historical romanticists, who represent him as party to an unnatural intrigue based on the alleged licentiousness and shamelessness of his consort, Princess Ino*kami*, a lady then in her fifty-sixth year with a hitherto blameless record. Momokawa, wishing to secure the succession to Prince Yamabe – afterwards Emperor Kwammu – brought about the deaths of the Empress Ino*kami*, Konin's consort, and her son, Osabe, the heir apparent. Stories injurious to the lady's reputation were circulated in justification of the murder. Certain it is, however, that to Momokawa's exertions the Emperor Kwammu owed his accession, as had his father, Konin. Kwammu was Konin's eldest son, and would have been named Prince Imperial on his father's ascent of the throne had not his mother, Takano, been deficient in qualifications of lineage. He had held the posts of president of the University and minister of the Central Department, and his career, alike in office and on the throne, bore witness to the wisdom of his supporters.

Momokawa, by way of promoting Prince Yamabe's interests, caused a statue to be made in his likeness, and, enshrining it in the temple Bonshaku-ji, ordered the priests to offer supplications in its behalf. The chronicle further relates that after the deaths of the Empress (Ino*kami*) and her son (Osabe), Momokawa and Emperor Konin were much troubled by the spirits of the deceased. Momokawa died before the accession of Kwammu, but to him was largely due the great influence subsequently wielded by the Fujiwara at Court.

The fact is that the Fujiwara were a natural outcome of the situation. The Tang systems, which Kamatari, the great founder of the family, had been chiefly instrumental in introducing, placed in the hands of the sovereign powers much too extensive to be safely entrusted to a monarch qualified only by heredity. Comprehending the logic of their organization, the Chinese made their monarchs' tenure of authority depend upon the verdict of the nation. But in Japan the title to the crown being divinely bequeathed, there could be no question of appeal to a popular tribunal.

The Fujiwara became a species of electoral college, not possessing, indeed, any recognized mandate from the nation, yet acting in the nation's behalf to secure worthy occupants for the throne. For a time this system worked satisfactorily, but ultimately the Fujiwara became flagrant abusers of the power handed down to them. Momokawa's immediate followers were worthy to wear his mantle. Tanetsugu, Korekimi, Tsugunawa – these are names that deserve to be printed in letters of gold on the pages of Japan's annals. They either prompted or presided over the reforms and retrenchments that marked Kwammu's reign, and personal ambition was never allowed to interfere with their duty to the State.

IMPERIAL PRINCES

Contemporaneously with the rise of the Fujiwara, an important alteration took place in the status of Imperial princes. According to the Daika legislation, not only sons of sovereigns but also their descendants to the fifth generation were classed as members of the Imperial family and inherited the title of "Prince". But no salaries were given to them; they had to support themselves with the proceeds of sustenance fiefs. The Emperor Kwammu was the first to break away from this time-honoured usage. He reduced two of his own sons, born of a non-Imperial lady, from the *Kwobetsu* class to the *Shimbetsu*, conferring on them the *uji* names of Nagaoka and Yoshimine, and he followed the same course with several of the Imperial grandsons, giving them the name of Taira.

Thenceforth, whenever a sovereign's offspring was numerous, it became customary to group them with the subject class under a family name. A prince thus reduced received the sixth official rank (*roku-i*), and was appointed to a corresponding office in the capital or a province, promotion following according to his ability and on successfully passing the examination prescribed for Court officials. Nevertheless, to be divested of the title of "Prince" did not mean less of princely prestige. Such nobles were always *primi inter pares*. The principal *uji* thus created were Nagaoka, Yoshimine, Ariwara, Taira, and Minamoto.

Uji No Choja and Gaku-in No Betto

The imperially descended *uji* spoken of above, each consisting of several houses, were grouped according to their names, and each group was under the supervision of a chief, called *uji no choja* or *uji no cho*. Usually, as has been already stated, the corresponding position in an ordinary *uji* was called *uji no Kami* and belonged to the first-born of the principal house, irrespective of his official rank. But in the case of the imperially descended *uji*, the chief was selected and nominated by the sovereign with regard to his administrative post. With the appointment was generally combined that of *Gaku-in no betto*, or commissioner of the academies established for the youths of the *uji*. The principal of these academies was the Kwangaku-in of the Fujiwara. Founded by Fujiwara Fuyutsugu, minister of the Left, in the year 821, and endowed with a substantial part of his estate in order to afford educational advantages for the poorer members of the great family, this institution rivalled even the Imperial University, to be presently spoken of. It was under the superintendence of a special commissioner (*benkwari*).

Next in importance was the Shogaku-in of the Minamoto, established by Ariwara Yukihira in the year 881. Ariwara being a grandson of the Emperor Saga, a member of the Saga Genji received the nomination of chief commissioner; but in the year 1140, the minister of the Right, Masasada, a member of the Murakami Genji, was appointed to the office, and thenceforth it remained in the hands of that house. Two other educational institutions were the Junna-in of the O-*uji* and the Gakukwan-in of the *Tachibana-uji*, the former dating from the year 834 and the latter from 820. It is not on record that there existed any special school under Taira auspices.

THE NARA ECONOMY

One of the principal duties of local governors from the time of the Daika reforms was to encourage agriculture and the practice of devoting attention to rice culture only and neglecting upland crops, was condemned. It was therefore ordered that barley and millet should be assiduously grown, and each farmer was required to lay down two *tan* (⅔ acre) annually of these upland cereals. Necessarily, as the population increased, corresponding extension of the cultivated area became desirable, and already, in the year 722, a work of reclamation on a grand scale was officially undertaken by organizing a body of peasants and sending them to bring under culture a million *cho* (two and a half million acres) of new land.

Private initiative was also liberally encouraged. An Imperial rescript promised that any farmer harvesting three thousand *koku* (fifteen thousand bushels) of cereals from land reclaimed by himself should receive the sixth class order of merit (*kun roku-to*). The Daika principle that the land was wholly the property of the Crown had thus to yield partially to the urgency of the situation, and during the third decade of the eighth century it was enacted that, if a man reclaimed land by utilizing aqueducts and reservoirs already in existence, the land should belong to him for his lifetime, while if the reservoirs and aqueducts were of his own construction, the right of property should be valid for three generations.

For a certain period the system of "three generations, or one life" worked smoothly enough; but subsequently it was found that as the limit of time approached, farmers neglected to till the land and suffered it to lie waste. Therefore, in the year 743, the Government enacted that all reclaimed land should be counted the perpetual property of the reclaimer, with one proviso, namely, that three years of neglect to cultivate should involve confiscation. The prime purpose of the legislators was achieved, since the people devoted themselves assiduously to land reclamation; but by free recourse to their power of commanding labour, the great families acquired estates largely in excess of the legal limit – evidently the effective operation of such a system predicated accurate surveys and strict supervision. Neither of these conditions existed in Japan at that remote period.

Trade and Industry

One of the unequivocal benefits bestowed on Japan by Buddhism was a strong industrial and artistic impulse. Architecture made notable progress owing to the construction of numerous massive and magnificent temples and pagodas. One of the latter, erected during the reign of Temmu, had a height of thirteen storeys. The arts of casting and of sculpture, both in metal and in wood, received great development, as did also the lacquer industry. Vermilion lacquer was invented in the time of Temmu, and soon five different colours could be produced, while to the Nara artisans belongs the inception of lacquer strewn with *makie*. Lacquer inlaid with mother-of-pearl was another beautiful concept of the Nara epoch. A special tint of red was obtained with powdered coral, and gold and silver were freely used in leaf or in plates.

Commerce with China and Korea was specially active throughout the eighth century, and domestic trade also nourished. In the capital there were two markets where people assembled at noon and dispersed at sunset. Men and women occupied different sections, and it would seem that transactions were subject to strict surveillance. Thus, if any articles of defective quality or adulterated were offered for sale, they were liable to be confiscated officially, and if a buyer found that short measure had been given, he was entitled to return his purchase. Market-rates had to be conformed with, and purchasers were required to pay promptly.

Architecture and Craft

The lofty, spacious Buddhist temple could not fail to impart an impetus to Japanese domestic architecture. Thus it is recorded that towards the close of the seventh century, tiled roofs and greater solidity of structure began to distinguish official buildings. But houses in general remained insignificant and simple.

In 742 the Emperor Shomu, responding to an appeal from the council of State, issued an edict that officials of the fifth rank and upwards and wealthy commoners should build residences with tiled roofs and walls plastered in red. This injunction was only partly obeyed: tiles came into more general use, but red walls offended the artistic instinct of the Japanese.

Of furniture the houses had very little as compared with Western customs. Neither chairs nor bedsteads existed; people sat and slept on the floor, separated from it only by mats made of rice-straw, by cushions or by woollen carpets, and in aristocratic houses there was a kind of stool to support the arm of the sitter, a lectern, and a dais for sitting on. Viands were served on tables a few inches high, and people sat while eating. From the middle of the seventh century a clepsydra of Chinese origin was used to mark the hours. When temple bells came into existence, the hours were struck on them for public information, and there is collateral evidence that some similar system of marking time had been resorted to from early eras.

In Japan bells of huge size and exquisite note were cast in apparent defiance of all the rules elaborated with so much difficulty in the West. One of the most remarkable hangs in the belfry of Todai-ji at Nara. It was cast in the year 732 when Shomu occupied the throne; it is 12 feet 9 inches high, 8 feet 10 inches in diameter, 10 inches thick, and weighs 49 tons. There are great bells also in the temples at Osaka and Kyoto, and it is to be noted that early Japanese bronze work was largely tributary and subsidiary to temple worship. Temple bells, vases, gongs, mirrors and lanterns are the principal items in this class of metal-working, until a much later period with its smaller ornaments.

At Nara, in Yamato province, near the temple of Todai-ji, a store house built of wood and called the *Shoso-in* was constructed in the Nara epoch, and it still stands housing a remarkable collection of furniture and ornaments from the Imperial palace. There is some question whether this collection is truly typical of the period, or even of the palace of the period; but the presence of many utensils from China, some from India (often with traces of Greek influence), and a few from Persia certainly shows the degree of cosmopolitan culture and elegance there was in the palace at Nara. Among the contents of this museum are: polished mirrors with repousse backs, kept in cases lined with brocaded silk; bronze vases; bronze censers; hicense-boxes made of Paulownia wood or of Chinese ware; two-edged swords, which were tied to the girdle, instead of being thrust through it; narrow leather belts with silver or jade decoration; bamboo flutes; lacquer writing-cases, etc.

Transport

During the reign of the Empress Gensho (715–723) the Nakasen-do, or Central Mountain road, was constructed. It runs from Nara to Kyoto and thence to the modern Tokyo, traversing six provinces *en route*. Neither history nor tradition tells whether it was wholly made in the days of Gensho or whether, as seems more probable, it was only commenced then and carried to completion in the reign of Shomu (724–748), when a large force of troops had to be sent northward against the rebellious Yemishi. Doubtless the custom of changing the capital on the accession of each sovereign had the effect of calling many roads into existence, but these were of insignificant length compared with a great trunk highway like the Nakasen-do.

Along these roads the lower classes travelled on foot; the higher on horseback, and the highest in carts drawn by bullocks. For equestrians who carried official permits, relays of horses could always be obtained at posting stations. Among the ox-carts which served for carriages, there was a curious type, distinguished by the fact that between the shafts immediately in front of the dashboard stood a figure whose outstretched arm perpetually pointed south. This compass-cart, known as the "south-pointing chariot," was introduced from China in the year 658.

EVERYDAY LIFE

During the last five years of the Emperor Temmu's reign – namely, from 681 – no less than nine sumptuary regulations were issued. The first was an edict, containing ninety-two articles, of which the prologue alone survives, "The costumes of all, from the princes of the Blood down to the common people, and the wearing of gold and silver, pearls and jewels, purple, brocade, embroidery, fine silks, together with woollen carpets, head-dresses, and girdles, as well as all kinds of coloured stuffs, are regulated according to a scale, the details of which are given in the written edict." In the next year (682), another edict forbids the wearing of caps of rank, aprons, broad girdles, and leggings by princes or public functionaries, as well as the use of shoulder-straps or mantillas by palace stewards or ladies-in-waiting. The shoulder-strap was a mark of manual labour, and its use in the presence of a superior has always been counted as rude in Japan.

A few days later, this meticulous monarch is found commanding men and women to tie up their hair, eight months being granted to make the change, and, at the same time, the practice of women riding astride on horseback came into vogue, showing that female costume had much in common with male. Caps of varnished gauze, after the Chinese type, began to be worn by both sexes simultaneously with the tying-up of the hair. Two years later, women of forty years or upwards were given the option of tying up their hair or letting it hang loose, and of riding astride or side-saddle as they pleased. At the same time, to both sexes, except on State occasions, liberty of choice was accorded in the matter of wearing sleeveless jackets fastened in front with silk cords and tassels, though in the matter of trousers, men had to gather theirs in at the bottom with a lace. By and by, the tying up of the hair by women was forbidden in its turn; the wearing of leggings was sanctioned, and the colours of Court costumes were strictly determined according to the rank of the wearer red, deep purple, light purple, dark green, light green, deep grape-colour and light grape-colour being the order from above downwards.

All this attention to costume is suggestive of much refinement. From the eighth century even greater care was devoted to the subject. We find three kinds of habiliments prescribed – full dress (*reifuku*), Court dress (*chofuku*) and uniform (*seifuku*) – with many minor distinctions according to the rank of the wearer. Broadly speaking, the principal garments were a paletot, trousers, and a narrow girdle tied in front. The sleeves of the paletot were studiously regulated. A nobleman wore them long enough to cover his hands, and their width – which in after ages became remarkable – was limited in the Nara epoch to one foot. The manner of folding the paletot over the breast seems to have perplexed the legislators for a time. At first they prescribed that the right should be folded over the left (*hidarimae*), but subsequently (719) an Imperial decree ordered that the left should be laid across the right (*migimae*), and since that day, nearly twelve hundred years ago, there has not been any departure from the latter rule. Court officials carried a baton (*shaku*), that, too, being a habit borrowed from China.

Food

When the influence of Buddhism became supreme in Court circles, all taking of life for purposes of food was interdicted. The Empress Shotoku (765–770) went so far as to forbid the keeping of dogs, falcons, or cormorants for hunting or fishing at Shinto ceremonials. But such vetoes were never effectually enforced. The great staple of diet was rice, steamed or boiled, and next in importance came millet, barley, fish of various kinds (fresh or salted), seaweed, vegetables, fruit (pears, chestnuts, etc.), and the flesh of fowl, deer, and wild boar. Salt, bean-sauce, and vinegar were used for seasoning. There were many kinds of dishes; among the commonest being soup (*atsumono*) and a preparation of raw fish in vinegar (*namasu*). In the reign of Kotoku (645–654), a Korean named Zena presented a milch cow to the Court, and from that time milk was recognized as specially hygienic diet. Thus, when the Daiho laws were published at the beginning of the eighth century, dairies were attached to the medical department, and certain provinces received orders to present butter (*gyuraku*) for the Court's use.

Funerary Rites

A mortuary chamber was provided for the corpse pending the preparation of the tomb is shown by the earliest annals; dirges were sung for eight days and eight nights, and that in the burial procession were marshalled bearers of viands to be offered at the grave, bearers of brooms to sweep the path, women who prepared the viands, and a body of hired mourners. From the days of the Emperor Bidatsu (572–585), we find the first mention of funeral orations, and although the contents of tombs bear witness to the fact that articles other than food were offered to the deceased, it is not until the burial of the Emperor's consort, Katachi, (612) that explicit mention is made of such a custom. By the end of the seventh century funerals had been invaded by Chinese customs, for it is recorded that "officials of the third rank were allowed at their funerals one hearse, forty drums, twenty great horns, forty little horns, two hundred flags, one metal gong, and one hand-bell, with lamentation for one day." At Temmu's obsequies (687) mention is made of an "ornamented chaplet," the first reference to the use of flowers, which constitute such a prominent feature of Buddhist obsequies.

But there is no evidence that Buddhist rites were employed at funerals until the death of the retired Emperor Shomu (756). Thereafter, the practice became common. It was also to a Buddhist priest, Dosho, that Japan owed the inception of cremation. Dying in the year 700, Dosho ordered his disciples to cremate his body at Kurihara, and, two years later, the Dowager Empress Jito willed that her corpse should be similarly disposed of. From the megalithic tombs of old Japan to the little urn that holds the handful of ashes representing a cremated body, the transition is immense. An edict issued in 706 shows that attending the resting place of the dead was still regarded as a sacred duty, for the edict ordered that, alike at the ancestral tombs of the *uji* and in the residential quarter of the common people, trees should be planted.

The Empress Gemmyo (d. 721) appears to have inaugurated the custom of erecting monuments with inscriptions, for she willed not only that evergreens should be planted at her grave but also that a tablet should be set up there. Some historians hold that the donning of special garments by way of mourning had its origin at that time, and that it was borrowed from the Tang code of etiquette. But the *Chronicles* state that in the year 312 CE, when the Prince Imperial committed suicide rather than occupy the throne, his brother, Osasagi, "put on plain unbleached garments and began mourning for him." White ultimately became the mourning colour, but in the eighth century it was dark, and mourning clothess were called *fuji-koromo*, because they were made from the bark of the wisteria (*fuji*).

Cultural Pastimes

The tendency of the Japanese has always been to accompany their feasting and merry-making with music, versifying, and dancing. At the time now under consideration there was the "winding-water fete" (*kyoku-sui no en*), when princes, high officials, courtiers, and noble ladies seated themselves by the banks of a rivulet meandering gently through some fair park, and launched tiny cups of mulled wine upon the current, each composing a stanza as the little messenger reached him, or drinking its contents by way of penalty for lack of poetic inspiration. There were also the flower festivals – that for the plum blossoms, that for the iris, and that for the lotus, all of which were instituted in this same Nara epoch – when the composition of couplets was quite as important as the viewing of the flowers. There was, further, the grand New Year's banquet in the Hall of Tranquillity at the Court, when all officials from the sixth grade downwards sang a stanza of loyal gratitude, accompanying themselves on the lute (*koto*). It was an era of refined effeminate amusements. Wrestling had now become the pursuit of professionals. Aristocrats engaged in no rougher pastime than equestrian archery, a species of football, hawking, and hunting. Everybody gambled. It was in vain that edicts were issued against dicing (*chobo* and *sugoroku*). The vice defied official restraint.

Having no books of its own, Japan naturally borrowed freely from the rich mine of Chinese literature. The advantages of education were, however, enjoyed by a comparatively small element of the population. During the Nara epoch, it does not appear that there were more than five thousand students attending the schools and colleges at one time. The aim of instruction was to prepare men for official posts rather than to impart general culture or to encourage scientific research. Students were therefore selected from the aristocrats or the official classes only. There were no printed books; everything had to be laboriously copied by hand, and thus the difficulties of learning were much enhanced. To be able to adapt the Chinese ideographs skilfully to the purposes of written Japanese was a feat achieved by comparatively few.

Much richer, however, is the realm of poetry. It was during the Nara epoch that the first Japanese anthology, the *Manyoshu* (*Collection of a Myriad Leaves*), was compiled. It remains to this day a revered classic, containing found poems dating nominally from the reigns of Yuryaku and Nintoku, as well as from the days of Shotoku Taishi, but much more numerous are those of Jomei's era (629–641) and especially those of the Nara epoch. The verses total 4496, in twenty volumes. Some make love their theme; some deal with sorrow; some are allegorical; some draw their inspiration from nature's beauties, and some have miscellaneous motives. Hitomaru, who flourished during the reign of the Empress Jito (690–697), and several of whose verses are to be found in the *Myriad Leaves*, has been counted by all generations the greatest of Japanese poets. Not far below him in fame is Akahito, who wrote in the days of Shomu (724–749).

Writing of poetry was a favourite pursuit in the Nara era. Guests bidden to a banquet were furnished with writing materials and invited to spend hours composing versicles on themes set by their hosts. But skill in writing verse was not merely a social gift; it came near to being a test of fitness for office.

At some remote date a Japanese maker of songs seems to have discovered that a peculiar and very fascinating rhythm is produced by lines containing five syllables and seven syllables alternately. That is Japanese poetry (*uta* or *tanka*). There are generally five lines: the first and third consisting of five syllables, the second, fourth and fifth of seven, making a total of 31 in all. The most attenuated form of all is the *hokku* (or *haikai* [*haiku*]) which consists of only three lines, namely, 17 syllables. Necessarily the ideas embodied in such a narrow vehicle must be fragmentary. Thus it results that Japanese poems are, for the most part, impressionist; they suggest a great deal more than they actually express. Here is an example:

> *Momiji-ha wo*
> *Kaze ni makasete*
> *Miru yori mo*
> *Hakanaki mono wa*
> *Inochi nari keri*

This may be translated: "More fleeting than the glint of withered leaf wind-blown, the thing called life."

The conventional and pictorial character of the literary form is illustrated again in the lines:

> *Shira-kumo ni*
> *Hane uchi-kawashi*
> *Tobu kari no*
> *Kazu sae miyuru*
> *Aki no yo no tsuki!*

which the same eminent scholar translates: "The moon on an autumn night making visible the very number of the wild-geese that fly past with wings intercrossed in the white clouds." It is to be noted that this last is, to Occidental notions, a mere poetic phrase and not a unit.

THE MILITARY SYSTEM

It **has been shown** that compulsory military service was introduced in 689, during the reign of the Empress Jito, one-fourth of all the able-bodied men in each province being required to serve a fixed time with the colours. It has also been noted that under the Daiho legislation the number was increased to one-third. This meant that no distinction existed between soldier and peasant. The plan worked ill. No sufficient provision of officers being made, the troops remained without training, and it frequently happened that, instead of military exercises, they were required to labour for the enrichment of a provincial governor.

The system, being thus discredited, fell into abeyance in the year 739, but that it was not abolished is shown by the fact that, in 780, we find the privy council alleging, in a memo to the Throne, that the conscripted men lacked training; that they were physically unfit; that they busied themselves devising pretexts for evasion; that their chief function was to perform fatigue-duty for local governors, and that to send such men into the field of battle would be to throw away their lives fruitlessly. The council recommended that indiscriminate conscription of peasants should be replaced by a system of selection, the choice being limited to men with some previous training; that the number taken should be in proportion to the size of the province, and that those not physically robust should be left to till the land. These recommendations were approved. They constituted the first step towards complete abolishment of compulsory service and towards the glorifying of the profession of arms above that of agriculture.

Experience quickly proved, however, that some more efficient management was necessary in the maritime provinces, and in 792, Kwammu being then on the throne, an edict abolished the provincial troops in all regions except those which, by their proximity to the continent of Asia, were exposed to danger, namely, *Dazai-fu* in Kyushu, and in Mutsu, Dewa, and Sado in the north. Some specially organized force was needed also for extraordinary service and for guarding official storehouses, offices, and places where post-bells (*suzu*) were kept. To that end the system previously practised during the reign of Shomu (724–749) was reverted to; that is to say, the most robust among the sons and younger brothers of provincial governors and local officials were enrolled in corps of strength varying with the duties to be performed. These were called *kondei* or *kenji*.

There is no record as to the exact dimensions of Japan's standing army in the ninth century, but if we observe that troops were raised in the eight littoral provinces only – six in the south and two in the north – and in the island of Sado, and that the total number in the six southern provinces was only nine thousand, it would seem reasonable to conclude that the aggregate did not exceed thirty thousand. There were also the *kondei* (or *kenji*), but these, since they served solely as guards or for special purposes, can scarcely be counted a part of the standing army. The inference is that the country had been reduced to a condition of comparative military weakness. As to that, however, clearer judgment may be formed in the context of the campaign – to be now spoken of – conducted by the Yamato against the Yemishi tribes throughout a great part of the eighth century and the early years of the ninth.

REVOLT OF THE YEMISHI

At the close of the third decade of the eighth century the capital was established at Nara amid conditions of great refinement, and saw the Court and the aristocracy absorbed in religious observances, while the provincial governments were, in many cases, corrupt and inefficient. In the year 724, the Yemishi of the east rose in arms and killed Koyamaro, warden of Mutsu, a region comprised of the five provinces of Iwaki, Iwashiro, Rikuzen, Rikuchu, and Mutsu – in other words, the whole of the northeastern and northern littoral of the main island. Similarly, the provinces now called Ugo and Uzen, which form the northwestern littoral, were comprised in the single term "Dewa." Nature has separated these two regions, Mutsu and Dewa, by a formidable chain of mountains, constituting the backbone of northern Japan. The aboriginal Yemishi had been held since Yamato-dake's signal campaign in the second century CE within Dewa, Mutsu, and the island of Yezo.

Umakai, grandson of the renowned Kamatari, set out at the head of thirty thousand men, levied from the eight Bando provinces, by which term Sagami, Musashi, Awa, Kazusa, Shimosa, Hitachi, Kotsuke, and Shimotsuke were designated. The expanded system of conscription established under the Daiho code was then in force, and thus a large body of troops could easily be assembled. Umakai's army did not experience any serious resistance. But neither did it achieve anything signal.

In the year 774, the Yemishi again took up arms, captured one (Mono) of the Japanese forts and drove out its garrison. Again the eight Bando provinces were ordered to send levies, and at the head of the army thus raised a Japanese general penetrated far into Mutsu and destroyed the Yemishi's chief stronghold. This success was followed by an aggressive policy on the part of the lord-warden, Ki no Hirozumi. He extended the chain of forts to Kabe in Dewa, and to Isawa in Mutsu. This was in 780. But there ensued a strong movement of reprisal on the part of the Yemishi.

The Court appointed Fujiwara Tsugunawa to take command of a punitive expedition, and once again Bando levies converged on the site of the dismantled castle of Taga. But beyond that point no advance was essayed, in spite of bitter reproaches from Nara. "In summer," wrote the Emperor (Konin), "you plead that the grass is too dry; in winter you allege that bran is too scant. You discourse adroitly but you get no nearer to the foe." Konin's death followed shortly afterwards, but his successor, Kwammu, zealously undertook the pursuit of the campaign.

The Emperor said in his decree that the barbarian tribes, when pursued, fled like birds; when unmolested, gathered like ants; that the conscripts from the Bando provinces were reported to be weak and unfit for campaigning, and that those skilled in archery and physically robust stood aloof from military service, forgetting that they all owed a common duty to their country and their sovereign. Therefore, his Majesty directed that the sons and younger brothers of all local officials or provincial magnates should be examined with a view to the selection of those suited for military service, who should be enrolled and drilled, to the number of not less than five hundred and not more than two thousand per province according to its size.

Thus, the eight Bando provinces must have furnished a force of from four to sixteen thousand men, all belonging to the aristocratic class. These formed the nucleus of the army. They were supplemented by 52,800 men, infantry and cavalry, collected from the provinces along the Eastern Sea (Tokai) and the Eastern Mountains (Tosan). so that the total force must have aggregated sixty thousand. The command in chief was conferred on Ki no Kosami. A sword was conferred on him by the Emperor, and he received authority to act on his own discretion without seeking instructions from the Throne.

Meanwhile, the province of Mutsu had been ordered to send provisions to Taga Castle. The troops were to be massed at Taga, and all the provisions and munitions were collected there by April, 789. Kosami moved out of Taga at the appointed time and pushed northward. But with every forward movement the difficulties multiplied. Snow in those regions lies many feet deep until the end of May, and the thaw ensuing brings down from the mountains heavy floods which convert the rivers into raging torrents and the roads into quagmires. On reaching the bank of the Koromo River, forty-five miles north of Taga, the troops halted. Their delay provoked much censure in the capital where the climatic conditions do not appear to have been fully understood or the transport difficulties appreciated. Urged by the Court to push on rapidly, Kosami resumed his march in June; failed to preserve efficient connexion between the parts of his army; had his van ambushed; fled precipitately himself, and suffered a heavy defeat, though only 2500 of his big army had come into action. His casualties were 25 killed, 245 wounded, and 1036 drowned. A truce was effected and the forces withdrew to Taga, while, as for Kosami, though he attempted to deceive the Court by a bombastic despatch, he was recalled and degraded together with all the senior officers of his army.

Kosami's discomfiture took place in 789 and the training of picked soldiers and the provision of arms and horses commenced at once. To the command-in-chief the Emperor (Kwammu) appointed Saka-no-ye no Tamuramaro, who in respect of personal prowess no less than strategical talent he was highly gifted. In June, 794, he invaded Mutsu at the head of a great army and, by a series of rapidly delivered blows, effectually crushed the aborigines, taking 457 heads, 100 prisoners, and 85 horses, and destroying the strongholds of 75 tribes. Thereafter, until the year of his death (811), he effectually held in check the spirit of revolt, crushing two other insurrections – in 801 and 804 – and virtually annihilating the insurgents. He transferred the garrison headquarters from Taga to Isawa, where he erected a castle, organizing a body of four thousand militia (*tonden-hei*) to guard it; and in the following year (803), he built the castle of Shiba at a point still further north.

A collateral result of these disturbances was to discredit the great Court nobles – the Otomo, the Tachibana, the Ki, and the Fujiwara – as leaders of armies, and to lay the foundation of the military houses (*buke*) which were destined to become feudal rulers of Japan in after ages. Ki no Hirozumi, Ki no Kosami, Otomo Yakamochi, Fujiwara Umakai, and Fujiwara Tsugunawa having all failed, the Court was compelled to have recourse to the representatives of a Chinese immigrant family, the Saka-no-ye. Another incidental issue of the situation was that conspicuous credit for fighting qualities attached to the troops specially organized in the Bando (Kwanto) provinces with the sons and younger brothers of local officials. These became the nucleus of a military class which ultimately monopolized the profession of arms.

RELATIONS WITH KOREA

During the eighth century relations of friendship were once more established with Koma. A Manchurian tribe, migrating from the valley of the Sungali River (then called the Sumo), settled on the east of the modern province of Shengking, and was there joined by a remnant of the Koma subjects after the fall of the latter kingdom. Ultimately receiving investiture at the hands of the Tang Court, the sovereign of the colony took the name of Tsuying, King of Pohai, and his son, Wu-i, sent an envoy to Japan in 727, when Shomu was on the throne. Where the embassy embarked there is no record, but, being blown out of their course, the boats finally made the coast of Dewa, where several of the envoy's suite were killed by the Yemishi. The envoy himself reached Nara safely, and, representing his sovereign as the successor of the Koma dynasty, was hospitably received, the usual interchange of gifts taking place.

Twenty-five years later (752), another envoy arrived. The Empress Koken then reigned at Nara, and her ministers insisted that, in the document presented by the ambassador, Pohai must distinctly occupy towards Japan the relation of vassal to suzerain, such having been the invariable custom observed by Koma in former times. The difficulty seems to have been met by substituting the name "Koma" for "Pohai," thus, by implication, admitting that the new kingdom held towards Japan the same status as that formerly held by Koma. This attitude was maintained throughout the whole of Japan's subsequent intercourse with the Pohai kingdom.

THE HEIAN EPOCH

During this longer epoch that spanned nearly 400 years, links with China weakened somewhat, with the Chinese system of government previously deemed a model to emulate falling into disarray. Cultural and commercial exchange continued to prosper, however, contributing to a perceived effeminacy and moral decay among the upper classes. This 'golden age' of Japanese literature was marred by the dominance of the Fujiwara clan and the outbreak of hostilities with the rival Minamoto and Taira clans. The conflict ultimately culminated in the eruption of a long civil war, in the aftermath of which the first Shogunate was established.

THE FIFTIETH SOVEREIGN, THE EMPEROR KWAMMU

The first ruler in the epoch was Kwammu (782–805). This monarch, as already shown, was specially selected by his father, Konin, at the instance of Fujiwara Momokawa, who observed in the young prince qualities essential to a ruler of men. Whether Kwammu's career as Emperor reached the full standard of his promise as prince, historians are not agreed.

Konin's reforms of local abuses showed at once courage and zeal. But he did not reach the root of the evil, nor did his son

Kwammu, though in the matter of intention and ardour there was nothing to choose between the two. The basic trouble was arbitrary and unjust oppression of the lower classes by the upper. These latter, probably educated in part by the be system, which tended to reduce the worker with his hands to a position of marked subservience, had learned to regard their own hereditary privileges as practically unlimited, and to conclude that well nigh any measure of forced labour was due to them from their inferiors. Konin could not correct this conception, and neither could Kwammu. Indeed, in the latter's case, the Throne was specially disqualified as a source of remonstrance, for the sovereign himself had to make extravagant demands upon the working classes on account of the transfer of the capital from Nara to Kyoto. Thus, although Kwammu's warnings and exhortations were earnest, and his dismissals and degradations of provincial officials frequent, he failed to achieve anything radical.

THE TRANSFER OF THE CAPITAL TO KYOTO

The reign of Kwammu is remarkable for two things: the conquest of the eastern Yemishi by Tamuramaro and the transfer of the capital from Nara to Kyoto. Nara is in the province of Yamato; Kyoto, in the neighbouring province of Yamashiro, and the two places lie twenty miles apart as the crow flies. It has been stated that to change the site of the capital on the accession of a sovereign was a common custom in Japan prior to the eighth century. In those early days the term *miyako*, though used in the sense of "metropolis," bore chiefly the meaning "Imperial residence," and to alter its locality did not originally suggest a national effort. But when Kwammu ascended the throne, Nara had been the capital during eight reigns, covering a period of seventy-five years, and had grown into a great city, a centre alike of religion and of trade. To transfer it involved a correspondingly signal sacrifice. What was Kwammu's motive? Some have conjectured a desire to shake off the priestly influences which permeated the atmosphere of Nara; others, that he found the Yamato city too small to satisfy his ambitious views or to suit the quickly developing dimensions and prosperity of the nation. Probably both explanations are correct. A ruler of Kwammu's sagacity must have appreciated that religious fanaticism, as practised at Nara, threatened to overshadow even the Imperial Court, and that the influence of the foreign creed tended to undermine the Shinto cult, which constituted the main bulwark of the Throne.

In 784, when Kwammu adopted the resolve to found a new capital, it was necessary to determine the place by sending out a search party under his most trusted minister, Fujiwara Tanetsugu. The choice of Tanetsugu fell, not upon Kyoto, but upon Nagaoka in the same province. There was no hesitation. The Emperor trusted Tanetsugu implicitly and appointed him chief commissioner of the building, which was commenced at once, a decree being issued that all taxes for the year should be paid at Nagaoka where also forced labourers were required to assemble and materials were collected. The *Records* state that the area of the site for the new palace measured 152 acres.

The palace was never finished. While it was still uncompleted, the Emperor took up his abode there, in the fall of 784, and efforts to hasten the work were redoubled. But a shocking incident occurred. The Crown Prince, Sagara, procured the elevation of a member of the Saeki family to the high post of State councillor (*sangi*), and having been impeached for this unprecedented act by Fujiwara Tanetsugu, was deprived of his title to the throne. Shortly afterwards, the Emperor repaired to Nara, and during the absence of the Court from Nagaoka, Prince Sagara ordered the assassination of Tanetsugu. Kwammu exacted stern vengeance for his favourite minister. He disgraced the prince and sent him into exile in the island of Awaji, which place he did not reach alive, as was perhaps designed.

These occurrences moved the Emperor so profoundly that Nagaoka became intolerable to him. Gradually the work of building was abandoned, and, in 792, a new site was selected by Wake no Kiyomaro at Uda in the same province. The Tang metropolis, Changan, was taken for model. Commenced in April, 794, the new metropolis was finished in December, 805.

The city was laid out with mathematical exactness in the form of a rectangle, nearly three and one-half miles long, from north to south, and about three miles wide, from east to west. In each direction were nine principal thoroughfares, those running east and west crossing the north and south streets at right angles. The east and west streets were numbered from 1 to 9, and, although the regularity of structure and plan of the city has been altered by fire and other causes in eleven hundred years, traces of this early system of nomenclature are still found in the streets of Kyoto, which is only a remnant of the ancient city; it was almost wholly destroyed by fire in the Onin war of 1467.

Running north from the centre of the south side was a great avenue, two hundred and eighty feet wide, which divided the city into two parts, the eastern, called "the left metropolis" (later Tokyo, "eastern capital"), and "the right metropolis" (or Saikyo, "western capital") – the left, as always in Japan, having precedence over the right, and the direction being taken not from the southern entrance gate but from the Imperial palace, to which this great avenue led and which was on the northern limits of the city and, as the reader will see, at the very centre of the north wall. Grouped around the palace were government buildings of the different administrative departments and assembly and audience halls.

The main streets, which have already been mentioned as connecting the gates in opposite walls, varied in width from 80 feet to 170 feet. They divided the city into nine districts, all of the same area except the ones immediately east of the palace. The subdivisions were as formal and precise. Each of the nine districts contained four divisions. Each division was made up of four streets. A street was made up of four rows, each row containing eight "house-units." The house-unit was 50 by 100 feet. The main streets in either direction were crossed at regular intervals by lanes or minor streets, all meeting at right angles.

The Imperial citadel in the north central part of the city was 4600 feet long (from north to south) and 3840 feet wide, and was surrounded by a fence roofed with tiles and pierced with three gates on either side. The palace was roofed with green tiles of Chinese manufacture and a few private dwellings had roofs made of slate-coloured tiles, but most of them were shingled. In the earlier period, it is to be remembered, tiles were used almost exclusively for temple roofs. The architecture of the new city was in general very simple and unpretentious. The old canons of Shinto temple architecture had some influence even in this city built on a Chinese model. Whatever display or ornament there was, appeared not on the exterior but in inner rooms, especially those giving on inner court yards. That these resources were severely taxed, however, cannot be doubted, especially when we remember that the campaign against the Yemishi was simultaneously conducted. History relates that three-fifths of the national revenues were appropriated for the building.

THE CHINESE INFLUENCE ON JAPANESE BUDDHISM

Intercourse with the Middle Kingdom was frequent and intimate. But although China under the Tang dynasty in the ninth century presented many industrial, artistic, and social features of an inspiring and attractive nature, its administrative methods had begun to fall into disorder, discrediting it in Japanese eyes. We find, therefore, that although renowned religionists went from Japan during the reign of Kwammu and familiarized themselves thoroughly with the Tang civilization, they did not, on their return, attempt to popularize the political system of China, but praised only its art, literature, and certain forms and conceptions of Buddhism which they found at Changan.

The most celebrated of these religionists were Saicho and Kukai – immortalized under their posthumous names of Dengyo Daishi and Kobo Daishi, respectively. The former went to Changan in the train of the ambassador, Sugawara Kiyokimi, in 802, and the latter accompanied Fujiwara Kuzunomaro, two years later. Saicho was specially sent to China by his sovereign to study Buddhism, in order that, on his return, he might become lord-abbot of a monastery which his Majesty had caused

to be built on Hie-no-yama – subsequently known as Hiei-zan –
a hill on the northeast of the new palace in Kyoto. Saicho also
brought from China many religious books.

Down to that time the Buddhist doctrine preached in Japan
had been of a very dispiriting nature. It taught that salvation
could not be reached except by efforts continued through
three immeasurable periods of time. But Saicho acquired a new
doctrine in China. From the monastery of Tientai (Japanese,
Tendai) he carried back to Hiei-zan a creed founded on the
"Lotus of the Good Law" – a creed that salvation is at once
attainable by a knowledge of the Buddha nature, and that such
knowledge may be acquired by meditation and wisdom. That
was the basic conception, but it underwent some modification
at Japanese hands.

The introduction of the Tendai belief has historical
importance. In the first place, it illustrates a fact that the
Japanese are never blind borrowers from foreign systems: their
habit is to adapt their borrowings into existing belief systems.
In the second place, the Tendai system became the parent of
nearly all the great sects subsequently born in Japan. In the
third place, the Buddhas of Contemplation, by whose aid the
meditation of absolute truth is rendered possible, suggested the
idea that they had frequently been incarnated for the welfare
of mankind, and from that theory it was but a short step to the
conviction that the ancient gods worshipped by the Japanese
worshipped were manifestations of these same mystical beings,
embodying Shinto into a higher and more universal system.
From that moment the triumph of Buddhism was secured and
the introduction of the Tendai creed into Japan constitutes a
landmark in Japanese history.

Contemporary with and even greater in the eyes of his countrymen than Dengyo Daishi, was Kobo Daishi (known as Kukai during his lifetime). He, too, visited China as a student of Buddhism, and on his return he founded the system of the True Word (*Shingori*), which has been practically identified with the Gnosticism of early Christian days. Kobo Daishi is the most famous of all Japanese Buddhist teachers; famous alike as a saint, as an artist, and as a calligraphist. His influence on the intellectual history of his country was marked, for he not only founded a religious system which to this day has a multitude of disciples, but he is also said to have invented, or at any rate to have materially improved, the Japanese syllabary (*hira-gana*).

That the disciples of the Shinto cult so readily endorsed a doctrine which relegated their creed to a subordinate place has suggested various explanations, but the simplest is the most convincing, namely, that Shinto possessed no intrinsic power to assert itself in the presence of a religion like Buddhism. At no period has Shinto produced a great propagandist. No Japanese sovereign ever thought of exchanging the tumultuous life of the Throne for the quiet of a Shinto shrine, nor did Shinto ever become a vehicle for the transmission of useful knowledge.

With Buddhism, the record is very different. Many of its followers were inspired by the prospect of using it as a stepping-stone to preferment rather than as a route to Nirvana. Official posts being practically monopolized by the aristocratic classes, those born in lowlier families found little opportunity to win honour and emoluments. But by embracing a religious career, a man might aspire to become an abbot or even a tutor to a prince or sovereign. On the other hand, it has been observed with much reason that as troublers of the people the Buddhist priests were not far behind the provincial governors. In fact, it fared with Buddhism as it commonly fares with all human institutions – success begot abuses. The tonsure became a means of escaping official exactions in the shape of taxes or forced labour, and the building of temples a device to acquire property and wealth as well as to evade fiscal burdens. Sometimes the Buddhist priests lent themselves to the deception of becoming nominal owners of large estates in order to enable the real owners to escape taxation. Buddhism in Japan ultimately became a great militant power, ready at all times to appeal to force.

THE FIFTY-FIRST SOVEREIGN, THE EMPEROR HEIJO

Heijo, the fifty-first sovereign (806–09), was the eldest son of Kwammu. The latter, warned by the distress that his own great expenditures on account of the new capital had produced, and fully sensible of the abuses practised by the provincial officials, urged upon the Crown Prince the imperative necessity of retrenchment, and Heijo, on ascending the throne, showed much resolution in discharging superfluous officials, curtailing all unneeded outlays, and simplifying administrative procedure. But physical weakness – he was a confirmed invalid – and the influence of an ambitious woman wrecked his career. While still Crown Prince, he fixed his affections on Kusu, daughter of Fujiwara Tanetsugu, who had been assassinated by Prince Sagara during Kwammu's reign, and when Heijo ascended the throne, this lady's influence made itself felt within and without the palace, while her brother, Nakanari, a haughty, headstrong man, trading on his relationship to her, usurped almost Imperial authority.

Heijo's ill-health, however, compelled him to abdicate after a reign of only three years. He retired to the old palace at Nara, entrusting the sceptre to his brother, Saga. This step was profoundly disappointing to Kusu and her brother. The former aimed at becoming Empress – she possessed only the title of consort – and Fujiwara Nakanari looked for the post of prime minister. They persuaded the ex-Emperor to intimate a desire of reascending the throne. Saga acquiesced and would have handed over the sceptre, but at the eleventh hour, Heijo's conscientious scruples, or his prudence, caused a delay, whereupon Kusu and her brother, becoming desperate, publicly proclaimed that Heijo wished to transfer the capital to Nara. Before they could consummate this programme, however, Saga secured the assistance of Tamuramaro, famous as the conqueror of the Yemishi, and by his aid Fujiwara Nakanari was seized and thrown into prison, the lady Kusu being deprived of her rank as consort and condemned to be banished from Court.

Heijo might have bowed to Nakanari's fate, but Kusu's sentence of degradation and exile overtaxed his patience. He raised an army and attempted to move to the eastern provinces. In Mino, his route was intercepted by a force under Tamuramaro, and the ex-Emperor's troops being shattered, no recourse offered except to retreat to Nara. Then the *Jo-o* (Heijo) took the tonsure, and his consort Kusu committed suicide. Those who had rallied to the ex-Emperor's standard were banished.

When Heijo ceded the throne to Saga, the former's son, Takaoka, was nominated Crown Prince, though Saga had sons of his own. On the day following Heijo's adoption of the tonsure, Takaoka was deprived of his rank. Entering the priesthood, he called himself Shinnyo, retired to Higashi-dera and studied the doctrine of the True Word (*Shingori*). In 836, he proceeded to China to prosecute his religious researches, and ultimately made his way to India (in his eighty-first year), where he was killed by a tiger in the district now known as the Laos States of Siam. This prince is believed to have been the first Japanese that travelled to India. His father, the ex-Emperor Heijo, was a student of the same Buddhist doctrine (Shingon) and received instruction in it from Kukai. Heijo died in 824, at the age of fifty-one.

THE FIFTY-SECOND SOVEREIGN, THE EMPEROR SAGA

It is memorable in the history of the ninth century that three brothers occupied the throne in succession, Heijo, Saga, and Junna. Saga (810–23), after a most useful reign of thirteen years, stepped down frankly in favour of his younger brother. During his brief tenure of power Heijo unflinchingly effected reforms of the most distasteful kind, as the dismissal of superfluous officials and the curtailing of expenses; and the latter's reign was distinguished by much useful legislation and organization. Heijo's abdication seems to have been due to genuine solicitude for the good of the State, and Saga's to a sense of reluctance to be outdone in magnanimity. Reciprocity of moral obligation (*giri*) has been a canon of Japanese conduct in all ages.

One of the earliest acts of Saga's reign was to establish the office of Court councillor (*sangi*) and to determine the number of these officials at eight. Another office, dating from the same time (810), was that of *kurando* (called also *kurodo*). This seems to have been mainly a product of the political situation. At the palace of the retired Emperor in Nara – the Inchu, as it was called – the ambitious Fujiwara Nakanari and the Imperial consort, Kusu, were arrogating a large share of administrative and judicial business, and were flagrantly abusing their usurped authority. Saga did not know whom to trust. He feared that the council of State (*Dajo-kwan*) might include some traitors to his cause, and he therefore instituted a special office to be the depository of all secret documents, to adjudicate suits at law, to promulgate Imperial rescripts and decrees, to act as a kind of palace cabinet, and to have charge of all supplies for the Court. Ultimately this last function became the most important of the *kurando*'s duties.

The necessity of revising the Dahio rules and regulations was appreciated by the Emperor Kwammu, but he did not live to witness the completion of the work, which he had entrusted to the *sa-daijin*, Fujiwara Uchimaro, and others. The task was therefore re-approached by a committee of which the *dainagon*, Fujiwara Fuyutsugu, was president, under orders from the Emperor Saga. Ten volumes of the rules and forty of the regulations were issued in 819, the former being a collection of all rescripts and decrees issued since the first year of Daiho (701), and the latter a synopsis of instructions given by various high officials and proved by practice since the same date. Here, then, was a sufficiently precise and comprehensive body of administrative guides. But men competent to utilize them were not readily forthcoming. The provincial governors and even the metropolitan officials, chosen from among men whose qualifications were generally limited to literary ability or aristocratic influence, showed themselves incapable of dealing with the lawless conditions existing in their districts.

A body of men called *kebiishi* was organized, upon whom devolved the duty of pursuing and arresting lawbreakers. At first this measure was on a small scale and of a tentative character. But its results proved so satisfactory that the system was extended from the capital to the provinces, and, in 830, a *Kebiishi-cho* (Board of *Kebiishi*) was duly formed, the number and duties of its staff being definitely fixed four years later. The importance attaching to the post of chief of this board is attested by the fact that the *bushi* (military men) in the hereditary service of the high dignitaries on the Board of *Kebiishi*, the *emon no Kami* and the *hyoye no Kami*, were entrusted – under the name of *tsuiho-shi* – with the duty of enforcing the law against all violators.

These *kebiishi* and *tsuiho-shi* have historical importance. They represent the unequivocal beginning of the military class which was destined ultimately to impose its sway over the whole of Japan. Their institution was also a distinct step towards transferring the conduct of affairs, both military and civil, from the direct control of the sovereign to the hands of officialdom.

Fujiwara Fuyutsugu, who took such an important part in the legislation of his era, was at once a statesman, a legislator, an historian, and a soldier. Serving the State loyally and assiduously, he reached the rank of first minister (*sa-daijiri*) though he died at the early age of fifty-two, and it is beyond question that to his ability must be attributed a large measure of the success achieved by his Imperial master, Saga. The story of his private life may be gathered from the fact that he established and richly endowed an asylum for the relief of his indigent relatives; a college (the

Kwangaku-iri) for the education of Fujiwara youths, and an *uji-tera* (*Nanyen-do*) at Nara for soliciting heaven's blessing on all that bore his name.

An interesting episode of Saga's reign was the compilation of a record of all the *uji* (family names). Originally the right to use a family name had been guarded as carefully as is a title of nobility in Europe. The *uji* was, in truth, a hereditary title. But, an *uji* was from time to time bestowed on families of aliens, and thus, in the course of ages, confusion gradually arose. From the middle of the eighth century, efforts to compile a trustworthy record were made, and in Kwammu's reign a genealogical bureau (*kankei-jo*) was actually organized, its labours resulting in a catalogue of titles (*seishi mokuroku*). This proved defective, however, as did a subsequent effort in Heijo's time. Finally, the Emperor Saga entrusted the task to Prince Mamta, who, with a large staff of assistants, laboured for ten years, and, in 814, produced the *Seishi-roku* (*Record of Uji*) in thirty volumes. This great work divided into three classes the whole body of *uji* – 1182 – enrolled in its pages: namely, *Kwobetsu*, or those of Imperial lineage; *Shimbetsu*, or those descended from the *Kami*, and *Bambetsu*, or those of alien origin (Chinese or Korean). A few who could not be clearly traced were placed in a "miscellaneous list."

THE FIFTY-THIRD SOVEREIGN, THE EMPEROR JUNNA

Junna (824–33) was Kwammu's third son. He ascended the throne on the abdication of his elder brother, Saga, and he himself abdicated in favour of the latter's son,

Nimmyo, nine years later. Junna's reign is not remarkable for any achievement. No special legislation was inaugurated nor any campaign against abuses undertaken. The three brothers, Heijo, Saga, and Junna, may be said to have devoted paramount attention to the study of Chinese literature. However that may be, the reign of Junna, though not subjectively distinguished, forms a landmark in Japanese history as the period which closed the independent exercise of sovereign authority. When Junna laid down the sceptre, it may be said, as we shall presently see, to have been taken up by the Fujiwara.

THE BEGINNING OF THE FUJIWARA SUPREMACY

In the year 834, Junna abdicated in favour of his elder brother Saga's second son, who is known in history as the fifty-fourth Sovereign, Emperor Nimmyo (834–850). The latter was married to Jun, daughter of Fujiwara Fuyutsugu, and had a son, Prince Michiyasu. But, in consideration of the fact that Junna had handed over the sceptre to Nimmyo, Nimmyo, in turn, set aside the claim of his own son, Michiyasu, and conferred the dignity of Prince Imperial on Prince Tsunesada, Junna's son. A double debt of gratitude was thus paid, for Tsunesada was not only Junna's son but also Saga's grandson, and thus the abdications of Saga and Junna were both compensated. The new Prince Imperial, however, being a man of much sagacity, foresaw trouble if he consented to supplant Nimmyo's son. He struggled to avoid the nomination, but finally yielded to the wishes of his father and his grandfather.

While these two ex-Emperors lived, things moved smoothly, to all appearances. On their demise trouble arose immediately. The Fujiwara family perceived its opportunity and decided to profit by it. Fujiwara Fuyutsugu had died, and it chanced that his son Yoshifusa was a man of boundless ambition. By him and his partisans a slander was framed to the effect that the Crown Prince, Tsunesada, harboured rebellious designs, and the Emperor, believing the story – having, it is said, a disposition to believe it – pronounced sentence of exile against Prince Tsunesada, as well as his friends, the celebrated scholar, Tachibana no Hayanari, and the able statesman, Tomo no Kowamine, together with a number of others. It is recorded that the sympathy of the people was with the exiles.

In the year 851, the fifty-fifth Emperor Montoku (851–858) ascended the throne, and Fujiwara Yoshifusa was appointed minister of the Right. Yoshifusa married Princess Kiyo, daughter of the Emperor Saga. She had been given the *uji* of Minamoto in order to legalize this union, and she bore to Yoshifusa a daughter who became Montoku's Empress under the name of Somedono. By her, Montoku had a son, Prince Korehito, whose chance of succeeding to the crown should have been very slender since he had three half-brothers, the oldest of whom, Prince Koretaka, had already attained his fourth year at the time of Korehito's birth, and was his father's favourite.

The baby, Korehito, was taken from the palace into Yoshifusa's mansion, and when only nine months old was nominated Crown Prince. The event enriched Japanese literature. For Montoku's first born, Prince Koretaka, seeing himself deprived of his birthright, went into seclusion in Ono at the foot of Mount Hiei, and there, in the shadow of the great

Tendai monastery, devoted his days to composing verselets. In that pastime he was frequently joined by Ariwara no Narihira, a grandson of the Emperor Heijo. In the celebrated Japanese anthology, the *Kokin-shu*, compiled at the beginning of the tenth century, there are found several couplets from the pens of Koretaka and Narihira.

It was in the days of Fujiwara Yoshifusa that the descendants of Kamatari first assumed the role of kingmakers. Yoshifusa obtained the position of minister of the Right on the accession of Montoku (851), and, six years later, he was appointed chancellor of the empire (*dajo daijin*) in the sequel of the intrigues which had procured for his own grandson (Korehito) the nomination of Prince Imperial. The latter, known in history as the 56th Emperor Seiwa (859–76), ascended the throne in the year 859. He was then a child of nine, and naturally the whole duty of administration devolved upon the chancellor. There had been many "chancellors" but few "regents" (*sessho*). In fact, the office of regent had always been practically confined to princes of the Blood. Yoshifusa did not possess any of the qualifications for holding the position, but he wielded power sufficient to dispense with them, and, in the year 866, he celebrated the Emperor's attainment of his majority by having himself named *sessho*. The appointment carried with it a sustenance fief of three thousand houses; the privilege of being constantly attended by squadrons of the Right and Left Imperial guards, and the honour of receiving the allowances and the treatment of the *Sangu*, that is to say, of an Empress, a Dowager Empress, or a Grand Dowager Empress. Husband of an Empress, father of an Empress Dowager, grandfather of a reigning Emperor, chancellor of the empire, and a regent – a subject could climb no higher. Yoshifusa died in 872 at the age of sixty-eight. Having no son of his own, he adopted his nephew, Mototsune, son of Fujiwara Nagara.

Seiwa abdicated in 876, at the age of twenty-seven. Some historians ascribe his abdication to a sentiment of remorse. He had ascended the throne in despite of the superior claims of his elder brother, Koretaka, and the usurpation weighed heavily on his conscience. But Seiwa was undoubtedly a good man as well as a zealous sovereign. One episode in his career deserves attention as illustrating the customs of the era. Mention has already been made of Ariwara no Narihira, a grandson of the Emperor Heijo and one of the most renowned among Japanese poets. He was a man of singular beauty, and his literary attainments, combined with the melancholy that marked his life of ignored rights, made him a specially interesting figure. He won the love of Taka, younger sister of Fujiwara Mototsune and niece of Yoshifusa. Their liaison was not hidden. But Yoshifusa, in default of a child of his own, was just then seeking some Fujiwara maiden suitable to be the consort of the young Emperor, Seiwa, in pursuance of the newly conceived policy of building the Fujiwara power on the influence of the ladies' apartments in the palace. Yoshifusa ordered the poet prince to cut his hair and go eastward in expiation of the crime of seeking to win Taka's affections, and having thus officially rehabilitated her reputation, he introduced her into the household of the Empress Dowager, his own daughter, through whose connivance the lady soon found her way to the young Emperor's chamber and became the mother of his successor, Yozei.

Though only a *Fujiwara*, Taka was subsequently raised to the rank of Empress (877–884). Ultimately, when Empress Dowager, her name was coupled with that of the priest Zenyu of Toko-ji, as the Empress Koken's had been with that of Dokyo, a hundred years previously, and she suffered deprivation of Imperial rank. As for Narihira, after a few years he was allowed to return from exile, but finding that all his hopes of preferment were vain, he abandoned himself to a life of indolence and debauchery.

YOZEI, UDA, AND THE KWAMPAKU

The fifty-seventh sovereign was Yozei (877–884), offspring of the Emperor Seiwa's union with the lady Taka. He ascended the throne in the year 877, at the age of ten, and Fujiwara Mototsune – Yoshifusa had died five years previously – became regent (sessho), holding also the post of chancellor (dajo-daijin). When Yozei was approaching his seventeenth year he was overtaken by an illness which left him a lunatic. The regent decided that he must be dethroned, and a council of State was convened to consider the matter. The ministers hesitated. Then one of the Fujiwara magnates (Morokuzu) loudly proclaimed that anyone dissenting from the chancellor's proposal would have to answer for his contumacy. Thereafter, no one hesitated – so overshadowing was the power of the Fujiwara. When carried to a special palace – thenceforth called Yozei-in – and informed that he had been dethroned, the young Emperor burst into a flood of tears.

No hesitation was shown in appointing Yozei's successor. Prince Tokiyasu, son of the Emperor Nimmyo, satisfied all the requirements. His mother, a daughter of Fujiwara Tsugunawa, was Mototsune's maternal aunt, and the Prince himself, already in his fifty-fifth year, had a son, Sadami, who was married to the daughter of Fujiwara Takafuji, a close relation to Mototsune. There can be no doubt that the latter had the whole programme in view when he proposed the dethronement of Yozei. Shortly after his accession, Prince Tokiyasu – known in history as the Emperor Koko (885–887) – fell ill, and at Mototsune's instance the sovereign's third son (Sadami) was nominated Prince Imperial. He succeeded to the throne as Emperor Uda (888–897) on the death of his father, after a reign of two years.

This event saw fresh extension of the Fujiwara's power. Uda was twenty-two years of age when he received the sceptre, but recognizing that he owed his elevation to Mototsune's influence and that his prospects of a peaceful reign depended upon retaining the Fujiwara's favour, his first act was to decree that the administration should be carried on wholly by the chancellor, the latter merely reporting to the Throne. This involved the exercise of power hitherto unprecedented. To meet the situation a new office had to be created, namely, that of kwampaku. The actual duties of this post were those of regent to a sovereign who had attained his majority, whereas sessho signified regent to a minor. Hence the kwampaku was obviously the more honourable office, since its incumbent officiated in lieu of an Emperor of mature years. Accordingly, the kwampaku – or mayor of the palace, as the term is usually translated – took precedence of all other officials. A subject could rise no higher without ceasing to yield allegiance.

As Mototsune was the first kwampaku, he has been called the most ambitious and the least scrupulous of the Fujiwara. But Mototsune merely stood at the pinnacle of an edifice, to the building of which many had contributed, and among those builders not a few fully deserved all they achieved. The names of such members of the Fujiwara family as Mimori, Otsugu, Yoshino, Sadanushi, Nagara, Yoshisuke, and Yasunori, who wrought and ruled in the period from Heijo and Saga to Montoku and Seiwa, might justly stand high in any record

The Affair of the Engi Era

The Emperor Uda not only possessed great literary knowledge but was also deeply sensible of the abuse that had grown out of the virtual usurpation of administrative authority by one family. As illustrating his desire to extend the circle of the Throne's servants and to enlist erudite men into the service of the State, it is recorded that he caused the interior of the palace to be decorated with portraits of renowned statesmen and literati from the annals of China. Fate seemed disposed to assist his design, for, in the year 891, the all-powerful Fujiwara Mototsune died, leaving three sons, Tokihira, Nakahira, and Tadahira, the eldest of whom was only twenty-one. During the life of Mototsune, to whom the Emperor owed everything, it would not have been politically or morally possible to contrive any radical change of system, and even after his death, the Fujiwara family's claim to the Throne's gratitude precluded any direct attempt on Uda's part to supplant them. Therefore, he formed the plan of abdicating in favour of his son, as soon as the latter should attain a suitable age – a plan inspired in some degree by his own feeble health and by a keen desire to pass the closing years of his life in comparative retirement. He carried out this design in the year 897, and was thenceforth known as Uda-in.

His son, Daigo, who now ascended the throne (898–930), was thirteen years old, but no Fujiwara regent was appointed, Tokihira, the one person eligible in respect of lineage, being precluded by youth. Therefore the office of minister of the Left was conferred on Tokihira, and Sugawara Michizane (called also Kwanko) became minister of the Right.

It was to this Michizane that the ex-Emperor looked for material assistance in the prosecution of his design. The Sugawara family traced its descent to Nomi no Sukune, the champion wrestler of the last century before Christ and the originator of clay substitutes for human sacrifices at burials, though the name "Sugawara" did not belong to the family until eight hundred years later, when the Emperor Konin bestowed it on the then representative in recognition of his great scholarship. Thenceforth, the name was borne by a succession of renowned literati, the most erudite and the most famous of all being Michizane.

The ex-Emperor, on the accession of his thirteen-year-old son, Daigo, handed to the latter an autograph document known in history as the Counsels of the Kwampei Era. Its gist was:

"Be just. Do not be swayed by love or hate. Study to think impartially. Control your emotion and never let it be externally visible. The *sa-daijin*, Fujiwara Tokihira, is the descendant of meritorious servants of the Crown. Though still young, he is already well versed in the administration of State affairs. You will consult him and be guided by his counsels. The *u-daijin*, Sugawara Michizane, is a man of profound literary knowledge. He is also acquainted with politics. Frequently I have profited by his admonitions. When I was elected Crown Prince I had but Michizane to advise me. Not only has he been a loyal servant to me, but he will be a loyal servant to my successor also."

Plainly the intention of the document was to place Michizane on a footing at least equal to that of Tokihira.

Michizane understood the perils of such preferment. He knew that the scion of a comparatively obscure family would not be tolerated as a rival by the Fujiwara. Three times he declined the high post offered to him. But the Emperor and the ex-Emperor had laid their plans, and Michizane was an indispensable factor.

Events moved rapidly. Two years later (900), the Emperor, in concert with the cloistered sovereign, proposed to raise Michizane to the post of chancellor and to entrust the whole administration to him. This was the signal for the Fujiwara to take action. One opportunity for slandering Michizane offered; his daughter had been married to Prince Tokiyo, the Emperor's younger brother. A rumour was busily circulated that this meant a plot for the dethronement of Daigo in favour of Tokiyo. Miyoshi Kiyotsura, an eminent scholar, acting subtly at the instance of the Fujiwara, addressed a seemingly friendly letter to Michizane, warning him that his career had become dangerously rapid and explaining that the stars presaged a revolution in the following year. At the same time, Minamoto Hikaru, son of the Emperor Nimmyo; Fujiwara Sadakuni, father-in-law of Daigo, and several others who were jealous of Michizane's preferment or of his scholarship, separately or jointly memorialized the Throne, impeaching Michizane as a traitor who plotted against his sovereign.

Supplemented by Miyoshi's "friendly" notice of a star-predicated cataclysm, this cumulative evidence convinced, and doubtless the number and rank of the accusers alarmed the Emperor, then only in his seventeenth year. Michizane was not invited to defend himself. In the first year (901) of the Engi era, a decree went out stripping him of all his high offices, and banishing him to the *Dazai-fu* in Kyushu as vice-governor. Many other officials were degraded as his partisans. The ex-Emperor, to whose pity he pleaded in a plaintive couplet, made a resolute attempt to aid him. His Majesty repaired to the palace for the purpose of remonstrating with his son, Daigo. The palace guards refused to admit the ex-Emperor, and, after waiting throughout a winter's day seated on a straw mat before the gate, Uda went away in the evening, sorehearted and profoundly humiliated.

Michizane's twenty-three children were banished to five places, and he himself, having only a nominal post, did not receive emoluments sufficient to support him in comfort. Even oil for a night-lamp was often unprocurable, and after spending twenty-five months in voluntary confinement with only the society of his sorrows, he expired (903) at the age of fifty-eight, and was buried in the temple Anraku-ji in Chikuzen.

His unjust fate and the idea that he suffered for his sovereign appealed powerfully to popular imagination. Moreover, lightning struck the palace in Kyoto, and the three principal contrivers of Michizane's disgrace, Fujiwara Tokihira, Fujiwara Sugane, and Minamoto Hikaru, all expired within a few years' interval. At that epoch a wide-spread belief existed in the powers of disembodied spirits for evil or for good. Such a creed grew logically out of the cult of ancestor worship. It began to be whispered abroad that Michizane's spirit was taking vengeance upon his enemies. The Emperor was the first to act upon this superstition. He restored Michizane's titles, raised him to the first grade of the second rank, and caused all the documents relating to his exile to be burned. Retribution did not stop there. Forty-five years after Michizane's death, the people of Kyoto erected to his memory the shrine of Temman *Tenjin*, and in the year 1004, the Emperor Ichijo not only conferred on him the posthumous office of chancellor with the unprecedented honour of first grade of the first rank, but also repaired in person to worship at the shrine. In later times, memorial shrines were built in various places, and to this day he is fervently worshipped as the deity of calligraphy, so high was he elevated by the Fujiwara's attempt to drag him down.

THE ENGI ERA

In the year 909, Fujiwara Tokihira died and was followed to the grave, in 913, by Minamoto Hikaru. For an interval of some years no minister of State was nominated; the Emperor Daigo himself administered affairs. For this interregnum in the sway of the Fujiwara, the Engi era is memorable.

It is memorable for other things also; notably for the compilation of documents which throw much light on the conditions then existing in Japan. The Emperor, in 914, called upon the Court officials to submit memorials which should supply materials for administrative reforms. The great scholar, Miyoshi Kiyotsura, responded with a statement.

As illustrating the state of the rural regions, the memorialist instanced the case of Bitchu, a province on the Inland Sea, where he held an official appointment in the year 893. The local records (*Fudoki*) showed that a levy made there about the middle of the seventh century had produced twenty thousand able-bodied soldiers, whereas a century later, there were found only nineteen hundred; yet another century afterwards, only seventy; at the close of the ninth century, nine, and in the year 911, not one. To such a state of desolation had the district been reduced in the space of 250 years, and its story might be taken as typical.

Passing to the question of religion, the memorialist declared that the Shinto ceremonials to secure good harvests had lost all sincerity. The officials behaved as though there were no such thing as deities. They used the offerings for their own private purposes, sold the sacred horses, and recited the rituals without the least show of reverence. As for Buddhist priests, before asking them to pray for the welfare of their parishioners, they must be asked to purge themselves of their own sins. The priests who ministered at the provincial temples had lost all sense of shame. They had wives, built houses, cultivated lands, and engaged in trade. Was it to be supposed that heaven would hearken to the intervention of such sinners?

Meanwhile, luxury and extravagance had reached an extreme degree. On one suit of clothes a patrimony was expended, and sometimes a year's income barely sufficed for a single banquet. At funeral services all classes launched into flagrant excesses. Feasts were prepared on such a scale that the trays of viands covered the entire floor of a temple. Thousands of pieces of gold were paid to the officiating priests, and a ceremony, begun in mourning, ended in revelry. Another abuse, prevalent according to Miyoshi Kiyotsura's testimony, was that accusations were falsely preferred by officials against their seniors. Provincial governors were said to have frequently indulged in this treacherous practice and to have been themselves at times the victims of similar attacks. The Court, on receipt of such charges, seldom scrutinized them closely, but at once despatched officers to deal with the incriminated persons, and in the sequel, men occupying exalted positions were obliged to plead on an equal footing with officials of low grade or even common people.

Miyoshi Kiyotsura urged that all petitioning and all resulting inquiries by specially appointed officials should be interdicted, except in matters relating to political crime, and that all offenders should be handed over to the duly constituted administrators of justice. As to these latter, he spoke very plainly. The *kebiishi*, he wrote, who, being appointed to the various provinces, have to preserve law and order within their jurisdictions, should be men specially versed in law, whereas a majority of those serving in that capacity are ignorant and incompetent persons who have purchased their offices.

It is against the Buddhist priests and the soldiers of the six guards that he inveighs most vehemently, however. He calls them "vicious and ferocious," Those who take the tonsure, he says, number from two to three thousand yearly, and about one-half of that total are wicked men – low fellows who, desiring to evade taxation and forced labour, have shaved their heads and donned priests vestments, aggregate two-thirds of the population. They marry, eat animal food, practise robbery, and carry on coining operations without any fear of punishment. If a provincial governor attempts to restrain them, they flock together and have recourse to violence.

As for the soldiers of the guards, instead of taking their monthly term of duty at the palace, they are scattered over the country, and being strong and audacious, they treat the people violently and the provincial governors with contumacy, sometimes even forming leagues to rob the latter and escaping to the capital when they are hard pressed. (These guardsmen had arms and horses of their own and called themselves *bushi*, a term destined to have wide vogue in Japan.) Miyoshi Kiyotsura says that instead of being "metropolitan tigers" to guard the palace, they were "rural wolves" to despoil the provinces.

Administration of the Emperor Daigo

The Emperor Daigo, who ruled thirty-two years – from 898 to 930 – is brought very close to us by the statement of a contemporary historian that he was "wise, intelligent, and kind-hearted," and that he always wore a smiling face, his own explanation of the latter habit being that he found it much easier to converse with men familiarly than solemnly. A celebrated incident of his career is that one winter's night he took off his wadded silk garment to evince sympathy with the poor who possessed no such protection against the cold. Partly because of his debonair manner and charitable impulses he is popularly remembered as "the wise Emperor of the Engi era." Yet the usurpations of the Fujiwara; the prostitution of Buddhism to evil ends; the growth of luxurious and dissipated habits, and the subordination of practical ability to pedantic scholarship – these four malignant growths upon the national life found no healing treatment at Daigo's hands.

The Classical Age of Literature

The Engi era and the intervals of three or four decades before and after it may be regarded as the classical age of literature in Japan. Prose composition of a certain class was wholly in Chinese. During the reigns of Uda and Daigo (888–930), Sugawara Michizane, Miyoshi Kiyotsura, Ki no Haseo, and Koze no Fumio, formed a quartet of famous masters of Chinese literature. Several littérateurs reached high office, as chief chamberlain, councillor of State, minister of Education, and so forth. Miyoshi Kiyotsura ranks next to Michizane among the scholars of that age. He was profoundly versed in jurisprudence, mathematics (such as they were at the time), the Chinese classics, and history. But whereas Michizane bequeathed to posterity ten volumes of poems and two hundred volumes of a valuable historical work, no production of Kiyotsura's pen has survived except his celebrated memorial referred to above. He received the post of minister of the Household in 917 and died in the following year.

It must be understood that the work of these scholars appealed to only a very limited number of their countrymen. Official notices and enactments were intelligible by few men of the trading classes and by no women. But a different record is found in the realm of high literature. Here there is much wealth. The Nara epoch gave to Japan the famous *Manyo-shu* (*Myriad Leaves*), and the Engi era gave the scarcely less celebrated *Kokin-shu*, an anthology of over eleven hundred poems, ancient and modern. The language had now attained to its full development. With its rich system of terminations and particles it was a pliant instrument in the writer's hands, and the vocabulary was varied and copious to a degree which is astonishing when we remember that it was drawn almost exclusively from native sources.

This Heian literature reflects the pleasure-loving, cultured and refined, character of the class of Japanese who produced it. It has no serious masculine qualities and may be described in one word as *belles-lettres* – poetry, fiction, diaries, and essays of a desultory kind. The lower classes of the people had no share in the literary activity of the time. A very large and important part of the best literature which Japan has produced was written by women. A good share of the Nara poetry is of feminine authorship, and, in the Heian period, women took a still more conspicuous part in maintaining the honour of the native literature. The two greatest works which have come down from Heian time, the *Genji Monogatari* by Murasaki Shikibu, and the *Makura Soshi* by Sei Shonagon, are both by women. The position of women in ancient Japan was very different from what it afterwards became when Chinese ideals were in the ascendant. The Japanese of this early period did not share the feeling common to most Eastern countries that women should be kept in subjection and as far as possible in seclusion.

The first notable specimen of prose in Japanese style (*wabun*) was the preface to the *Kokin-shu*, written by Ki no Tsurayuki, who contended, and his own composition proved, that the introduction of Chinese words might well be dispensed with in writing Japanese. But what may be called the classical form of Japanese prose was fixed by the *Taketori Monogatari*, an anonymous work which appeared at the beginning of the Engi era (901), and was quickly followed by others.

In short, an extraordinary love of literature and of all that pertained to it swayed the minds of Japan throughout the Nara and the Heian epochs. The ninth and tenth centuries produced such poets as Ariwara no Yukihira and his younger brother, Narihira; Otomo no Kuronushi, Ochikochi no Mitsune, Sojo Henjo, and the poetess Ono no Komachi; gave us three anthologies (*Sandai-shu*), the *Kokin-shu*, the *Gosen-shu*, and the *Shui-shu*, as well as five of the *Six National Histories* (*Roku Kokushi*), the *Zoku Nihonki*, the *Nihon Koki*, the *Zoku Nihon Koki*, the *Montoku Jitsuroku*, and the *Sandai Jitsuroku*; and saw a bureau of poetry (*Waka-dokoro*) established in Kyoto. Fine art also was cultivated, and it is significant that calligraphy and painting were coupled together in the current expression (*shogwa*) for products of pictorial art. Kudara no Kawanari and Koze no Kanaoka, the first Japanese painters to achieve great renown, flourished in the ninth and tenth centuries, as did also a famous architect, Hida no Takumi.

THE CAPITAL AND THE PROVINCES

There were four chief causes for the existence of *shoen*, or manors. The first was reclamation. In the year 723, it was decreed that persons who reclaimed land should acquire a *de facto* title of tenure for three generations, and, twenty years later, the tenure of title was made perpetual, limits of area being fixed, however – 1250 acres for princes and nobles of the first rank, and thereafter by various gradations, to twenty-five acres for a commoner. But these limits were not enforced, and in the year 767 it became necessary to issue a decree prohibiting further reclamation, which was followed, seventeen years later, by a rescript forbidding provincial governors to exact forced labour for tilling their manors.

That this did not check the evil is proved by an official record, compiled in 797, from which it appears that princes and influential nobles possessed manors of great extent; that they appointed intendants to manage them; that these intendants themselves engaged in operations of reclamation; that they abused their power by despoiling the peasants, and that dishonest farmers made a practice of evading taxes and tribute by settling within the bounds of a manor. These abuses reached their acme during the reigns of Uda and Daigo (888–930), when people living in the vicinity of a manor were ruthlessly robbed and plundered by the intendant and his servants, and when it became habitual to elude the payment of taxes by making spurious assignments of lands to influential officials in the capital. Thus the *shoen* grew in number and extent.

The second factor which contributed to the extension of manors was the bestowal of estates in perpetuity on persons of conspicuous ability, and afterwards on men who enjoyed Imperial favour. Land thus granted was called *shiden* and enjoyed immunity from taxation. Then there were tracts given in recognition of public merit. These *koden* were originally of limited tenure, but that condition soon ceased to be observed, and the *koden* fell into the same category with manors (*shoen*).

Finally we have the *jiden*, or temple lands. These, too, were at the outset granted for fixed terms, but when Buddhism became powerful the limitation ceased to be operative, and moreover, in defiance of the law, private persons presented tracts, large or small, to the temples where the mortuary tablets of their families were preserved, and the temples, on their own account, acquired estates by purchase or by reclamation. The *jiden*, like the other three kinds of land enumerated above, were exempt from taxation. Owned by powerful nobles or influential families, the *shoen* were largely cultivated by forced labour, and as in many cases it paid the farmers better to rent such land; and thus escape all fiscal obligations, than to till their own fields.

During the last quarter of the tenth century peremptory edicts were issued to check this state of affairs, but the power of the Court to exact obedience had then dwindled almost to cipher. The salient features of the era were virtual abrogation of the Daiho laws imposing restrictions upon the area and period of land-ownership; rapid growth of tax-free manors and consequent impoverishment of the Court in Kyoto; the appearance of provincial magnates who yielded scant obedience to the Crown, and the organization of military classes which acknowledged the authority of their own leaders only.

REVOLT OF TAIRA NO MASAKADO

In the year 930, the Emperor Daigo died and was succeeded by his son Shujaku, a child of eight, whose mother was a daughter of Fujiwara Mototsune. In accordance with the system now fully established, Fujiwara Tadahira became regent. History depicts this Tadahira as an effeminate dilettante, but as representative of the chief aristocratic family in an age when to be a Fujiwara was to possess a title superior to that conferred by ability in any form and however conspicuous, his right to administer the government in the capacity of regent obtained universal recognition.

It had become the custom at that time for the provincial magnates to send their sons to Kyoto, where they served in the corps of guards, became acquainted with refined life, and established relations of friendship with the Taira and the Minamoto, the former descended from the Emperor Kwammu, the latter from the Emperor Seiwa. Thus, at the time of Daigo's death, a scion of the Taira, by name Masakado, was serving under Tadahira in the capital. Believing himself endowed with high military capacity, Masakado aspired to be appointed *kebiishi* of his native province, Shimosa. But his archery, his horsemanship, and his fencing elicited no applause in Kyoto, whereas a relative, Sadabumi, attracted admiration by a licentious life.

Masakado finally retired to Shimosa in an angry mood. His military career began with family feuds, and after he had killed one of his uncles on account of a dispute about the boundaries of a manor, and sacked the residence of another in consequence of a trouble about a woman, he did not hesitate to obey a summons to Kyoto to answer for his acts of violence. Masakado was acquitted after the formality of investigation had been satisfied. Naturally this judgment did not prove a deterrent; on the contrary, it amounted to a mandate.

On his return to Kwanto, Masakado was soon found once more in the arena. A raid that Masakado made into Musashi province is memorable as the occasion of the first collision between the Taira and the Minamoto, which great families were destined ultimately to convert all Japan into a battlefield. Finally, Masakado carried his raids so far that he allowed himself to be persuaded of the hopelessness of pardon. It was then that he resolved to revolt. Overrunning the whole eight provinces of the Kwanto, he appointed his own partisans to all posts of importance and set up a court after the Kyoto model.

Had it rested with Kyoto to subdue this revolt, Masakado might have attained his goal. But chance and the curious spirit of the time fought for the Court. A trifling breach of etiquette on the part of Masakado – not pausing to bind up his hair before receiving a visitor – forfeited the co-operation of a great soldier, Fujiwara Hidesato (afterwards known as Tawara Toda), and the latter, joining forces with Taira Sadamori, whose father Masakado had killed, attacked the rebels in a moment of elated carelessness, shattered them completely, and sent Masakado's head to the capital. The whole affair teaches that the Fujiwara aristocrats, ruling in Kyoto, had neither power nor inclination to meddle with provincial administration, and that the districts distant from the metropolis wore practically under the sway of military magnates in whose eyes might constituted right.

THE REVOLT OF FUJIWARA SUMITOMO

Another event, characteristic of the time, occurred in Nankai-do (the four provinces of the island of Shikoku) contemporaneously with the revolt of Masakado. During the Shohei era (931–937) the ravages of pirates became so frequent in those waters that Fujiwara no Sumitomo was specially despatched from Kyoto to restrain them. This he effected without difficulty. But instead of returning to the capital, he collected a number of armed men together with a squadron of vessels, and conducted a campaign of spoliation and outrage in the waters of the Inland Sea as well as the channels of Kii and Bungo. An expedition was despatched against Sumitomo under the command of Ono no Yoshifuru, general of the guards.

Yoshifuru mustered only two hundred ships whereas Sumitomo had fifteen hundred. The issue might have been foretold had not the pirate chief's lieutenant gone over to the Imperial forces. Sumitomo, after an obstinate resistance and after one signal success, was finally routed and killed. In a memorandum presented (946) by Ono Yoshifuru on his return from the Sumitomo campaign he says:

"My information is that those who pursue irregular courses are not necessarily sons of provincial governors alone. Many others make lawless use of power and authority; form confederacies; engage daily in military exercises; collect and maintain men and horses under pretext of hunting game; menace the district governors; plunder the common people; violate their wives and daughters, and steal their beasts of burden and employ them for their own purposes, thus interrupting agricultural operations. Yesterday, they were outcasts, with barely sufficient clothes to cover their nakedness; to-day, they ride on horseback and don rich raiment. Meanwhile the country falls into a state of decay, and the homesteads are desolate. My appeal is that, with the exception of provincial governors' envoys, any who enter a province at the head of parties carrying bows and arrows, intimidate the inhabitants, and rob them of their property, shall be recognized as common bandits and thrown into prison on apprehension."

THE SIXTY-SECOND SOVEREIGN, THE EMPEROR MURAKAMI

Murakami (947–67), son of Daigo by the daughter of the regent, Fujiwara Mototsune, ascended the throne in succession to Shujaku, and Fujiwara Tadahira held the post of regent, as he had done in Shujaku's time, his three sons, Saneyori, Morosuke, and Morotada, giving their daughters; one, Morosuke's offspring, to be Empress, the other two to be consorts of the sovereign. Moreover, Morosuke's second daughter was married to the Emperor's younger brother, Prince Takaaki, who afterwards descended from princely rank to take the family name of Minamoto. Saneyori, Morosuke, and

Takaaki took a prominent part in the administration of State affairs, and thus the Fujiwara held a supreme place.

Murakami has a high position among Japan's model sovereigns. He showed keen and intelligent interest in politics; he sought to employ able officials; he endeavoured to check luxury, and he solicited frank guidance from his elders. But whatever may have been the personal qualities of Murakami, however conspicuous his poetical ability and however sincere his solicitude for the welfare of his subjects, he failed signally to correct the effeminate tendency of Kyoto society or to protect the lives and property of his people. Bandits raided the capital, broke into the palace itself, set fire to it, and committed frequent depredations unrestrained. An age when the machinery for preserving law and order was practically paralyzed scarcely deserves the eulogies of posterity.

The lady with whom Murakami first consorted was a daughter of Fujiwara Motokata, who represented a comparatively obscure branch of the great family, and had attained the office of chief councillor of State (*dainagori*) only. She bore to his Majesty a son, Hirohira, and the boy's grandfather confidently looked to see him named Prince Imperial. But presently the daughter of Fujiwara Morosuke, minister of the Right, entered the palace, and although her Court rank was not at first superior to that of the *dainagon*'s daughter, her child had barely reached its third month when, through Morosuke's irresistible influence, it was nominated heir to the throne. Motokata's disappointment proved so keen that his health became impaired and he finally died – of chagrin, the people said.

A more substantial calamity resulted, however, from the habit of ignoring the right of primogeniture in favour of arbitrary selection. Murakami, seeing that the Crown Prince (*Reizei*) had an exceedingly feeble physique, deemed it expedient to transfer the succession to his younger brother, Tamehira. But the latter, having married into the Minamoto family, had thus become ineligible for the throne in Fujiwara eyes. The Emperor hesitated, therefore, to give open expression to his views, and while he waited, he himself fell mortally ill. On his death-bed he issued the necessary instruction, but the Fujiwara deliberately ignored it, being determined that a consort of their own blood must be the leading lady in every Imperial household. Then the indignation of the other great families, the Minamoto and the Taira, blazed out. Mitsunaka, representing the former, and Shigenobu the latter, entered into a conspiracy to collect an army in the Kwanto and march against Kyoto with the sole object of compelling obedience to Murakami's dying behest.

The plot was divulged by Minamoto Mitsunaka in the sequel of a quarrel with Taira no Shigenobu; the plotters were all exiled, and Takaaki, youngest son of the Emperor Daigo, though wholly ignorant of the conspiracy, was falsely accused to the Throne by Fujiwara Morotada, deprived of his post of minister of the Left, to which his accuser was nominated, and sent to that retreat for disgraced officials, the *Dazai-fu*. Another instance is here furnished of the readiness with which political rivals slandered one another in old Japan, and another instance, also, of the sway exercised over the sovereign by his Fujiwara ministers.

REIZEI AND ENYU

The reigns of **Reizei** (968–69) and **Enyu** (970–84) are remarkable for quarrels among the members of the Fujiwara family. After one year's reign, Reizei, who suffered from brain disease, abdicated in favour of his younger brother, Enyu, then only in his eleventh year. Fujiwara Saneyori acted as regent, but, dying shortly afterwards, was succeeded in that office by his nephew, Koretada, who also had to resign on account of illness.

Between this latter's two brothers, Kanemichi and Kaneiye, keen competition for the regency now sprang up. Kanemichi's eldest daughter was the Empress of Enyu, but his Majesty favoured Kaneiye, who thus attained much higher rank than his elder brother. Kanemichi, however, had another source of influence. His sister was Murakami's Empress and mother of the reigning sovereign, Enyu. This Imperial lady, writing to his Majesty Enyu at Kanemichi's dictation, conjured the Emperor to be guided by primogeniture in appointing a regent, and Enyu, though he bitterly disliked Kanemichi, could not gainsay his mother. Thus Kanemichi became chancellor and acting regent.

The struggle was not concluded, however. It ended in the palace itself, whither the two brothers repaired almost simultaneously, Kanemichi rising from his sick-bed for the purpose. In the presence of the boy Emperor, Kanemichi arbitrarily transferred his own office of *kwampaku* to Fujiwara Yoritada and degraded his brother, Kaneiye, to a comparatively insignificant post. The sovereign acquiesced; he had no choice. A few months later, this dictator died. It is related of him that his residence was more gorgeous than the palace and his manner of life more sumptuous than the sovereign's.

KWAZAN AND ICHIJO

The eldest son of the Emperor Reizei, Kwazan (985–86) ascended the throne in 985. and nominated Enyu's son to be Crown Prince, instead of conferring the position on his own brother, Prince Okisada (afterwards Sanjo). Now the Crown Prince was the son of Kaneiye's daughter, and that ambitious noble determined to compass the sovereign's abdication without delay. Kwazan, originally a fickle lover, had ultimately conceived an absorbing passion for the lady Tsuneko. He could not be induced to part with her even at the time of her pregnancy. When Tsuneko died in labour Kwazan, distraught with grief, was approached by Kaneiye's son, Michikane, who urged him to retire from the world and seek in Buddhism the perfect peace thus alone attainable. Michikane declared his own intention of entering the "path," and on a moonlight night the two men, leaving the palace, repaired to the temple Gwangyo-ji to take the tonsure. There, Michikane, pretending he wished to bid final farewell to his family, departed to return no more, and the Emperor understood that he had been deceived.

Retreat was now impossible, however. He abdicated in favour of Ichijo (987–1011), a child of seven, and Kaneiye became regent and chancellor. He emulated the magnificence of his deceased brother and rival, Kanemichi. He had five sons, the most remarkable of whom were Michitaka, Michikane, and Michinaga. On the death of Kaneiye the office of *kwampaku* fell to his eldest son, Michitaka, and, in 993, the latter being seriously ill, his son, Korechika, looked to be his successor. But the honour fell to Michitaka's brother, Michikane. Seven days after his nomination, Michikane died, and, as a matter of course, men said that he had been done to death by the incantations of his ambitious nephew. Again, however, the latter was disappointed. Kaneiye's third son, Michinaga, succeeded to the regency.

Almost immediately, the new regent seems to have determined that his daughter should be Empress. But the daughter of his elder brother, the late Michitaka, already held that position. Michinaga "required" the Empress to abandon the world, shave her head, and remove to a secluded palace (the Kokideri), where-after he caused his own daughter to become the Imperial consort.

It is not to be imagined that with such a despotic regent, the Emperor himself exercised any real authority. The annals show that Ichijo was of benevolent disposition; that he sympathized with his people; that he excelled in prose composition and possessed much skill in music. Further, during his reign of twenty-four years many able men graced the era. But neither their capacity nor his own found opportunity for exercise in the presence of Michinaga's proteges, and, while profoundly disliking the Fujiwara autocrat, Ichijo was constrained to suffer him.

SANJO AND GO-ICHIJO

Prince Okisada, younger brother of the Emperor Kwazan, ascended the throne at the age of thirty-six, on the abdication of Ichijo, and is known in history as Sanjo (1012–17). Before his accession he had married the daughter of Fujiwara Naritoki, to whom he was much attached, but with the crown he had to accept the second daughter of Michinaga as *chugu*, his former consort becoming Empress. His Majesty had to acquiesce in another arbitrary arrangement also. It has been shown above that Michinaga's eldest daughter had been given the title of *chugu* (imperial consort) in the palace of Ichijo, to whom she bore two sons, Atsunari and Atsunaga. Neither of these had any right to be nominated Crown Prince in preference to Sanjo's offspring. Michinaga, however, caused Atsunari to be appointed Prince Imperial, ignoring Sanjo's son, since his mother belonged to an inferior branch of the Fujiwara. Further, it did not suit the regent's convenience that a ruler of mature age should occupy the throne. An eye disease from which Sanjo suffered became the pretext for pressing him to abdicate, and, in 1017, Atsunari, then in his ninth year, took the sceptre as Emperor Go-Ichijo, or Ichijo II (1017–36). Michinaga continued to act as regent, holding, at the same time, the office of minister of the Left, but he subsequently handed over the regency to his son, Yorimichi, becoming himself chancellor.

Go-Ichijo was constrained to endure at Michinaga's hands the same despotic treatment as that previously meted out to Sanjo. The legitimate claim of his offspring to the throne was ignored in favour of his brother, Atsunaga, who received for consort the fourth daughter of Michinaga. Thus, this imperious noble had controlled the administration for thirty years; had given his daughters to three Emperors; had appointed his son to be regent in his place, and had the Crown Prince for grandson. He held the empire in the hollow of his hand.

His estates far exceeded those of the Crown; the presents offered to him by all ranks reached an enormous total; he built for himself a splendid mansion (Jotomon) with forced labour requisitioned from the provinces. At the approach of illness he took refuge in Buddhism, but even here the gorgeous ostentation of his life was not abated. He planned the building of a monastery which should prove a worthy retreat for his declining years. Michinaga retired there to die, and on his death-bed he received a visit from the Emperor, who ordered three months' Court mourning on his decease.

The Minamoto were steadily taking the lead in the science of war. Already, indeed, the Fujiwara in the capital were beginning to recognize the power of the Minamoto. It has been related above that one of the rebel Masakado's earliest opponents was a Minamoto, vice-governor of Musashi. His son, Mitsunaka, a redoubtable warrior, assisted the Fujiwara in Kyoto, and Mitsunaka's sons, Yorimitsu and Yorinobu, contributed materially to the autocracy of the regent Michinaga. Yorimitsu was appointed by the regent to command the cavalry of the guard, and he is said to have brought that corps to a state of great efficiency.

There was, indeed, much need of a strong hand. One had only to emerge from the palace gates to find oneself among the haunts of bandits. The names of such robber chiefs as Hakamadare no Yasusuke, Kidomaru, Oeyama Shutendoji, and Ibaraki-doji have been handed down as the heroes in many a strange adventure and the perpetrators of many heinous crimes. Even the Fujiwara residences were not secure against the torches of these plunderers, and during the reign of Ichijo the palace itself was frequently fired by them. In Go-Ichijo's tune, an edict was issued forbidding men to carry bows and arrows in the streets, but had there been power to enforce such a veto, its enactment would not have been necessary. Its immediate sequel was that the bandits broke into Government offices and murdered officials there.

THE TOI INVASION

In the spring of 1019, when Go-Ichijo occupied the throne, a large host of invaders suddenly poured into the island of Tsushima, which lies half-way between the south of Korea and the northeast of Kyushu, distant about sixty miles from either coast.

The invaders were the Toi, originally called Sushen or Moho, under the former of which names they make their appearance in Japanese history in the middle of the sixth century. They inhabited that part of the Asiatic continent which lies opposite to the island of Ezo, but there is nothing to show what impulse they obeyed in making this sudden descent upon Japan. Their fleet comprised some fifty vessels only, each from forty to sixty feet long and propelled by thirty or forty oars, but of how many fighting men the whole force consisted, no record has been preserved. As to arms, they carried swords, bows, spears, and shields, and in their tactical formation spearmen occupied the front rank, then came swordsmen, and finally bowmen. Every man had a shield. Their arrows were short, measuring little over a foot, but their bows were powerful, and they seem to have fought with fierce courage.

At first they carried everything before them. The governor of Tsushima, being without any means of defence, fled to the *Dazai-fu* in Kyushu, and the inhabitants were left to the mercy of the invaders, who then pushed on to the island of Iki. There the governor, Fujiwara Masatada, made a desperate resistance, losing his own life in the battle.

Ten days after their first appearance off Tsushima, the Toi effected a landing in Chikuzen and marched towards

Hakata, plundering, burning, massacring old folks and children, making prisoners of adults, and slaughtering cattle and horses for food. It happened, fortunately, that Takaiye, younger brother of Fujiwara Korechika, was in command at the *Dazai-fu*. He met the crisis with the utmost coolness, and made such skilful dispositions for defence that, after three days' fighting, in which the Japanese lost heavily, Hakata remained uncaptured.

High winds and rough seas now held the invaders at bay, and in that interval the coast defences were repaired and garrisoned, and a fleet of thirty-eight boats having been assembled, the Japanese assumed the offensive, ultimately driving the Toi to put to sea. A final attempt was made to effect a landing at Matsuura in the neighbouring province of Hizen, but, after fierce fighting, the invaders had to withdraw altogether. The whole affair had lasted sixteen days, and the Japanese losses were 382 killed and 1280 taken prisoners.

The rewards handed out to the brave defenders were insignificant, and the event clearly illustrates the policy of the Central Government – a policy already noted in connexion with the revolt of Masakado – namely, that any emergency dealt with prior to the receipt of an Imperial rescript must be regarded as private, whatever its nature, and therefore beyond the purview of the law. Inevitably, under such a system, the provincial magnates settled matters to their own liking without reference to Kyoto, and equipped themselves with armed retinues. In truth, it is not too much to say that, from the tenth century, Japan outside the capital became an arena of excursions and alarms, the preservation of peace being wholly dependent on the ambitions of local magnates.

A prominent conflict in this era is the struggle between the Taira and the Minamoto in the Kwanto. For generations the family of Taira Tadatsune had ruled in the province of Shimosa and had commanded the allegiance of all the *bushi* of the region. Tadatsune held at one time the post of vice-governor of the neighbouring province of Kazusa, where he acquired large manors (*shoen*). In the year 1028, he seized the chief town of the latter province, and pushing on into Awa, killed the governor and obtained complete control of the province. The Court, on receiving news of these events, ordered Minamoto Yorinobu, governor of Kai, and several other provincial governors to attack the Taira chief.

Yorinobu did not wait for his associates. Setting out with his son, Yoriyoshi, in 1031, he moved at once against Tadatsune's castle, which stood on the seashore of Shimosa, protected by moats and palisades, and supposed to be unapproachable from the sea except by boats, of which Tadatsune had taken care that there should not be any supply available. But the Minamoto general learned that the shore sloped very slowly on the castle front, and marching his men boldly through the water, he delivered a crushing attack.

For this exploit, which won loud plaudits, he was appointed commandant of the local government office. The same post was subsequently bestowed on Yorinobu's son, Yoriyoshi, and on the latter's son, Yoshiiye, known by posterity as "Hachiman Taro," Japan's most renowned archer, to whom the pre-eminence of the Minamoto family was mainly due. The chief importance of these events is that they laid the foundation of the Minamoto family's supremacy in the Kwanto, and thus permanently influenced the course of Japanese history.

THE BUSHI

When great provincial magnates began, about the tenth century, to support a number of armed retainers, these gradually came to be distinguished as *bushi*. In modern times the ethics of the *bushi* have been analysed under the name *bushido* (the way of the warrior), but of course no such term or any such complete code existed in ancient days. Although the *bushi* figured mainly on the provincial stage, he acted an important part in the capital also. There, the Throne and its Fujiwara entourage were constrained to enlist the co-operation of the military nobles for the purpose of controlling the lawless elements of the population. The Minamoto family were conspicuous in that respect. Indeed, the Minamoto were commonly spoken of as the "claws" of the Fujiwara.

In fact, the empire outside the capital was practically divided between the Minamoto, the Taira, and the Fujiwara families, so that anything like a feud could scarcely fail to have wide ramifications. The eleventh century may be said to have been the beginning of such tumults. Not long after the affair of Taira Tadatsune, there occurred the much larger campaign known as *Zen-kunen no Sodo*, or the "Prior Nine Years' Commotion." The scene of this struggle was the vast province of Mutsu in the extreme north of the main island. For several generations the Abe family had exercised sway there, and the Court deputed Minamoto Yoriyoshi to restore order. The Abe magnate was killed by a stray arrow at an early stage of the campaign, but his son, Sadato, made a splendid resistance.

Yoriyoshi's eldest son, Yoshiiye, one of the most skilful bowmen Japan ever produced. Nine years were needed to finish the campaign, and, in its sequel, Yoriyoshi was appointed governor of Iyo, and Yoshiiye, governor of Mutsu.

Sadato was ultimately killed, but his younger brother Muneto had the affection and full confidence of Yoshiiye. Muneto, however, remembered his brother's fate and cherished a desire to take vengeance on Yoshiiye, which mood also was recognized as becoming to a model *bushi*. One night, the two men went out together, and Muneto decided that the opportunity for vengeance had come. Drawing his sword, he looked into the ox-carriage containing Yoshiiye and found him sound asleep. The idea of behaving treacherously in the face of such trust was unendurable, and thereafter Muneto served Yoshiiye with faith and friendship. The confidence that the Minamoto hero reposed in the brother of his old enemy and the way it was requited – these, too, are claimed as traits of the *bushi*.

Yet another canon is furnished by Yoshiiye's career – the canon of humility. Oye no Masafusa was overheard remarking that Yoshiiye had some high qualities but was unfortunately ignorant of strategy. This being repeated to Yoshiiye, he showed no resentment but begged to become Masafusa's pupil. Yet he was already conqueror of the Abe and governor of Dewa.

THE GO-SANNEN CAMPAIGN

Thereafter the provinces of Mutsu and Dewa were again the scene of another fierce struggle which, called the "After Three-years War." 1089–91). It was a family quarrel between the scions of Kiyowara Takenori, a magnate of Mutsu who had rendered conclusive assistance to Yoshiiye in the Nine-years'

War; and as a great landowner of Dewa, Kimiko Hidetake, took part, the whole north of Japan may be said to have been involved. It fell to Yoshiiye, as governor of Mutsu, to quell the disturbance, and very difficult the task proved, so difficult that the issue might have been different had not Fujiwara Kiyohira – who will be presently spoken of – espoused the Minamoto cause.

When news of the struggle reached Kyoto, Yoshiiye's younger brother, Yoshimitsu, who held the much coveted post of *kebiishi*, applied for permission to proceed at once to his brother's assistance. The Court refused his application, whereupon he resigned his office and, like a true *bushi*, hastened to the war. Yoshimitsu was a skilled performer upon a musical instrument called the *sho*. He had studied under a celebrated master, Toyohara Tokimoto, now no more, and, on setting out for the field of battle in the far north, he became apprehensive lest the secrets imparted to him by his teacher should die with him. He therefore invited Tokimoto's son, Tokiaki, to bear him company during the first part of his journey, and to him he conveyed all the knowledge he possessed. The spectacle of this renowned soldier giving instruction in the art of music to the son of his deceased teacher on moonlit nights as he travelled towards the battlefield, has always appealed strongly to Japanese conception of a perfect samurai, and has been the motive of many a picture.

When Yoshiiye reported to the Throne the issue of this bloody battle, Kyoto replied that the war had been a private feud and that no reward or distinctions would be conferred. Yoshiiye therefore devoted the greater part of his own manors to recompensing those that had followed his standard. He thus won universal respect throughout the Kwanto. It is easy to comprehend that in the Kwanto it became a common saying, "Better serve the Minamoto than the sovereign."

THE FUJIWARA OF THE NORTH

Fujiwara **Kiyohira** was descended from Hidesato, the conqueror of Masakado. After the *Go-sannen* outbreak he succeeded to the six districts of Mutsu which had been held by the insurgent chiefs. This vast domain descended to his son Motohira, and to the latter's son, Hidehira, whose name we shall presently find in large letters on a page of Japanese history.

The Mutsu branch of the Fujiwara wielded paramount sway in the north for several generations. Near Hiraizumi, in the province of Rikuchu, may still be seen four buildings forming the monastery Chuson-ji. In one of these edifices repose the remains of Kiyohira, Motohira, and Hidehira. The ceiling, floor and four walls of this *Konjiki-do* (golden hall) were originally covered with powdered gold, and its interior pillars are inlaid with mother-of-pearl on which are traced the outlines of twelve Arhats. In the days of Kiyohira the monastery consisted of forty buildings and was inhabited by three hundred priests.

THE REASSERTION OF THE AUTHORITY OF THE THRONE

During **two centuries** the administrative power remained in the hands of the Fujiwara. They lost it by their own timidity rather than through the machinations of their enemies. When the Emperor Go-Shujaku (1037–45) was mortally ill, he appointed his eldest son, Go-Reizei (1046–68), to be his successor, and signified his desire that the latter's half-brother, Takahito, should be nominated Crown Prince. Fujiwara Yorimichi was then regent (*kwampaku*). To him, also, the dying sovereign made known his wishes. Now Takahito had not been born of a Fujiwara mother. The regent, therefore, while complying at once in Go-Reizei's case, said that the matter of the Crown Prince might be deferred, his purpose being to wait until a Fujiwara lady should bear a son to Go-Reizei.

In thus acting, Yorimichi obeyed the policy from which his family had never swerved through many generations, and which had now become an unwritten law of the State. But his brother, Yoshinobu, read the signs of the times in a sinister light. He argued that the real power had passed to the military magnates, and that by attempting to stem the current the Fujiwara might be swept away altogether. He therefore repaired to the palace, and simulating ignorance of what had passed between the late sovereign and the *kwampaku*, inquired whether it was intended that Prince Takahito should enter a monastery. Go-Reizei replied emphatically in the negative and related the facts, whereupon Yoshinobu declared that the prince should be nominated forthwith. It was done, and thus for the first time in a long series of years a successor to the throne was proclaimed who had not the qualification of a Fujiwara mother.

During more than twenty years of probation as Crown Prince, this sovereign, Go-Sanjo, had ample opportunity of observing the arbitrary conduct of the Fujiwara, and when he held the sceptre he neglected no means of asserting the authority of the Crown, one conspicuous step being to take a daughter of

Go-Ichijo into the palace as *chugu*, a position created for a Fujiwara and never previously occupied by any save a Fujiwara.

Altogether, Go-Sanjo (1069–72) stands an imposing figure in the annals of his country. Erudition he possessed in no small degree, and it was supplemented by diligence, high moral courage and a sincere love of justice. He also set to his people an example of frugality. It is related that, observing as he passed through the streets one day, an ox-carriage with gold mountings, he stopped his cortege and caused the gold to be stripped off. Side by side with this record may be placed his solicitude about the system of measures, which had fallen into disorder. With his own hands he fashioned a standard which was known to later generations as the *senshi-masu* of the Enkyu era (1069–1074). The question of tax-free manors (*shoen*) also received much attention. He established a legislative office where all titles to *shoen* had to be examined and recorded, the Daiho system of State ownership being restored, so that all rights of private property required official sanction, the Court also becoming the judge in all disputes as to validity of tenure.

Another abuse with which Go-Sanjo sought to deal drastically was the sale of offices and ranks. Although the bestowal of rank in return for a money payment was interdicted during the reign of Kwammu, in the days of Ichijo, the acquisition of tax-free manors increased rapidly and the treasury's income diminished correspondingly, so that it became inevitable, in times of State need, that recourse should be had to private contributions, the contributors being held to have shown "merit" entitling them to rank or office or both.

Go-Sanjo strictly interdicted all such transactions. But this action brought him into sharp collision with the then *kwampaku,* Fujiwara Norimichi. The latter built within the enclosure of Kofuku-ji at Nara an octagonal edifice containing two colossal images of Kwannon. On this *nanen-do* the regent spent a large sum, part of which was contributed by the governor of the province. Norimichi therefore applied to the Emperor for an extension of the governor's term of office. Go-Sanjo refused his assent. But Norimichi insisted. Finally the Emperor, growing indignant, declared that the *kwampaku*'s sole title to respect being derived from his maternal relationship to the sovereign, he deserved no consideration at the hands of an Emperor whose mother was not a Fujiwara. It was a supreme moment in the fortunes of the Fujiwara.

Their obviously selfish device of seating a minor on the throne and replacing him as soon as he reached years of discretion, had been gradually invested by the Fujiwara with an element of spurious altruism. Go-Sanjo held, however, that such a system not only impaired the Imperial authority but also was unnatural. No father, he argued, could be content to divest himself of all practical interest in the affairs of his family, and to condemn the occupant of the throne to sit with folded hands was to reduce him to the rank of a puppet. Therefore, even though a sovereign abdicated, he should continue to take an active part in the administration of State affairs. Go-Sanjo proposed to substitute camera government (*Insei*) for control by a *kwampaku*. But he was forced to abdicate, owing to ill health, in 1073, and died the following year.

The Seventy-Second Emperor, Shirakawa

Go-Sanjo was succeeded by his eldest son, Shirakawa (1073–86). He had taken for consort Kenko, the daughter of Fujiwara

Yorimichi. Shirakawa modelled himself on his father. He personally administered affairs of State, displaying assiduity and ability but not justice. Unlike his father he allowed himself to be swayed by favour and affection, arbitrarily ignored time-honoured rules, and was guilty of great extravagance in matters of religion. But he carried into full effect the camera (or cloistered) system of government, thereafter known as *Insei*. For, in 1086, after thirteen years' reign, he resigned the sceptre to an eight-year-old boy, Horikawa, his son by the *chugu*, Kenko. He took the tonsure and the religious title of *Ho-o* (pontiff), but in the Toba palace, his new residence, he organized an administrative machine on the exact lines of that of the Court.

Thenceforth the functions of Imperialism were limited to matters of etiquette and ceremony, all important State business being transacted by the *Ho-o* and his camera entourage. If the decrees of the Court clashed with those of the cloister, as was occasionally inevitable, the former had to give way. The earnest efforts made by Go-Sanjo to check the abuse of sales of rank and office as well as the alienation of State lands into private manors, were rendered wholly abortive under the sway of Shirakawa. The cloistered Emperor was a slave of superstition. He caused no less than six temples to be built of special grandeur, and to the principal of these (Hosho-ji) he made frequent visits in state, on which occasions gorgeous ceremonies were performed.

His respect for Buddhism was so extreme that he strictly interdicted the taking of life in any form, a veto which involved the destruction of eight thousand fishing nets and the loss of their means of sustenance to innumerable fishermen, as well as the release of all falcons kept for hawking. On one occasion, when rain prevented a contemplated progress to Hosho-ji, he sentenced the rain to imprisonment and caused a quantity to be confined in a vessel. To the nation, however, all this meant something very much more than a mere freak. It meant that the treasury was depleted and that revenue had to be obtained by recourse to the abuses which Go-Sanjo had struggled so earnestly to check, the sale of offices and ranks, even in perpetuity, and the inclusion of great tracts of State land in private manors.

The Seventy-Fourth Emperor, Toba

Horikawa died in 1107, after a reign of twenty years, and was succeeded by his son Toba (1108–23), a child of five. Affairs of State continued to be directed by the cloistered sovereign, and he chose for his grandson's consort Taiken-mon-in, who bore to him a son, the future Emperor Sutoku. Toba abdicated, after a reign of fifteen years, on the very day of Sutoku's nomination as heir apparent, and, six years later, Shirakawa died (1128), having administered the empire from the cloister during a space of forty-three years.

As a device to wrest the governing power from the grasp of the Fujiwara, Go-Sanjo's plan was certainly successful, and had he lived to put it into operation himself, the results must have been different. But in the greatly inferior hands of Shirakawa this new division of Imperial authority and the segregation of its source undoubtedly conspired to prepare the path for military feudalism and for curtained Emperors.

Toba, with the title of Ho-o, took the tonsure and administered from the cloister after Shirakawa's death. One of his first acts after abdication was to take another consort, a daughter of Fujiwara Tadazane, whom he made Empress under the name of Kaya-no-in; but as she bore him no offspring, he placed in the Toba palace a second Fujiwara lady, Bifuku-mon-in, daughter of Nagazane. By her he had (1139) a son whom he caused to be adopted by the Empress, preparatory to placing him on the throne as Emperor Konoe, at the age of three. Thus, the cloistered sovereigns followed faithfully in the footsteps of the Fujiwara.

Soldier-Priests

A phenomenon which became conspicuous during the reign of Shirakawa was recourse to violence by Buddhist priests. This abuse had its origin in the acquisition of large manors by temples and the consequent employment of soldiers to act as guards. Ultimately, great monasteries like Kofuku-ji, Onjo-ji, and Enryaku-ji came to possess thousands of these armed men, and consequently wielded temporal power. A fierce feud raged between Onjo-ji and Enryaku-ji monasteries; the latter accused the former of causing the death of Prince Atsubumi through incantations In the year 1081, the priest-soldiers of Enryaku-ji set the torch to Onjo-ji, and, flocking to Kyoto in thousands, threw the capital into disorder. Twelve years later (1093), thousands of cenobites (soldier-priests), carrying the sacred tree of the Kasuga shrine, marched from Nara to Kyoto, clamouring for vengeance on the governor of Omi, whom they charged with arresting and killing the officials of the shrine. This became a precedent. Thereafter, whenever the priests had a grievance, they flocked to the palace carrying the sacred tree of some temple or shrine. Instances of such turbulence were not infrequent, and they account in part for the reckless prodigality shown by Shirakawa in building and furnishing temples. The cenobites did not confine themselves to demonstrations at the palace; they had their own quarrels also.

MANNERS AND CUSTOMS OF THE HEIAN EPOCH

The Heian epoch was marked by an increasing luxury and artificiality, due largely to the adoption of Chinese customs. The capital city was built on a Chinese pattern and the salient characteristics of the Court during the period named from the new capital are on the Chinese pattern too. The Chinese idea of a civil service in which worth was tested by examinations was carried to a pedantic extreme both in administration and in society. In these examinations the important paper was in Chinese prose composition, which was much as if Latin prose were the main subject to prove the fitness of a candidate for an English or American administrative post. And the tests of social standing and the means of gaining fame at Court were skill in verse-writing, in music and dancing, in calligraphy and other forms of drawing, and in taste in landscape gardening.

If the men of the court were effeminate and emotional, sexual morality and wifely fidelity seems to have been lightly esteemed amongst the women. The Fujiwara working for the control of the Throne through Imperial consorts induced, even forced, the Emperors to set a bad example in such matters. But over all this vice there was a veneer of elaborate etiquette. Even in the field a breach of etiquette was a deadly insult. At Court, etiquette and ceremony became the only functions of the nominal monarch after the camera government of the cloistered ex-Emperors had begun. And aristocratic women, though they might be notoriously unfaithful, kept up a show of modesty, covering their faces in public, refusing to speak to a stranger, going abroad in closed carriages or heavily veiled with hoods, and talking to men with their faces hid by a fan, a screen, or a sliding door, these degrees of intimacy being nicely adjusted to the rank and station of the person addressed. Love-making and wooing were governed by strict and conventional etiquette, and an interchange of letters of a very literary and artificial type and of poems usually took the place of personal meetings. Indeed, literary skill and appreciation of Chinese poetry and art were the main things sought for in a wife.

Amusements

The pastimes of Court society in these years differed not so much in kind as in degree from those of the Nara epoch. In amusement, as in all else, there was extravagance and elaboration. What has already been said of the passion for literature would lead us to expect to find in the period an extreme development of the couplet-tournament (*uta awase*) which had had a certain vogue in the Nara epoch and was now a furore at Court. The Emperor Koko and other Emperors in the first half of the Heian epoch gave splendid verse-making parties, when the palace was richly decorated, often with beautiful flowers. In this earlier part of the period the gentlemen and ladies of the Court were separated, sitting on opposite sides of the room in which the party was held. Later in the Heian epoch the composition of love letters was a favorite competitive amusement, and although canons of elegant phraseology were implicitly followed, the actual contents of these fictitious letters were frankly indecent.

Other literary pastimes were: "incense-comparing," a combination of poetical dilletantism and skill in recognizing the fragrance of different kinds of incense burned separately or in different combinations; supplying famous stanzas of which only a word or so was given; making riddles in verse; writing verse or drawing pictures on fans – testing literary and artistic skill; and making up lists of related ideographs. The love of flowers was carried to extravagant lengths. The camera Court in particular organized magnificent picnics to see the cherry-trees of Hosho-ji and the snowy forest at Koya. There were spring festivals of sunrise at Sagano and autumn moonlight excursions to the Oi River. The taste of the time was typified in such vagaries as covering trees with artificial flowers in winter and in piling up snow so that some traces of snowy landscapes might still be seen in spring or summer. Other favourite amusements at Court included hawking, a kind of backgammon called *sugoroku*, and different forms of gambling. Football was played, a Chinese game in which the winner was he who kicked the ball highest and kept it longest from touching the ground.

Another rage was keeping animals as pets, especially cats and dogs, which received human names and official titles and, when they died, elaborate funerals. Kittens born at the palace at the close of the tenth century were treated with consideration comparable to that bestowed on Imperial infants. To the cat-mother the courtiers sent the ceremonial presents after childbirth, and one of the ladies-in-waiting was honoured by an appointment as guardian to the young kittens.

With the growth of luxury in the Heian epoch and the increase of extravagant entertainment and amusement, there was a remarkable development of music and the dance. Besides the six-stringed harp or *wagon*, much more complex harps or lutes of thirteen or twenty-five strings were used, and in general there was a great increase in the number and variety of instruments. Indeed, we may list as many as twenty kinds of musical instruments and three or four times as many varieties of dance in the Heian epoch. Most of the dances were foreign in their origin, some being Hindu, more Korean, and still more Chinese, according to the usual classification. But imported dances, adaptations of foreign dances, and the older native styles were all more or less pantomimic.

ARCHITECTURE AND LANDSCAPE GARDENING

Except in the new capital city with its formal plan there were no great innovations in architecture. Parks around large houses and willows and cherry-trees planted along the streets of Kyoto relieved this stiffness of the great city. Landscape-gardening became an art. Gardens were laid out in front of the row of buildings that made up the home of each noble or Court official.

Convention was nearly as rigid here as it was in Court etiquette. In the centre of this formal garden was a miniature lake with bridges leading to an island; there was a waterfall feeding the lake, usually at its southern end; and at the eastern and western limits of the garden, respectively, a grotto for angling and a "hermitage of spring water" – a sort of picnic ground frequented on summer evenings.

There was less temple building than in the Nara epoch and more attention was given to the construction of elegant palaces for court officials and nobles. But these were built of wood and were far from being massive or imposing. As in other periods of Japanese architecture, the exterior was sacrificed to the interior where there were choice woodworking and joinery in beautiful woods, and occasionally screen-or wall-painting as decoration.

There was still little house-furnishing. Mats (*tatami*), fitted together so as to cover the floor evenly, were not used until the very close of the period; and then, too, sliding doors began to be used as partitions. The coverings of these doors, silk or paper, were the "walls" for Japanese mural paintings of the period. As the *tatami* came into more general use, the bedstead of the earlier period, which was itself a low dais covered with mats and with posts on which curtains and nets might be hung, went out of use, being replaced by silken quilts spread on the floor-mats. Cushions and arm-rests were the only other important pieces of furniture.

The development of interior decoration in temples, monasteries, and palaces was due to progress on the part of lacquerers and painters. Gold lacquer, lacquer with a gold-dust surface (called *nashi-ji*), and lacquer inlaid with mother-of-pearl were increasingly used. Thanks in part to the painters' bureau (*E-dokoro*) in the palace, Japanese painters began to be ranked with their Chinese teachers. Koze Kanaoka was the first to be thus honored, and it is on record that he was engaged to paint figures of arhats on the sliding doors of the palace. The epoch also boasted Fujiwara Tame*uji*, founder of the Takuma family of artists, and Fujiwara Motomitsu, founder of the Tosa academy. The sculpture of the time showed greater skill, but less grandeur of conception, than the work of the Nara masters. Sculpture in wood was important, dating especially from the 11th century. Jocho, possibly the greatest of the workers in this medium, followed Chinese models, and carved a famous Buddha for Michinaga's temple of Hosho-ji (1022).

Two minor forms of sculpture call for special attention. The decoration of armour reached a high pitch of elaboration; and the beautiful armour of Minamoto Yoshitsune is still preserved at Kasuga, Nara. And masks to be used in mimetic dances, such as the *No*, received attention from many great glyptic artists.

THE HEIAN ECONOMY

In the year 799, cotton-seed, carried by an Indian junk which drifted to the coast of Mikawa, was sown in the provinces of Nankai-do and Saikai-do, and fifteen years later, when Saga reigned, tea plants were brought from overseas and were set out in several provinces. The Emperor Nimmyo (834–850) had buckwheat sown in the home provinces (Kinai), and the same sovereign encouraged the cultivation of sorghum, panic-grass, barley, wheat, large white beans, small red beans, and sesame. It was at this time that the *ina-hata* (paddy-loom) was devised for drying sheaves of rice before winnowing. Although it was a very simple implement, it nevertheless proved of such great value that an Imperial command was issued urging its wide use. In short, in the early years of the Heian epoch, the Throne took an active part in promoting agriculture, but this wholesome interest gradually declined in proportion to the extension of tax-free manors (*shoen*).

The story of trade resembled that of agriculture prosperous development at the beginning of the era, followed by stagnation and decline. Under Kwummu (782–805) and his immediate successors, canals and roads were opened, irrigation works were undertaken, and coins were frequently cast. But coins were slow in finding their way into circulation, and taxes were generally paid in kind. Nevertheless, for purposes of trade, prices of staples were fixed in terms of coin. Yet in actual practice, commodities were often assessed in terms of silk or rice. Goods were packed in stores (*kura*) or disposed on shelves in shops (*machi-ya*), and at ports where merchantmen assembled there were houses called *tsuya* (afterwards *toiya*) where wholesale transactions were conducted on the commission system.

The city of Kyoto was divided into two parts, an eastern capital (Tokyo) and a western capital (Saikyo). During the first half of every month all commercial transactions were conducted in the eastern capital, where fifty-one kinds of commodities were sold in fifty-one shops; and during the second half the western capital alone was frequented, with its thirty-three shops and thirty-three classes of goods. After the abolition of embassies to China, at the close of the ninth century, oversea trade declined for a time. But the inhabitants of Tsukushi and Naniwa, which were favourably located for voyages, continued to visit China and Korea, whence they are reported to have obtained articles of value. Other ports frequented by foreign-going ships were Kanzaki, Eguchi, Kaya, Otsu, and Hakata.

EDUCATION

There was, of course, no organized system of schools in this period, but education was not neglected. A university was established in the newly built capital, and there were five family schools or academies for the youth of the separate *uji*. A school and hospital, founded by Fujiwara Fuyutsugu in 825, received an Imperial endowment. At almost exactly the same time (823) the Bunsho-in was founded by Sugawara. The Sogaku-in was founded in 831 by Arihara Yukihara. In 850 the consort of the emperor Saga built the Gakkwan-in for the Tachibana family; and in 841 the palace of Junna became a school. And there was one quasi-public school, opened in 828, in the Toji monastery south of the capital, which was not limited to any family and was open to commoners.

SUPERSTITION

The notable increase in superstition during this period was due in part at least to the growth in Japan of the power of Buddhism, and, be it understood, of Buddhism of a degraded and debased form. The effort to combine Buddhism and Shinto probably robbed the latter of any power it might otherwise have had to withstand superstition. Although men of the greatest ability went into the Buddhist monasteries, including many Imperial princes, their eminence did not make them better leaders and guides of the people, but rather aided them in misleading and befooling the laity.

Near the end of the ninth century one Emperor made a gift of 500,000 yen for prayers that seemed to have saved the life of a favourite minister. Prayers for rain, for prolonged life, for victory over an enemy, were implicitly believed to be efficient, and priests received large bribes to make these prayers. Or they received other rewards: the privilege of coming to Court in a carriage was granted to one priest for bringing rain after a long drought and to another for saving the life of a sick prince in

981. As men got along in years they had masses said for the prolongation of their lives – with an increase in the premium each year for such life insurance. Thus, at forty, a man had masses said in forty shrines, but ten years later at fifty shrines in all.

In this matter, as in others, the influence of the Fujiwara was great. They were in a close alliance with the priests, and they controlled the Throne through consorts and kept the people in check through priests and superstitions.

With the widespread belief in the power of priestly prayer there was prevalent a fear of spirits and demons. Emperor Kwammu made efforts to placate the spirit of his younger brother whom he had exiled and killed. Kwammu, fearing that death was coming upon him, built a temple to the shade of this brother. A cloud over the palace of another Emperor was interpreted as a portentous monster, half monkey and half snake, and one of the Minamoto warriors won fame for his daring in shooting an arrow at the cloud, which then vanished. Equally foolhardy and marvellous was the deed of Fujiwara Michinaga, who alone of a band of courtiers in the palace dared one dark night to go unattended and without lights from one end of the palace to the other.

When the new city of Kyoto was built, a Buddhist temple was put near the northeast gate to protect the capital from demons, since the northeast quarter of the sky belonged to the demons; and on a hill a clay statue was erected, eight feet high and armed with bow, arrows and cuirass, to guard the city. So implicit was the belief in the power of this colossal charm that it was said that it moved and shouted to warn the city of danger.

THE SUPREMACY OF THE MILITARY CLASS

The Japanese term *monobe* (or *mononofu*), meaning soldiers, was expressed by Chinese ideographs having the sound, *bushi*. What tenets constituted the soldier's code in old Japan? Our first guide is the celebrated anthology, *Manyo-shu*, compiled in the ninth century and containing some poems that date from the sixth. From this we learn that the Yamato *monobe* (or *monono-fu*) believed himself to have inherited the duty of dying for his sovereign if occasion required. In that cause he must be prepared at all times to find a grave, whether upon the desolate moor or in the stormy sea. The dictates of filial piety ranked next in the ethical scale. The soldier was required to remember that his body had been given to him by his parents, and that he must never bring disgrace upon his family name or ever disregard the dictates of honour. Loyalty to the Throne, however, took precedence among moral obligations. Parent, wife, and child must all be abandoned at the call of patriotism. Such, as revealed in the pages of the *Myriad Leaves*, were the simple ethics of the early Japanese soldier.

The *Fujiwara*, earnest disciples of Chinese civilization, looked down on the soldier, and delegated to him alone the use of brute force and control of the criminal classes, reserving for themselves the management of civil government and the pursuit of literature, and even leaving politics and law in the hands of the schoolmen.

In these circumstances the military families of Minamoto (*Gen*) and Taira (*Hei*), performing the duties of guards and of police, gradually acquired influence; were trusted by the Court on all occasions demanding an appeal to force, and spared no pains to develop the qualities that distinguished them – the qualities of the *bushi*. Thus, as we turn the pages of history, we find the ethics of the soldier developing into a recognized code. His sword becomes an object of profound veneration. That the *bushi*'s word must be sacred and irrevocable is established by the conduct of Minamoto Yorinobu who, having promised to save the life of a bandit if the latter restore a child taken as a hostage, refuses subsequently to inflict any punishment whatever on the robber. That a *bushi* must prefer death to surrender is a principle observed in thousands of cases, and that his family name must be carefully guarded against every shadow of reproach is proved by his habit of prefacing a duel on the battle-field with a recitation of the titles and deeds of his ancestors.

To hold to his purpose in spite of evil report; to rise superior to poverty and hardship; not to rest until vengeance is exacted for wrong done to a benefactor or a relation; never to draw his sword except in deadly earnest – these are all familiar features of the *bushi*'s practice, though the order and times of their evolution cannot be precisely traced.

As for tactics, individual prowess was the beginning and the end of all contests, and strategy consisted mainly of deceptions, surprises, and ambushes. Outflanking methods were always to be pursued against an adversary holding high ground, and the aim should be to sever the communications of an army having a mountain or a river on its rear. When the enemy selected a position involving victory or death, he was to be held, not attacked, and when it was possible to surround a foe, one avenue of escape should always be left to him, since desperate men fight fiercely. In crossing a river, much space should separate the van from the rear of the crossing army, and an enemy crossing was not to be attacked until his forces had become well engaged in the operation. Birds soaring in alarm should suggest an ambush, and beasts breaking cover, an approaching attack. There was much spying. A soldier who could win the trust of the enemy, sojourn in his midst, and create dissensions in his camp, was called a hero.

Bushido taught a vassal to sacrifice his own interest and his own life on the altar of loyalty, but it did not teach a ruler to recognize and respect the rights of the ruled. It taught a wife to efface herself for her husband's sake, but it did not teach a husband any corresponding obligation towards a wife. In a word, it expounded the relation of the whole to its parts, but left unexpounded the relation of the parts to one another.

There was practically no ladder for the commoner – the farmer, the artisan, and the merchant – to ascend into the circle of the *samurai*. It can not be doubted that by closing the door of rank in the face of merit, *bushido* checked the development of the nation. Another defect in the *bushido* was indifference to intellectual investigation. The schoolmen of Kyoto, who alone received honour for their moral attainments, were not investigators but imitators, not scientists but classicists. The ethics of the *bushi* are charged with inculcating the principles of private morality only and ignoring those of public morality.

Military Families and their Retainers

It has been noticed that the disposition of the Central Government was to leave the provincial nobles severely alone, treating their feuds and conflicts as wholly private affairs. Thus, these nobles being cast upon their own resources for the protection of their lives and properties, retained the services of *bushi,* arming them well and drilling them assiduously, to serve as guards in time of peace and as soldiers in war. One result of this demand for military material was that the helots of former days were relieved from the badge of slavery and became hereditary retainers of provincial nobles, nothing of their old bondage remaining except that their lives were at the mercy of their masters.

As the provincial families grew in numbers and influence they naturally extended their estates, so that the landed property of a great sept sometimes stretched over parts, or even the whole, of several provinces. In these circumstances it became convenient to distinguish branches of a clan by the names of their respective localities and thusthere came into existence a territorial name (*myoji* or *shi*). For example, when the descendants of Minamoto no Yoshiiye acquired great properties at Nitta and Ashikaga in the provinces of Kotsuke and Shimotsuke, they took the territorial names of Nitta and Ashikaga, remaining always Minamoto.

While the names of the great *uji* were few, the territorial cognomens were very numerous. It will readily be conceived that although the territorial sections of the same *uji* sometimes quarrelled among themselves, the general practice was that all claiming common descent supported each other in war.

In its attitude towards these two families the Court showed short-sighted shrewdness. It pitted one against the other; if the Taira showed turbulence, the aid of the Minamoto was enlisted; and when a Minamoto rebelled, a Taira received a commission to deal with him. Thus, the Throne purchased peace for a time at the cost of sowing, between the two great military clans, seeds of discord destined to shake even the Crown. In the capital the *bushi* served as palace guards; in the provinces they were practically independent. Such was the state of affairs on the eve of a fierce struggle known in history as the tumult of the Hogen and Heiji eras (1150–1160).

THE HOGEN INSURRECTION

We have related how Taiken-mon-in, consort of the Emperor Toba, was chosen for the latter by his grandfather, the cloistered Emperor Shirakawa, and that she bore to Toba a son who ultimately ascended the throne as Sutoku. But, rightly or wrongly, Toba learned to suspect that before she became his wife, the lady's relations with Shirakawa had been over-intimate and that Sutoku was illegitimate. Therefore, immediately after Shirakawa's demise, Toba took to himself an Empress, Kaya-no-in, daughter of Fujiwara Tadazane; and failing offspring by her, chose another Fujiwara lady, Bifuku-mon-in, daughter of Nagazane. For this, his third consort, he conceived a strong affection, and when she bore to him a prince, Toba placed the latter on the throne at the age of three, compelling Sutoku to resign. This happened in the year 1141, and there were thenceforth two cloistered Emperors, Toba and Sutoku, standing to each other in the relation of grandfather and grandson. The baby sovereign was called Konoe (1142–55), and Fujiwara Tadamichi, brother of Bifu-ku-mon-in, became *kwampaku*.

Between this Tadamichi and his younger brother, Yorinaga, who held the post of *sa-daijin*, there existed acute rivalry. Their father's sympathies were wholly with Yorinaga, and he ultimately went so far as to depose Tadamichi from his hereditary position as *o-uji* of the Fujiwara. Thus, the enmity between Tadamichi and Yorinaga needed only an opportunity to burst into flame, and that opportunity was soon furnished.

The Emperor Konoe died (1155) at the early age of seventeen, and the cloistered sovereign, Sutoku (sought to secure the throne for his son Shigehito, whom Toba's suspicions had disqualified. But Bifuku-mon-in, believing, or pretending to believe, that the premature death of her son had been caused by Sutoku's incantations, persuaded the cloistered Emperor, Toba, in that sense, and having secured the co-operation of the *kwampaku*, Tadamichi, she set upon the throne Toba's fourth son, under the name of Go-Shirakawa (1156–1158), the latter's son, Morihito, being nominated Crown Prince, to the complete exclusion of Sutoku's offspring.

So long as Toba lived the arrangement remained undisturbed, but on his death in the following year (1156), Sutoku, supported by the *sa-daijin*, Yorinaga, planned to ascend the throne again, and there ensued a desperate struggle. This was not merely a quarrel for the succession, but was fuelled by the jealousies of the Fujiwara brothers, Yorinaga and Tadamichi, and importance from the association of the Minamoto and the Taira families. For when Sutoku appealed to arms against the Go-Shirakawa faction, he was incited by Fujiwara Yorinaga and his father Tadazane, and supported by Taira Tadamasa as well as by jthe two Minamoto, Tameyoshi and Tametomo; while Go-Shirakawa's cause was espoused by Fujiwara Tadamichi, by Taira no Kiyomori, and by Minamoto Yoshitomo.

Among this group of notables the most memorable in a historical sense are Minamoto Tametomo and Taira Kiyomori.

Of the latter there will presently be occasion to speak again. The former was a born warrior. Eighth son of Minamoto Tameyoshi, he showed himself so masterful, physically and morally, that his father deemed it wise to provide a distant field for the exercise of his energies and to that end sent him to Bungo in the island of Kyushu. Tametomo was then only thirteen. In two years he had established his sway over nearly the whole island, and the ceaseless excursions and alarms caused by his doings having attracted the attention of the Court, and futile orders for his chastisement were issued. Tameyoshi, his father, was then removed from office as a punishment for his son's contumacy, and thereupon Tametomo, esteeming filial piety as one of the *bushi*'s first obligations, hastened to the capital, taking with him only twenty-five of his principal retainers. His age was then seventeen; his height seven feet; his muscular development enormous, and he could draw a bow eight feet nine inches in length. His intention was to purchase his father's pardon by his own surrender, but on reaching Kyoto he found the Hogen tumult just breaking out, and, of course, he joined his father's party.

Sutoku's party occupied the Shirakawa palace. Unfortunately for the ex-Emperor the conduct of the struggle was entrusted to Fujiwara Yorinaga, and he, in defiance of Tametomo's advice, decided to remain on the defensive; an evil choice, since it entailed the tenure of highly inflammable wooden buildings. Yoshitomo and Kiyomori took full advantage of this strategical error. They forced the Shirakawa palace, and after a desperate struggle, the defenders took to flight. Sutoku was exiled to Sanuki, and hastened his demise by self-inflicted privations – he died (1164) eight years after being sent into exile – the evils of the time were attributed to his unquiet spirit and a shrine was built to his memory.

Not less heartless was the treatment of the vanquished nobles. The Fujiwara alone escaped. Yorinaga had the good fortune to fall on the field of battle, and his father, Tadazane, was saved by the intercession of his elder son, Tadamichi, of whose dislike he had long been a victim. But this was the sole spot of light on the sombre page. By the Emperor's orders, the Taira chief, Kiyomori, executed his uncle, Tadamasa; by the Emperor's orders, though not without protest, the Minamoto chief, Yoshitomo, put to death his father, Tameyoshi; by the Emperor's orders all the relatives of Yorinaga were sent into exile; by the Emperor's orders his nephew, Prince Shigehito, was compelled to take the tonsure, and by the Emperor's orders the sinews of Tametomo's bow-arm were cut and he was banished to the Izu island.

THE SEVENTY-SEVENTH EMPEROR, GO-SHIRAKAWA

Go-Shirakawa occupied the throne during two years only (1156–1158), but he made his influence felt from the cloister throughout the long period of thirty-four years (1158 to 1192), directing the administration from his "camera palace" (*Inchu*) during the reigns of five Emperors. Ambition impelled him to tread in the footsteps of Go-Sanjo. He re-opened the Office of *Records* (*Kiroku-jo*), which that great sovereign had established for the purpose of centralizing the powers of the State, and he sought to recover for the Throne its administrative functions. But his independence was purely nominal, for in everything he took counsel of Fujiwara Michinori (Shinzei) and obeyed that statesman's guidance. Michinori's character is not to be implicitly inferred from the cruel courses suggested by him after the Hogen tumult. He was a man of keen intelligence and profound learning Michinori devoted a great part of his life to arts and culture, and when, in 1140, that is to say, sixteen years before the Hogen disturbance, he received the tonsure, all prospect of an official career seemed to be closed to him. But the accession of Go-Shirakawa gave him an opportunity. The Emperor trusted him, and he abused the trust to the further unhappiness of the nation.

THE HEIJI TUMULT

Go-Shirakawa's son, Morihito, ascended the throne in 1159 and is known in history as Nijo, the seventy-eighth sovereign of Japan. From the very outset he resented the ex-Emperor's attempt to interfere in the administration of affairs, and the two Courts fell into a state of discord, Fujiwara Shinzei inciting the cloistered Emperor to assert himself, and two other Fujiwara nobles, Tsunemune and Korekata, prompting Nijo to resist. These two, observing that another noble of their clan, Fujiwara Nobuyori; was on bad terms with Shinzei, approached Nobuyori and proposed a union against their common enemy.

Shinzei had committed one great error; he had alienated the Minamoto family. In the Hogen struggle, Yoshitomo, the Minamoto chief, an able captain and a brave soldier, had suggested the strategy which secured victory for Go-Shirakawa's forces. But in the subsequent distribution of rewards, Yoshitomo's claims received scant consideration, his merits being underrated by Shinzei.

This had been followed by a still more painful slight. To Yoshitomo's formal proposal of a marriage between his daughter and Shinzei's son, not only had a refusal been given, but also the nuptials of the youth with the daughter of the Taira chief, Kiyomori, had been subsequently celebrated with much eclat. In short, Shinzei chose between the two great military clans, and had erred egregiously in failing to recognize that the day had passed when the military clans could be thus employed as Fujiwara tools. Approached by Nobuyori, Yoshitomo joined hands with the plotters, and the Minamoto troops, forcing their way into the Sanjo palace, set fire to the edifice and killed Shinzei (1159). The Taira chief, Kiyomori, happened to be then absent in Kumano, and Yoshitomo's plan was to attack him on his way back to Kyoto before the Taira forces had mustered. But just as Fujiwara Yorinaga had wrecked his cause in the Hogen tumult by ignoring Minamoto Tametomo's advice, so in the Heiji disturbance, Fujiwara Nobuyori courted defeat by rejecting Minamoto Yoshitomo's strategy. The Taira, thus accorded leisure to assemble their troops, won such a signal victory that during many years the Minamoto disappeared almost completely from the political stage, and the Taira held the empire in the hollow of their hands.

Shinzei's record shows him to have been cruel, jealous, and self-seeking, but it has to be admitted that the conditions of the time were calculated to educate men of his type, as is shown by the story of the Hogen insurrection. For when Sutoku's partisans assembled at the palace of Shirakawa, Minamoto Tametomo addressed them thus:

"I fought twenty battles and two hundred minor engagements to win Kyushu, and I say that when an enemy is outnumbered, its best plan is a night attack. If we fire the Takamatsu palace on three sides to-night and assault it from the fourth, the foe will surely be broken. I see on the other side only one man worthy to be called an enemy. It is my brother Yoshitomo, and with a single arrow I can lay him low. As for Taira Kiyomori, he will fall if I do but shake the sleeve of my armour. Before dawn we shall be victors."

Fujiwara Yorinaga's refusal to follow Tametomo's advice and Fujiwara Nobuyori's rejection of Yoshitomo's counsels were wholly responsible for the disasters that ensued, and were also illustrative of the contempt in which the Fujiwara held the military magnates, who, in turn, were well aware of the impotence of the Court nobles on the battle-field.

Yoshitomo had many sons but only four of them escaped from the Heiji tumult. The eldest of these was Yoritomo, then only fourteen. After killing two men who attempted to intercept his flight, he was finally banished to Izu, whence, a few years later, he emerged to the destruction of the Taira. A still younger son, Yoshitsune, was destined to prove the most renowned warrior Japan ever produced. His mother, Tokiwa, one of Yoshitomo's mistresses, a woman of rare beauty, fled from the Minamoto mansion during a snow-storm after the Heiji disaster, and, with her three children, succeeded in reaching a village in Yamato, where she might have lain concealed had not her mother fallen into the hands of Kiyomori's agents. Tokiwa was then required to choose between giving herself up and suffering her mother to be executed. Her beauty saved the situation. Kiyomori had no sooner seen her face than he offered to have mercy if she entered his household and if she consented to have her three sons educated for the priesthood. Thus, Yoshitsune survived, and in after ages people were wont to say of Kiyomori's passion and its result that his blissful dream of one night had brought ruin on his house.

THE TAIRA AND THE FUJIWARA

The most prominent features of Taira no Kiyomori's character were unbridled ambition, intolerance of opposition, and unscrupulous pursuit of visible ends. He did not initiate anything but was content to follow in the footsteps of the Fujiwara. It has been recorded that in 1158 – after the Hogen tumult, but before that of Heiji – he married his daughter to a son of Fujiwara Shinzeoi. In that transaction, however, Shinzei's will dominated. Two years later, the Minamoto's power having been shattered, Kiyomori gave another of his daughters to be the mistress of the *kwampaku*, Fujiwara Motozane. There was no offspring of this union, and when, in 1166, Motozane died, he left a five-year-old son, Motomichi, born of his wife, a Fujiwara lady. This boy was too young to succeed to the office of regent, and therefore had no title to any of the property accruing to the holder of that post, who had always been recognized as *de jure* head of the Fujiwara family. Nevertheless, Kiyomori, having contrived that the child should be entrusted to his daughter's care, asserted its claims so strenuously that many of the Fujiwara manors and all the heirlooms were handed over to it, the result being a visible weakening of the great family's influence.

The most signal result of the Hogen and Heiji insurrections was to transfer the administrative power from the Court nobles to the military chiefs. In no country were class distinctions more scrupulously observed than in Japan. All officials of the fifth rank and upwards must belong to the families of the Court nobility, and no office carrying with it rank higher than the sixth might be occupied by a military man.

The social positions of the two groups were even more rigidly differentiated; those of the fifth rank and upwards being termed *tenjo-bito*, or men having the privilege of entree to the palace and to the Imperial presence; while the lower group (from the sixth downwards) had no such privilege and were consequently termed *chige-bito*, or groundlings. The three highest offices (spoken of as *san-ko*) could not be held by any save members of the Fujiwara or Kuga families. All this was changed after the Heiji commotion. The Fujiwara had used the military leaders for their own ends; Kiyomori supplemented his military strength with Fujiwara methods. He caused himself to be appointed *sangi* (councillor of State) and to be raised to the first grade of the third rank, and he procured for his friends and relations posts as provincial governors, so that they were able to organize throughout the empire military forces devoted to the Taira cause.

These steps were mere preludes to his ambitious programme. He married his wife's elder sister to the ex-Emperor, Go-Shirakawa, and the fruit of this union was a prince who subsequently ascended the throne as Takakura. The Emperor Nijo had died in 1166, after five years of effort, only partially successful, to restrain his father, Go-Shirakawa's, interference in the administration. Nijo was succeeded by his son, Rokujo, a baby of two years; and, a few months later, Takakura, then in his seventh year, was proclaimed Prince Imperial. Rokujo (the seventy-ninth sovereign) was not given time to learn the meaning of the title "Emperor." In three years he was deposed by Go-Shirakawa with Kiyomori's co-operation, and Takakura (eightieth sovereign) ascended the throne in 1169, occupying it until 1180. Thus, Kiyomori found himself uncle of an Emperor only ten years of age.

On the nomination of Takakura to be Crown Prince the Taira leader was appointed – appointed himself would be a more accurate form of speech – to the office of *nai-daijin*, and within a very brief period he ascended to the chancellorship, overleaping the two intervening posts of *u-daijin* and *sa-daijin*. This was in the fiftieth year of his life. At fifty-one, he fell seriously ill and took the tonsure by way of soliciting heaven's aid. Recovering, he developed a mood of increased arrogance. His residence at Rokuhara was a magnificent pile of building, as architecture then went, standing in a park of great extent and beauty. There he administered State affairs with all the pomp and circumstance of an Imperial court. He introduced his daughter, Toku, into the Household and very soon she was made Empress, under the name of Kenrei-mon-in.

The Fujiwara had been beaten at their own game. A majority of the highest posts were filled by Kiyomori's kinsmen. Their manors were to be found in five hundred places, and their fields were innumerable. Their mansions were full of splendid garments and rich robes like flowers, and the spaces before their portals were so thronged with ox-carriages and horses that markets were often held there.

It is necessary to note, too, with regard to these manors, that many of them were tax-free lands (*koderi*) granted in perpetuity. Such grants, as has been already shown, were not infrequent, but the *koden* bestowed on Taira officers were, in effect, military fiefs. It is true that similar fiefs existed in the north and in the south, but their number was so greatly increased in the days of Taira ascendancy as almost to constitute a new departure. Kiyomori was, in truth, one of the most despotic rulers that ever held sway in Japan. He organized a band of three hundred youths whose business was to go about Kyoto and listen to the citizens' talk. If anyone was reported by these spies as having spoken ill of the Taira, he was seized and punished.

Plots Against the Taira: Kiyomori's Last Years

All these arbitrary acts provoked indignation among every class of the people. A conspiracy known in history as the "Shishi-ga-tani plot," from the name of the place where the conspirators met to consult, was organized in 1177, having for object a general uprising against the Taira. In the Shishi-ga-tani plot the part assigned to the priest Saiko was to induce Go-Shirakawa to take active interest in the conspiracy and to issue a mandate to the Minamoto *bushi* throughout the country. No such mandate was issued, nor does it appear that the ex-Emperor attended any of the meetings in Shishi-ga-tani, but there can be no doubt that he had full cognizance of, and sympathized with, what was in progress.

The conspiracy never matured. It was betrayed by Minamoto Yukitsuna. Saiko and his two sons were beheaded; Narichika was exiled and subsequently put to death, and all the rest were banished. The great question was, how to deal with His Majesty Go-Shirakawa. Kiyomori was for leading troops to arrest his

Majesty, and to escort him as a prisoner to the Toba palace or the Taira mansion. None of the despot's kinsmen or adherents ventured to gainsay this purpose until Kiyomori's eldest son, Shigemori, appeared upon the scene. Shigemori had contributed much to the signal success of the Taira. Dowered with all the strategical skill and political sagacity which his father lacked, he had won victories for the family arms, and again and again had restrained the rash exercise of Kiyomori's impetuous arrogance.

Shigemori declared that he would not survive any violence done to Go-Shirakawa, Kiyomori left the council chamber, bidding Shigemori to manage the matter as he thought fit. Thus, Go-Shirakawa escaped all the consequences of his association with the conspirators. But Kiyomori took care that a copy of the bonze Saiko's confession, extracted under torture and fully incriminating his Majesty, should come into the Imperial hands.

A final rupture between the ex-Emperor and the Taira leader became daily imminent. Two events contributed to precipitate it. One was that in the year following the Shishi-ga-tani conspiracy, Kiyomori's daughter, Toku, bore to Takakura a prince – the future Emperor Antoku (eighty-first sovereign). The Taira chief thus found himself grandfather of an heir to the throne, a fact which did not tend to abate his arrogance. The second was the death of Shigemori, which took place in 1179.

Shigemori's record shows him to have been at once a statesman and a general. He never hesitated to check his father's extravagances, though from first to last he remained the same short-sighted, passion-driven, impetuous despot and finally the evil possibilities of the situation weighed so heavily on Shigemori's nerves that he publicly repaired to a temple to pray for release from life. As though in answer to his prayer he was attacked by a disease which carried him off at the age of forty-two. Certainly a sense of impotence to save his father and his family from the calamities he clearly saw approaching was the proximate cause of his breakdown.

Results soon became apparent. The ex-Emperor, who had truly estimated Shigemori's value as a pillar of Taira power, judged that an opportunity for revolt had now arrived, and the Taira chief, deprived of his son's restraining influence, became less competent than ever to manage the great machine which fortune had entrusted to his direction. The first challenge came from the ex-Emperor's side. It has been related above that one of Kiyomori's politic acts after the Heiji insurrection was to give his daughter to the regent; that, on the latter's death, his child, Motomichi, by a Fujiwara, was entrusted to the care of the Taira lady; that a large part of the Fujiwara estates were diverted from the regent and settled upon Motomichi, and that the latter was taken into a Taira mansion. The regent who suffered by this arbitrary procedure was Fujiwara Motofusa, who was ready to join hands with Go-Shirakawa in any anti-Taira procedure.

Therefore, in 1179, on the death of Kiyomori's daughter, to whose care Motomichi had been entrusted in his childhood, the ex-Emperor, at the instance of Motofusa, appropriated all her manors and those of Motomichi. Moreover, on the death of Shigemori shortly afterwards, the same course was pursued with his landed property, and further, Motomichi, though lawful head of the Fujiwara family, son-in-law of Kiyomori, and of full age, had been refused the post of *chunagon*, the claim of a twelve year-old son of Motofusa being preferred. Kiyomori saw that the gauntlet had been thrown in his face. Hastening from his villa of Fukuhara, in Settsu, at the head of a large force of troops, he placed the ex-Emperor in strict confinement in the Toba palace, segregating him completely from the official world and depriving him of all administrative functions; he banished the *kwampaku*, Motofusa, and the chancellor, Fujiwara Moronaga; he degraded and deprived of their posts thirty-nine high officials who had formed the entourage of Go-Shirakawa; he raised Motomichi to the office of *kwampaku*, and he conferred on his son, Munemori, the function of guarding Kyoto, strong bodies of soldiers being posted in the two Taira mansions of Rokuhara on the north and south of the capital.

The Yorimasa Conspiracy

In 1180, at the instance of Kiyomori, no doubt, the Emperor Takakura, then in his twentieth year, resigned the throne in favour of Kiyomori's grandson, Antoku (eighty-first sovereign), a child of three. This was the culmination of the Taira's fortunes. There was at that time among the Kyoto officials a Minamoto named Yorimasa, who was an expert bowman, a skilled soldier, and an adept versifier, accomplishments not infrequently combined in one person during the Heian epoch. Go-Shirakawa, appreciating Yorimasa's abilities, nominated him director of the Imperial Estates Bureau (*Kurando*) and afterwards made him governor of Hyogo.

But it was not until he had reached the age of seventy-five that, on Kiyomori's recommendation, he received promotion, in 1178, to the second grade of the third rank (*ju-sammi*), thus for the first time obtaining the privilege of access to the Imperial presence. In the year of Heiji, he held his little band of *bushi* in the leash until the issue of the battle could be clearly forseen, and then he threw in his lot with the Taira. Such shallow fealty seldom wins its way to high place. Men did not forget Yorimasa's record. His belated admission to the ranks of the *tenjo-bito* provoked some derision and he was commonly spoken of as *Gen-sammi* (the Minamoto third rank).

But even for one constitutionally so cautious, the pretensions of the Taira became intolerable. Yorimasa determined to strike a blow for the Minamoto cause, and looking round for a figure-head, he fixed upon Prince Mochihito, elder brother of Takakura. This prince, being the son of a concubine, had never reached Imperial rank, though he was thirty years of age, but he possessed some capacity, and a noted physiognomist had recognized in him a future Emperor. In 1170, at Yorimasa's instance, Prince Mochihito secretly sent to all the Minamoto families throughout the empire, especially to Yoritomo at his place of exile in Izu, a document impeaching the conduct of the Taira and exhorting the Minamoto to muster and attack them.

Yorimasa's story shows that he would not have embarked upon this enterprise had he not seen solid hope of success. But one of the aids he counted on proved unsound. That aid was the Buddhist priesthood. Kiyomori had offended the great monasteries by bestowing special favour on the insignificant shrine of Itsukushima-Myojin. A revelation received in a dream having persuaded him that his fortunes were intimately connected with this shrine, he not only rebuilt it on a scale of much magnificence, but also persuaded Go-Shirakawa to make three solemn progresses thither.

A monster demonstration on the part of three great, and overlooked monasteries – Enryaku (Hiei-zan), Kofuku (Nara), or Onjo (Miidera) – was temporarily quieted, but deep umbrage rankled in the bosoms of the priests, and Yorimasa counted on their co-operation with his insurrection. He forgot, however, that no bond could be trusted to hold them permanently together in the face of their habitual rivalry, and it was here that his scheme ultimately broke down. At an early stage, some vague news of the plot reached Kiyomori's ears but he entertained no conception of Yorimasa's complicity. Thus, while removing Go-Shirakawa to Rokuhara and despatching a force to seize Mochihito, he entrusted the direction of the latter measure to Yorimasa's son, Kanetsuna, who, it need scarcely be said, failed to apprehend the prince or to elicit any information from his followers.

Presently Kiyomori learned that the prince had escaped to Onjo-ji (Miidera). Kiyomori's trust in Yorimasa remained still unshaken, Yorimasa believed that immediate aid would be furnished from Hiei-zan. But before his appeal reached the latter, Kiyomori's overtures had been accepted. Nothing now remained for Yorimasa and Mochihito except to make a desperate rush on Kyoto or to ride away south to Nara, where temporary refuge offered. The latter course was chosen, in spite of Yorimasa's advice. On the banks of the Uji River in a dense fog they were overtaken by the Taira force, the latter numbering twenty thousand, the fugitives three or four hundred. The Minamoto made a gallant and skilful resistance, and finally Yorimasa rode off with a handful of followers, hoping to carry Mochihito to a place of safety. Before they passed out of range an arrow struck the old warrior. Struggling back to Byodo-in, where the fight was still in progress, he seated himself on his iron war-fan and, having calmly composed his death-song, committed suicide.

The Death of Kiyomori

These things happened in May, 1180, and in the following month Kiyomori carried out a design entertained by him for some time. He transferred the capital from Kyoto to Fukuhara, in Settsu, where the modern town of Kobe stands. Kiyomori seems to have thought that as the centres of Taira strength lay in the south and west of the empire, the province of Settsu would be a more convenient citadel than Kyoto. Hence he built at Fukuhara a spacious villa and took various steps to improve the harbour. But Fukuhara is fifty miles from Kyoto, and to reach the latter quickly from the former in an emergency was a serious task in the twelfth century. Moreover, Kyoto was devastated in 1177 by a conflagration which reduced one-third of the city to ashes, and in April of 1180 by a tornado of most destructive force, so that superstitious folk, who abounded in that age, began to speak *omi*nously of the city's doom.

What weighed most with the Taira leader, however, was the propinquity of the three great monasteries; Hiei-zan on the north, Miidera on the east, and Nara on the south. In fact, the city lay at the mercy of the soldier-priests. At any moment they might combine, descend upon the capital, and burn it before adequate succour could be marshalled.

Kiyomori carried with him to Fukuhara the boy-Emperor (Antoku), the ex-Emperor (Takakura), the cloistered Emperor (Go-Shirakawa), the *kwampaku* (Motomichi), and all the high Court officials with rare exceptions. The work of construction at Fukuhara not being yet complete, Go-Shirakawa had to be lodged in a building thirty feet square, to which men gave the name of the "jail palace." Kyoto, of course, was thrown into a state of consternation. Remonstrances, petitions, and complaints poured into the Fukuhara mansion. Meanwhile the Minamoto rose. In August of 1180, their white flag was hoisted, and Kiyomori did not underrate its meaning.

At the close of the year, he decided to abandon the Fukuhara scheme and carry the Court back to Kyoto. On the eve of his return he found an opportunity of dealing a heavy blow to the monasteries of Miidera and Nara. For, it having been discovered that they were in collusion with the newly risen Minamoto, Kiyomori sent his sons, Tomomori and Shigehira, at the head of a force which sacked and burned Onjo-ji, Todai-ji, and Kofuku-ji. Thereafter a terrible time ensued for Kyoto, for the home provinces (Kinai), and for the west of the empire. During the greater part of three years, from 1180 to 1182 inclusive, the people suffered, first from famine and afterwards from pestilence. Pitiful accounts are given by contemporary writers. Men were reduced to the direst straits. Hundreds perished of starvation in the streets of Kyoto, and as, in many cases, the corpses lay unburied, pestilence of course ensued. It is stated that in Kyoto alone during two months there were forty-two thousand deaths.

The eastern and western regions, however, enjoyed comparative immunity. By the priests and the political enemies of the Taira these cruel calamities were attributed to the evil deeds of Kiyomori and his fellow clansmen, so that the once omnipotent family gradually became an object of popular execration. Kiyomori, however, did not live to witness the ruin of his house. He expired at the age of sixty in March, 1181, just three months after the restoration of Kyoto to metropolitan rank. Since August of the preceding year, the Minamoto had shown signs of troublesome activity, but as yet it seemed hardly possible that their puny onsets should shake, still less pull down, the imposing edifice of power raised by the Taira during twenty years of unprecedented success. Nevertheless, Kiyomori, impatient of all reverses, bitterly upbraided his sons and his officers for incompetence, and when, after seven days' sickness, he saw the end approaching, his last commission was that neither tomb nor temple should be raised to his memory until Yoritomo's head had been placed on his grave.

The Opening of the Conflict

When, after the great struggle of 1160, fourteen-year-old Yoritomo, the eldest of Yoshitomo's surviving sons, had been exiled to Izu, the eastern regions were infested by Minamoto kinsmen and partisans. But Kiyomori did not act blindly. He was placed in the hands of two: one a Fujiwara, Ito Sukechika, and a Taira, who, taking the name Hojo from the locality of his manor, called himself Hojo Tokimasa. [...] Sukechika might have been expected to sympathize with his ward in consideration of the sufferings of the Fujiwara at Kiyomori's hands. Tokimasa, as a Taira, should have been wholly antipathetic. Yet had Tokimasa shared Sukechika's mood, the Minamoto's sun would never have risen over the Kwanto.

The explanation is that Tokimasa belonged to a large group of provincial Taira who were at once discontented because their claims to promotion had been ignored, and deeply resentful of indignities and ridicule to which their rustic manners and customs had exposed them at the hands of their upstart kinsmen in Kyoto. While remaining Yoritomo's ostensible warden, he became his confidant and abettor. With Tokimasa he found security and established relations with Masa, his warden's eldest daughter. In all Yoritomo's career there is not one instance of a sacrifice of expediency or ambition on the altar of sentiment or affection. He was a cold, calculating man. It is in the last degree improbable that he risked his political hopes for the sake of a trivial amour. At any rate the event suggests crafty deliberation rather than a passing passion. For though Tokimasa simulated ignorance of the liaison and publicly proceeded with his previous engagement to wed Masa to Taira Kanetaka, lieutenant-governor of Izu, he privately connived at her flight and subsequent concealment.

This incident is said to have determined Yoritomo. He disclosed all his ambitions to Hojo Tokimasa, and found in him an able coadjutor. Yoritomo now began to open secret communications with several of the military families in Izu and the neighbouring provinces. In making these selections and approaches, the Minamoto exile was guided and assisted by Tokimasa. Confidences were not by any means confined to men of Minamoto lineage. The kith and kin of the Fujiwara, and even of the Taira themselves, were drawn into the conspiracy.

In May, or June, 1180, the mandate of Prince Mochihito reached Yoritomo, carried by his uncle, Minamoto Yukiiye, whose figure thenceforth appears frequently upon the scene. Yoritomo showed the mandate to Tokimasa, and the two men were taking measures to obey when they received intelligence of the deaths of Mochihito and Yorimasa and of the fatal battle on the banks of the Uji.

Yoritomo would probably have deferred conclusive action in such circumstances had he not been warned that the Taira were planning to exterminate the remnant of the Minamoto and that Yoritomo's name stood first on the black-list. Moreover, the advisability of taking the field at once was strongly and incessantly urged by a priest, Mongaku, who, after a brief acquaintance, had impressed Yoritomo favourably.

The First Stage of the Struggle

The campaign was opened by Hojo Tokimasa on the 8th of September, 1180. He attacked the residence of the lieutenant-governor of Izu, Taira Kanetaka, burned the mansion, and killed Kanetaka, whose abortive nuptials with the lady Masa had been celebrated a few months previously. Yoritomo himself at the head of a force of three hundred men, crossed the Hakone Pass three days later *en route* for Sagami, and encamped at Ishibashi-yama. This first essay of the Minamoto showed no military caution whatever. It was a march into space. It is true that many Taira magnates of the Kwanto were pledged to draw the sword in the Minamoto cause. They had found the selfish tyranny of Kiyomori not at all to their taste or their profit. Yoritomo may possibly have entertained some hope that the Oba army would not prove a serious menace.

Whatever the explanation may be, the little Minamoto band were attacked in front and rear simultaneously during a stormy night. The remnants of the Minamoto sought shelter in a cryptomeria grove, where Yoritomo proved himself a powerful bowman. But when he found his followers reduced to six men. These, at the suggestion of Doi Sanehira, he ordered to scatter and seek safety in flight, while he himself with Sanehira hid in a hollow tree. Their hiding-place was discovered by Kajiwara Kagetoki, a member of the Oba family, whose sympathies were with the Minamoto. He placed himself before the tree and signalled that the fugitives had taken another direction. Presently, Oba Kagechika, riding up, thrust his bow into the hollow tree, and as two pigeons flew out, he concluded that there was no human being within.

From the time of this hairbreadth escape, Yoritomo's fortunes rose rapidly. After some days of concealment among the Hakone mountains, he reached the shore of Yedo Bay, and crossing from Izu to Awa, was joined by Tokimasa and others. Sympathizers began to flock in. Eight provinces of the Kwanto responded like an echo to Yoritomo's call, and, by the time he had made his circuit of Yedo Bay, some twenty-five thousand men were marshalled under his standard. Kamakura, on the seacoast a few miles south of the present Yokohama, was chosen for headquarters, and one of the first steps taken was to establish there a grand shrine to Hachiman, the god of War and tutelary deity of the Minamoto.

Meanwhile, Tokimasa had secured the allegiance of the Takeda family of Kai, and was about to send a strong force to join Yoritomo's army. But by this time the Taira were in motion. Kiyomori had despatched a body of fifty thousand men under Koremori, and Yoritomo had decided to meet this army on the banks of the Fuji river. It became necessary, therefore, to remove all potential foes from the Minamoto rear, and accordingly Hojo Tokimasa received orders to overrun Suruga and then to direct his movements with a view to concentration on the Fuji. Thither Yoritomo marched from Kamakura, and by the beginning of November, 1180, fifty thousand Taira troops were encamped on the south bank of the river and twenty-seven thousand Minamoto on the north. A decisive battle must be fought in the space of a few days. In fact, the 13th of November had been indicated as the probable date.

But the battle was never fought. The Taira officers seem to have been thrown into a state of nervous prostration by the unexpected magnitude of the Minamoto's uprising. They were debating, and had nearly recognized the propriety of falling back without challenging a combat or venturing their heads further into the tiger's mouth, when something – a flight of water-birds, a reconnaissance in force, a rumour, or what not – produced a panic, and before a blow had been struck, the Taira army was in full retreat for Kyoto.

Yoshitsune

In the Minamoto camp there was some talk of pursuing the fugitive Taira, but it was ultimately decided that the allegiance of the whole Kwanto must be definitely secured first. Therefore the army was withdrawn to a more convenient position on the Kiso River, and steps, ultimately successful, were taken to win over the powerful Minamoto families of Satake and Nitta.

It was at this time that there arrived in Yoritomo's camp a youth of twenty-one with about a score of followers. Of medium stature and of frame more remarkable for grace than for strength, he attracted attention chiefly by his piercing eyes and by the dignified intelligence of his countenance. This was Yoshitsune, the youngest son of Yoshitomo. Placed in the monastery of Kurama, as stipulated by Kiyomori, Yoshitsune had no sooner learned to think than he became inspired with an absorbing desire to restore the fortunes of his family. At the age of fifteen he managed to effect his escape to the north of Japan. The agent of his flight was an iron-merchant who habitually visited the monastery on matters of business, and whose dealings took him occasionally to Mutsu.

At the time of Yoshitsune's novitiate in the Kurama temple, the political power in Japan may be said to have been divided between the Taira, the provincial Minamoto, the Buddhist priests, and the Fujiwara, and of the last the only branch that had suffered no eclipse during the storms of Hogen and Heiji had been the Fujiwara of Mutsu. After these conflicts, Fujiwara Kiyohira succeeded to the six districts of Mutsu, which constituted the largest estate in the hands of any one Japanese noble. That estate was in the possession of Hidehira, grandson of Kiyohira, at the time when the Minamoto family suffered its heavy reverses. Yoshitsune expected, therefore, that at least an asylum would be assured, could he find his way to Mutsu. He was not mistaken. Hidehira received him with all hospitality, and as Mutsu was practically beyond the control of Kyoto, the Minamoto fugitive could lead there the life of a *bushi*, and openly study everything pertaining to military art. He made such excellent use of these opportunities that, by the time the Minamoto standard was raised anew in Izu, Yoshitsune had earned the reputation of being the best swordsman in the whole of northern Japan.

When Yoshitsune rode into Yoritomo's camp on a November day in the year 1180, he was accompanied by a score of followers, several who subsequently earned undying fame, but one deserves special mention here. Benkei, the giant halberdier, had turned his back upon the priesthood, and, becoming a free lance, conceived the ambition of forcibly collecting a thousand swords from their wearers. He wielded the halberd with extraordinary skill, and such a huge weapon in the hand of a man with seven feet of stalwart stature constituted a menace before which a solitary wayfarer did not hesitate to surrender his sword. The giant Benkei had sworn allegiance to Yoshitsune, an oath which he kept so faithfully as to become the type of soldierly fidelity for all subsequent generations of his countrymen.

In the provinces of Shinano and Kotsuke a powerful Minamoto resurrection synchronized with, but was independent of, the Yoritomo movement The hero of the Shinano-Kotsuke drama was Minamoto no Yoshinaka, commonly called Kiso Yoshinaka, because his youth was passed among the mountains where the Kiso River has its source – he had been rescued as a baby of two when his father fell in battle. Yoshinaka attained an immense stature as well as signal skill in archery and horsemanship. Like Yoritomo and Yoshitsune, he brooded much on the evil fortunes of the Minamoto, and paid frequent visits to Kyoto to observe the course of events. In the year 1180, the mandate of Prince Mochihito reached him, and learning that Yoritomo had taken the field, he gathered a force in Shinano. Yoshinaka gained a signal victory over the Taira forces marshalled against him by the governor of Shinano, and pushing thence eastward into Kotsuke, obtained the allegiance of the Ashikaga of Shimotsuke and of the Takeda of Kai. Thus, the year 1180 closed upon a disastrous state of affairs for the Taira, no less than ten provinces in the east having fallen practically under Minamoto sway.

Kiyomori expired in March, 1181, as already related. His last behest, that the head of Yoritomo should be laid on his grave, nerved his successors to fresh efforts. But Kiyomori's son, Munemori, upon whom devolved the direction of the Taira clan's affairs, was wholly incompetent for such a trust. Now the home provinces and the west fell into the horrors of famine and pestilence, as described above; and in such circumstances to place armies in the field and to maintain them there became impossible. The Taira had to desist from all warlike enterprises until the summer of 1182, when a great effort was made to crush the rapidly growing power of the Minamoto. But when Jo no Nagashige, a powerful Taira magnate of Echigo Nagashige, set in motion against Yoshinaka a strong force, swelled by a contingent from Kyoto under Michimori the results were signal defeat for the Taira and the carrying of the white flag by Yoshinaka into Echigo, Etchu, Noto, and Kaga.

Dissensions among the Minamoto

Meanwhile discord had declared itself between Yoritomo and Yoshinaka. In view of Yoshinaka's brilliant successes, Takeda Nobumitsu of Kai province proposed a marriage between his daughter and Yoshinaka's son, Yoshitaka. This union was declined by Yoshinaka, whereupon Nobumitsu suggested to Yoritomo that Yoshinaka's real purpose was to ally his house with the Taira by marriage. A rupture between the two Minamoto chiefs was presaged by Yoritomo's entourage and things gradually shaped themselves in accordance with that forecast.

The malcontents in Yoritomo's camp or his discomfited opponents began to transfer their allegiance to Yoshinaka, a tendency which culminated when Yoritomo's uncle, Yukiiye, taking umbrage because a provincial governorship was not given to him, rode off at the head of a thousand cavalry to join Yoshinaka. Early in the year 1183, Yoritomo sent a force into Shinano with orders to exterminate Yoshinaka. But the latter declined the combat. Quoting a popular saying that the worst enemies of the Minamoto were their own dissensions, he directed his troops to withdraw into Echigo, leaving to Yoritomo a free hand in Shinano. When this was reported to Yoritomo, he recalled his troops from Shinano, and asked Yoshinaka to send a hostage. Yoshinaka replied by sending his son Yoshitaka. He was now wedded to Yoritomo's daughter, and the two Minamoto chiefs seemed to have been effectually reconciled.

Advance on Kyoto and the Taira Retreat

At this point the Taira leaders were straining every nerve to beat back the westward-rolling tide of Minamoto conquest. In May, 1183, this decisive phase of the contest was opened; the Taira were said to have mustered a force that was one hundred thousand strong. At first, things fared badly with the Minamoto. They lost an important fortress at Hiuchi-yama, but when the main army of the Minamoto came into action, the complexion of affairs changed at once. In a great battle fought at Tonami-yama in Echizen, Yoshinaka won a signal victory by the manoeuvre of launching at the Taira a herd of oxen having torches fastened to their horns. Thousands of the Taira perished, including many leaders.

Other victories at Kurikara and Shinowara opened the road to Kyoto. Yoshinaka pushed on until the capital lay at the mercy of Yoshinaka's armies. The latter stages of the Minamoto march had been unopposed. The cloistered Emperor, Go-Shirakawa, secretly made his way to Hiei-zan and placed himself under the protection of Yoshinaka, rejoicing at the opportunity to shake off the Taira yoke.

On August 14, 1183, the evacuation of Kyoto took place. Munemori, refusing to listen to the counsels of the more resolute among his officers, applied the torch to the Taira mansions at northern and southern Rokuhara, and, taking with him the Emperor Antoku, then in his sixth year, his Majesty's younger brother, and their mother, together with the regalia – the mirror, the sword, and the gem – retired westward, followed by the whole remnant of his clan.

The Taira leaders having carried off the Emperor Antoku, there was no actually reigning sovereign in Kyoto, whither the cloistered Emperor now returned, an imposing guard of honour being furnished by Yoshinaka. Go-Shirakawa therefore resumed the administration of State affairs, Yoshinaka being given the privilege of access to the Presence and entrusted with the duty of guarding the capital. Out of the five hundred manors of the Taira, one hundred and fifty were given to Yoshinaka and Yukiiye, and over two hundred prominent Taira officials were stripped of their posts and their Court ranks.

Fujiwara Kanezane, minister of the Right, notified the Court that, as Antoku had left the capital, another occupant to the throne should be appointed, in spite of the absence of the regalia. It is plain that the proposal made by the minister of the Right had for motive the convenience of the Minamoto, whose cause lacked legitimacy so long as the sovereign and the regalia were in the camp of the Taira.

But the minister's advice had a disastrous sequel. Yoshinaka was resolutely bent on securing the succession for the son of Prince Mochihito, known as Prince Hokuriku,. But Go-Shirakawa would not pay any attention to these representations. He held that Prince Hokuriku was ineligible, since his father had been born out of wedlock; the truth being that the ex-Emperor had determined to obtain the crown for one of his own grandsons, younger brothers of Antoku, who thenceforth became the Emperor Go-Toba (1184–98).

The Fall of Yoshinaka

Yoshinaka's fortunes began to ebb from the time of his failure to obtain the nomination of Prince Hokuriku. A force despatched to Bitchu with the object of arresting the abduction of Antoku. He and his officers found that their rustic ways and illiterate education exposed them constantly to the thinly veiled sneers of the dilettanti and pundits who gave the tone to metropolitan society. The soldiers resented these insults with increasing roughness and recourse to violence, so that the coming of Yoritomo began to be much desired. Go-Shirakawa sent two messages at a brief interval to invite the Kamakura chief's presence in the capital. Yoritomo replied with a memorial which won for him golden opinions, but he showed no sign of visiting Kyoto. His absorbing purpose was to consolidate his base in the east, and he had already begun to appreciate that the military and the Imperial capitals should be distinct.

Naturally, when the fact of these pressing invitations to Yoritomo reached Yoshinaka's ears, he felt some resentment, and this was reflected in the demeanour of his soldiers, outrages against the lives and properties of the citizens becoming more and more frequent. Even the private domains of the cloistered Emperor himself, to say nothing of the manors of the courtiers, were freely entered and plundered, so that public indignation reached a high pitch. The umbrage thus engendered was accentuated by treachery. Driven from Kyushu, the Taira chiefs had obtained a footing in Shikoku and had built fortifications at Yashima in Sanuki, which became thenceforth their headquarters. They had also collected on the opposite coast of the Inland Sea a following which seemed likely to grow in dimensions, and, with the idea of checking that result, it was proposed to send troops to the Sanyo-do under Minamoto Yukiiye, who had been named governor of Bizen. Taught, however, by experience that disaster was likely to be the outcome of Yukiiye's generalship, Yoshinaka interfered to prevent his appointment, and Yukiiye, resenting this slight, became thenceforth a secret foe of Yoshinaka.

Yukiiye seems to have been an unscrupulous schemer. Serving originally under Yoritomo, who quickly took his measure, he concluded that nothing substantial was to be gained in that quarter. Therefore, he passed over to Yoshinaka, who welcomed him, not as an enemy of Yoritomo, but as a Minamoto. Thenceforth Yukiiye's aim was to cause a collision between the two cousins and to raise his own house on the ruins of both.

Yoshinaka, however, had too frank a disposition to be suspicious. He believed until the end that Yukiiye's heart was in the Minamoto cause and took Yukiiye into his confidence. That was the traitor's opportunity. He secretly informed the ex-Emperor that Yoshinaka had planned a retreat to the east, carrying his Majesty with him, and this information induced Go-Shirakawa to obtain from Hiei-zan and Miidera armed monks to form a palace-guard under the command of the *kebiishi*, Taira Tomoyasu, a declared enemy of Yoshinaka. At once Yoshinaka despatched a force to the palace; seized the persons of Go-Shirakawa and Go-Toba; removed Motomichi from the regency, appointing Moroie, a boy of twelve, in his place, and dismissed a number of Court officials.

In this strait, Go-Shirakawa, whose record is one long series of undignified manoeuvres to keep his own head above water, applied himself to placate Yoshinaka while privately relying on Yoritomo. His Majesty granted to the former the control of all the domains previously held by the Taira and commissioned him to attack Yoritomo while, at the same time, the latter was secretly encouraged to destroy his cousin. At that moment (February, 1184), Yoritomo's two younger brothers, Yoshitsune and Noriyori, were *en route* for Kyoto, where they had been ordered to convey the Kwanto taxes. They had a force of five hundred men only, but these were quickly transformed into the van of an army of fifty or sixty thousand, which Yoritomo, with extraordinary expedition, sent from Kamakura to attack Yoshinaka.

The "Morning Sun *shogun*" (Asahi-*shogun*), as Yoshinaka was commonly called with reference to his brilliant career, now at last saw himself confronted by the peril which had long disturbed his thoughts. At a distance of three hundred miles from his own base, with powerful foes on either flank and in a city whose population was hostile to him, his situation seemed almost desperate. He took a step dictated by dire necessity – made overtures to the Taira, asking that a daughter of the house of Kiyomori be given him for wife. Munemori refused. The fortunes of the Taira at that moment appeared to be again in the ascendant. They were once more supreme in Kyushu; the west of the main island from coast to coast was in their hands; they had re-established themselves in Fukuhara, and at any moment they might move against Kyoto.

In fact, the situation was almost hopeless for Yoshinaka. All that he could do was to arrest momentarily the tide of onset by planting handfuls of men to guard the chief avenues at Uji and Seta where, four years previously, Yorimasa had died for the Minamoto cause. To the Uji bridge, Nenoi Yukichika was sent with three hundred men; to the Seta bridge, Imai Kanehira with five hundred. The names of these men and of their brothers, Higuchi Kanemitsu and Tate Chikatada, are immortal in Japanese history. They were the four sons of Nakahara Kaneto, by whom Yoshinaka had been reared, and their constant attendance on his person, their splendid devotion to him and their military prowess caused people to speak of them as Yoshinaka's *Shi-tenno* – the four guardian deities of Buddhist temples.

Their sister, Tomoe, is even more famous. Strong and brave as she was beautiful, she became the consort of Yoshinaka, with whom she had been brought up, and she accompanied him in all his campaigns, fighting by his side and leading a body of troops in all his battles. She was with him when he made his final retreat and she killed a gigantic warrior, Uchida Ieyoshi, who attempted to seize her on that occasion. Yoshinaka compelled her to leave him at the supreme moment, being unwilling that she should fall into the enemy's hands; and after his death she became a nun, devoting the rest of her days to prayers for his spirit.

But Yoshinaka did not repay this noble devotion with equal sincerity. Attracted by rumours of the beauty of the daughter of the *kwampaku*, Fujiwara Motofusa, he compelled her to enter his household in Kyoto, and when news came that the armies of Yoshitsune and Noriyori were approaching the capital, this great captain, instead of marshalling his forces and making dispositions for defence, went to bid farewell to the beautiful girl who resided in his Gojo mansion. Hours of invaluable time passed, until finally, two of his faithful comrades, Echigo Chuta and Tsuwata Saburo, seated themselves in front of the mansion and committed suicide to recall their leader to his senses. Yoshinaka emerged, but it was too late. He could not muster more than three hundred men, and in a short time Yoshitsune rode into the city at the head of a large body of cavalry.

Yoshitsune had approached by way of Uji. He was not at all deterred by the fact that the enemy had destroyed the bridge. His mounted bowmen dashed into the river and crossed it with little loss. A few hours brought them to Kyoto, where they made small account of the feeble resistance that Yoshinaka was able to offer. Wounded and with little more than half a score of followers, Yoshinaka rode off, and reaching the plain of Awazu, met Imai Kanehira with the remnant of his five hundred men who had gallantly resisted Noriyori's army of thirty thousand. Imai counselled instant flight eastward. In Shinano, Yoshinaka would find safety and a dominion, while to cover his retreat, Imai would sacrifice his own life. Such noble deeds were the normal duty of every true *bushi*. Yoshinaka galloped away, but, riding into a marsh, disabled his horse and was shot down. Meanwhile Imai, in whose quiver there remained only eight arrows, had killed as many of the pursuing horsemen, and then placing the point of his sword in his mouth, had thrown himself headlong from his horse.

Battle of Ichi-no-Tani

The victory of the armies led by Noriyori and Yoshitsune brought Kamakura and Fukuhara into direct conflict, and it was speedily decided that these armies should at once move westward to attack the Taira. Within ten days of the death of Yoshinaka this same army, augmented to seventy-six thousand, began to move westward from Kyoto (March 19, 1184).

The Taira, as noted above, had by this time largely recovered from the disasters suffered in their first encounters with Yoshinaka's forces. In the western provinces of the main island, in Shikoku, and in Kyushu, scions of the clan had served as governors in former times, so that ties of close intimacy had been established with the inhabitants. Since the first flight to Kyushu in August, 1183, their generals, Shigehira, Michimori, Noritsune, and others had defeated the forces of Yoshinaka at Mizushima and those of Yukiiye at Muroyama, so that no less than fourteen provinces of the Sanyo-do and the Nankai-do owned Taira sway, and by the beginning of 1184 they had re-occupied the Fukuhara district, establishing themselves at a position of great natural strength called Ichi-no-tani in the province of Harima. Their lines extended several miles, over which space one hundred thousand men were distributed. They lay within a semi-circle of mountains supposed to be inaccessible from the north; their camp was washed on the south by the sea where a thousand war-vessels were assembled; the east flank rested on a forest, and the west was strongly fortified.

On March 21, 1184, the Kamakura armies delivered their assault on this position; Noriyori with fifty-six thousand men against the east flank at Ikuta; Yoshitsune's lieutenants with twenty thousand men against the west at Suma. Little progress was made. Defence and attack were equally obstinate, and the advantage of position as well Yoshitsune selected seventy-five men to deliver an assault by descending the northern rampart of mountains at the undefended Hiyodori Pass, among them being Benkei, Hatakeyama Shigetada, and others of his most trusted comrades. They succeeded in riding down the steep declivity, and they rushed at the Taira position, setting fire to everything inflammable.

Taken completely by surprise, the Taira weakened, and the Minamoto, pouring in at either flank, completed the rout which had already commenced. Munemori was among the first of the fugitives. He embarked with the Emperor Antoku and the regalia, and steered for Yashima, whither he was quickly followed by the remnants of his force. Okabe Tadazumi, a Minamoto captain, took the head of Tadanori but could not identify it. In the lining of the helmet, however, was found a roll of poems and among them one signed "Tadanori":

> Twilight upon my path,
> And for mine inn to-night
> The shadow of a tree,
> And for mine host, a flower.

This little gem of thought has gleamed on Tadanori's memory through all the centuries and has brought vicarious fame even to his slayer, Tadazumi.

Battle of Yashima

The battle of Ichi-no-tani was not by any means conclusive. It drove the Taira out of Harima and the four provinces on the immediate west of the latter, but it did not disturb them in Shikoku or Kyushu, nor did it in any way cripple the great fleet which gave them a signal advantage. Noriyori returned to Kamakura to consult Yoritomo, but the latter and his military advisers could not plan anything except the obvious course of marching an army from Harima westward to the Strait of Shimonoseki, and thereafter collecting boats to carry it across to Kyushu. Yoshitsune was not consulted. He remained in Kyoto instead of repairing to Kamakura, and he thereby roused the suspicion of Yoritomo, who began to see in him a second Yoshinaka. Hence, in presenting a list of names for reward in connexion with the campaign against the "Morning Sun *shogun*," Yoritomo made no mention of Yoshitsune, and the brilliant soldier would have remained entirely without recognition had not the cloistered Emperor specially appointed him to the post of *kebiishi*.

Noriyori pushed westward steadily, but not without difficulty. He halted for a time in the province of Suwo, and finally, in March, 1185, five months after moving out of Harima, he contrived to transfer the main part of his force across Shimonoseki Strait and to marshall them in Bungo in the north of Kyushu. The position then was this: first, a Taira army strongly posted at Yashima in Sanuki (Shikoku), and another Taira army strongly posted on Hikoshima, an island west of Shimonoseki Strait. Evidently, in such conditions, no advance into Kyushu could be made by Noriyori without inviting capital risks. The key of the situation for the Minamoto was to wrest the command of the sea from the Taira and to drive them from Shikoku preparatory to the final assault upon Kyushu. This was recognized after a time, and Kajiwara Kagetoki received orders to collect or construct a fleet with all possible expedition, which orders he applied himself to carry out at Watanabe, in Settsu, near the eastern entrance to the Inland Sea.

Meanwhile, Yoshitsune had been chafing in Kyoto. He obtained from the cloistered Emperor the commission of *tai-shogun* (great general) and hastened to Settsu to take command.

Complications ensued at once. Kagetoki objected to be relegated to a secondary place, and Go-Shirakawa was induced to recall Yoshitsune. But the latter refused to return to Kyoto, and, of course, his relations with Kagetoki were not cordial.

The 21st of March, 1185, was a day of tempest. Yoshitsune saw his opportunity. He proposed to run over to the opposite coast and attack Yashima under cover of the storm. Kagetoki objected that no vessel could live in such weather. Yoshitsune then called for volunteers. About one hundred and fifty daring spirits responded. They embarked in five war-junks. Yoshitsune and his little band of heroic men landed safely on the Awa coast, and dashed at once to the assault of the Taira, who were taken wholly by surprise, never imagining that any forces could have essayed such an enterprise in such a tempest. Some fought resolutely, but the evening of the 23rd of March saw the Taira fleet congregated in Shido Bay and crowded with fugitives. There they were attacked at dawn on the 24th by Yoshitsune, to whom there had arrived on the previous evening a re-enforcement of thirty war-junks, sent, not by Kagetoki, but by a Minamoto supporter who had been driven from the province of Iyo some time previously by the Taira.

As usual, the impetuosity of Yoshitsune's onset carried everything before it. Soon the Taira fleet was flying down the Inland Sea, and when Kajiwara Kagetoki, having at length completed his preparations, arrived off Yashima on the 25th of March with some four hundred war-vessels, he found only the ashes of the Taira palaces and palisades. Munemori, with the boy Emperor and all the survivors of the Taira, had fled by sea to join Tomomori at Hikoshima. During three consecutive days, with a mere handful of one hundred and fifty followers,

Yoshitsune had engaged a powerful Taira army on shore, and on the fourth day he had attacked and routed them at sea, where the disparity of force must have been evident and where no adventitious natural aids were available.

Battle of Dan-No-Ura

The fight at Yashima was followed by a month during which time the two clans prepared for final action. The Taira would have withdrawn altogether into Kyushu, but such a course must have been preceded by the dislodging of Noriyori, with his army of thirty thousand men, from Bungo province, which they had occupied since the beginning of March. The Taira generals dared not enter Kyushu so long as a strong Minamoto force was planted on the left flank of their route.

Ever since the Ichi-no-tani fight, the Minamoto generals, especially Kajiwara Kagetoki, had been actively engaged in building, or otherwise acquiring, war-junks. By April, 1185, they had brought together a squadron of seven to eight hundred; whereas, in the sequel of Yashima and minor engagements, the Taira fleet had been reduced to some five hundred. The war-junk of those days was not a complicated machine. Propelled by oars, it had no fighting capacities of its own, its main purpose being to carry its occupants within bow-range or sword-reach of their adversaries. Naval tactics consisted solely in getting the wind-gage for archery purposes.

By the 22nd of April, 1185, the whole of the Minamoto fleet had assembled at Oshima, an island lying off the southeast of Suwo, the Taira vessels, with the exception of the Hikoshima contingent, being anchored at Dan-no-ura. On that day, a strong squadron, sent out by Yoshitsune for reconnoitring purposes, marshalled itself at a distance of about two miles from the Taira array, and this fact having been signalled to the Taira general, Tomomori, at Hikoshima, he at once passed the strait and joined forces with the main fleet at Dan-no-ura. Yoshitsune's design had been to deliver a general attack immediately after the despatch of the reconnoitring squadron, but this was prevented by a deluge of blinding rain which lasted until the night of the 24th.

Thus, it was not until the 25th that the battle took place. It commenced with an inconclusive archery duel at long range, whereafter the two fleets closed up and a desperate hand-to-hand struggle ensued. Neither side could claim any decisive advantage until Taguchi Shigeyoshi deserted from the Taira and passed over with all his ships to the Minamoto. This Taguchi had been originally an influential magnate of Iyo in Shikoku, whence he had accompanied the Taira retreat to Nagato, leaving his son with three thousand men to defend the family manors in Iyo. The son was so generously treated by the Minamoto that he threw in his lot with them and sent letters urging his father to adopt the same cause. Taguchi not only followed his son's advice but also chose the moment most disastrous for the Taira.

His defection was followed quickly by a complete rout. A resolute attempt was made to defend the ship containing the young Emperor, his mother, his grandmother, and several other Taira ladies; but the vessel finally passed into Minamoto possession, but not before a terrible tragedy occurred. Kiyomori's widow, the *Ni-i-no-ama*, grandmother of Antoku, took the six-year old child in her arms and jumped into the sea, followed by Antoku's mother, the Empress Dowager (*Kenrei-mon-in*), carrying the regalia, and by other court ladies. The Empress Dowager was rescued, as were also the sacred mirror and the gem, but the sword was irrevocably lost.

The Taira leader, Munemori, and his son, Kiyomune, were taken prisoner, but Tomomori, Noritsune, and seven other Taira generals were drowned. Munemori and his son were executed finally at Omi. It may here be noted that, although several of the Taira leaders who took the field against the Minamoto were killed in the campaign or executed or exiled after it, the punitory measures adopted by Yoritomo were not by any means wholesale. To be a Taira did not necessarily involve Kamakura's enmity. On the contrary, not only was clemency extended to several prominent members of Kiyomori's kith and kin, but also many local magnates of Taira origin whose estates lay in the Kwanto were from first to last staunch supporters and friends of the Minamoto.

The record of Munemori, whose leadership proved fatal to the Taira cause, stamps him as something very rare among Japanese *bushi* – a coward. He was the first to fly from every battle-field. Tradition alleges that in this final fight Munemori's reputed mother, *Ni-i-no-ama*, before throwing herself into the sea with the Emperor in her arms, confessed that Munemori was not her son. Her motives in drowning the young emepror are said to have been two. One was to fix upon the Minamoto the heinous crime of having done a sovereign to death, so that some avenger might rise in future years; the other was to hide the fact that Antoku was in reality a girl whose sex had been concealed in the interest of the child's maternal grandfather, Kiyomori.

Yoshitsune's Fate

Japan accords to Yoshitsune the first place among its great captains. Pursued by the relentless anger of his own brother, whose cause he had so splendidly championed, he was forced to fly for refuge to the north, and was ultimately done to death. While Yoritomo is execrated as an inhuman, selfish tyrant, Yoshitsune is worshipped as a faultless hero. Yet, Yoritomo's keen insight discerned in his half-brother's attitude something more than mere rivalry. He discovered the possible establishment of special relations between the Imperial Court and a section of the Minamoto.

Yoshitsune's failure to repair to Kamakura after the battle of Ichi-no-tani inspired Yoritomo's first doubts. Yoshitsune remained at Kyoto, and that by so doing he should have suggested some suspicions to Yoritomo was unavoidable. The secret of the Court nobles' ability to exclude the military magnates from any share in State administration was no secret in Yoritomo's eyes. He saw clearly that this differentiation had been effected by playing off one military party against the other, or by dividing the same party against itself; and he saw clearly that opportunities for such measures had been furnished by subjecting the military leaders to constant contact with the Court nobility.

Therefore, he determined to keep two aims always in view. One was to establish a military and executive capital entirely apart from, and independent of, the Imperial and administrative metropolis; the other, to preserve the unity of the Minamoto clan in all circumstances. Both of these aims seemed to be threatened with failure when Yoshitsune preferred the Court in Kyoto to the camp in Kamakura; still more so when he accepted from Go-Shirakawa rank and office for which Yoritomo had not recommended him, and yet further when he obtained from the ex-Emperor a commission to lead the Minamoto armies westward without any reference to, and in despite of, the obvious intention of the Minamoto chief at Kamakura.

All these acts could scarcely fail to be interpreted by Yoritomo as preluding the very results which he particularly desired to avert, namely, a house of Minamoto divided against itself and the re-establishment of Court influence over a strong military party in Kyoto. His apprehensions received confirmation from reports furnished by Kajiwara Kagetoki. He seems from the first to have entertained doubts of Yoshitsune's loyalty to Yoritomo, and warned Kamakura in very strong terms against the brilliant young general who was then the idol of Kyoto, and thus, when Yoshitsune, in June, 1185, repaired to Kamakura to hand over the prisoners taken in the battle of Dan-no-ura and to pay his respects to Yoritomo, he was met at Koshigoe, a village in the vicinity, by Hojo Tokimasa, who conveyed to him Yoritomo's veto against his entry to Kamakura. A letter addressed by Yoshitsune to his brother on that occasion ran, in part, as follows:

Here am I, weeping crimson tears in vain at thy displeasure. Well was it said that good medicine tastes bitter in the mouth, and true words ring harsh in the ear. This is why the slanders that men speak of me remain unproved, why I am kept out of Kamakura unable to lay bare my heart. These many days I have lain here and could not gaze upon my brother's face. The bond of our blood-brotherhood is sundered.

But a short season after I was born, my honoured sire passed to another world, and I was left fatherless. Clasped in my mother's bosom, I was carried down to Yamato, and since that day I have not known a moment free from care and danger. Though it was but to drag out a useless life, we wandered round the capital suffering hardship, hid in all manner of rustic spots, dwelt in remote and distant provinces, whose rough inhabitants did treat us with contumely. But at last I was summoned to assist in overthrowing the Taira house, and in this conflict I first laid Kiso Yoshinaka low. Then, so that I might demolish the Taira men, I spurred my steed on frowning precipices. Careless of death in the face of the foe, I braved the dangers of wind and wave, not recking that my body might sink to the bottom of the sea, and be devoured by monsters of the deep. My pillow was my harness, arms my trade....

Translated by W. G. Aston

But Yoritomo steadily refused to cancel his veto, and after an abortive sojourn of twenty days at Koshigoe, Yoshitsune returned to Kyoto where his conduct won for him increasing popularity. Minamoto Yukiiye, learning of these strained relations, emerged from hiding and applied himself to win the friendship of Yoshitsune, who received his advances graciously. Yoritomo, much incensed at this development commissioned a Nara bonze, Tosabo Shoshun, whose physical endowments had brought him into prominence at Kamakura, to do away with him. After a fierce defence by Yoshitsune, who had only seven men to hold his mansion against sixty, Shoshun was killed.

After this event there could be no concealments between the two brothers. With difficulty and not without some menaces, Yoshitsune obtained from Go-Shirakawa a formal commission to proceed against Yoritomo by force of arms. Matters now moved with great rapidity. Yoritomo, always prescient, had fully foreseen the course of events. Shoshun's abortive attack on the Horikawa mansion took place on November 10, 1185, and before the close of the month three strong columns of Kamakura troops were converging on Kyoto. In that interval, Yoshitsune, failing to muster any considerable force in the capital or its environs, had decided to turn his back on Kyoto and proceed westward; he himself to Kyushu, and Yukiiye to Shikoku. They embarked on November 29th, but scarcely had they put to sea when they encountered a gale which shattered their squadron. Yoshitsune and Yukiiye both landed on the Izumi coast, each ignorant of the other's fate. The latter was captured and beheaded a few months later, but the former made his way to Yamato and found hiding-places among the valleys and mountains of Yoshino. The hero of Ichi-no-tani and Yashima was now a proscribed fugitive. Go-Shirakawa, whose fate was always to obey circumstances rather than to control them, had issued a new mandate on the arrival of Yoritomo's forces at Kyoto, and Kamakura was now authorized to exterminate Yoshitsune with all his partisans, wherever they could be found.

Meanwhile, Yoshitsune had been passing from one place of concealment to another in the three contiguous provinces of Izumi, Yamato, and Kii. Finally, in the spring of 1187, Yoshitsune and his followers, disguised as mendicant friars, made their way up the west coast, and, after hairbreadth escapes, found asylum in the domain of Fujiwara Hidehira, who had protected Yoshitsune in his youth. Hidehira owned and administered the whole of the two provinces of Mutsu and Dewa, which in those days covered some thirty thousand square miles and could easily furnish an army of a hundred thousand men.

The attitude of this great fief had always been an object of keen solicitude to Yoritomo. At one time there were rumours that Hidehira intended to throw in his lot with Yoshinaka; at another, that he was about to join hands with the Taira. When Hidehira died, in his ninety-first year, he h committed to his son, Yasuhira, the duty of guarding Yoshitsune. Hence, when, in the spring of 1188, Kamakura became aware of Yoshitsune's presence in Mutsu, two consecutive messages were sent thither, one from Yoritomo, the other from the Court, ordering Yoshitsune's execution. Yasuhira paid no attention, and Go-Shirakawa commissioned Yoritomo to punish the northern chief's contumacy. Yasuhira now became alarmed. He sent a large force to attack Yoshitsune at Koromo-gawa. Benkei and the little band of comrades who had followed Yoshitsune's fortunes continuously during eight years, died to a man fighting for him, and Yoshitsune, having killed his wife and children, committed suicide. His head was sent to Kamakura.

But this did not satisfy Yoritomo. He wanted something more than Yoshitsune's head; he wanted the great northern fief, and he had no idea of losing his opportunity. Three armies soon marched northward. They are said to have aggregated 284,000 of all arms. One moved up the western littoral; another up the eastern, and the third, under Yoritomo himself, marched by the inland route. The men of Mutsu fought stoutly, but after a campaign of some two months, Yasuhira, finding himself in a hopeless position, opened negotiations for surrender. His overtures being incontinently rejected, he appreciated the truth, namely, that Yoritomo was bent upon exterminating the Fujiwara of the north and taking possession of their vast estates. Then Yasuhira fled to Ezo, where, shortly afterwards, one of his own soldiers assassinated him and carried his head to Yoritomo. Thus, from 1189, Yoritomo's sway may be said to have extended throughout the length and breadth of Japan. In the storehouses of the Fujiwara, who, since the days of Kiyohira had ruled for a hundred years in the north, there were found piles of gold, silver, and precious stuffs with which Yoritomo recompensed his troops.

Yoritomo's victory marked the beginning of the Kamakura period (1185–1333), during which Japan was ruled by the Kamakura shogunate (officially established in 1192), from the new military capital of Kamakura. The system of government established by Yaritomo towards the close of the twelfth century and kept in continuous operation thereafter until the middle of the nineteenth, was known as the Bakufu, a word literally signifying "camp office," and intended to convey the fact that the affairs of the empire were in the hands of the military. The selection of Kamakura for capital was the first step towards solution. Kamakura certainly has topographical advantages. It is surrounded by mountains except on one face, which is washed by the sea. His father, Yoshitomo, had chosen Kamakura as a place of residence when he exercised military sway in the Kwanto, and Yoritomo wished to preserve the tradition of Minamoto power. He wished, also, to select a site so far from Kyoto that the debilitating and demoralizing influence of the Imperial metropolitan society might be powerless to reach the military capital. Kamakura was then only a fishing hamlet, but at the zenith of its prosperity it had grown to be a city of at least a quarter of a million of inhabitants. During a period of one hundred and fifty years it remained the centre of military society and the focus of a civilization radically different from that of Kyoto.

ANCIENT
KINGS & LEADERS

Ancient cultures often traded with and influenced
each other, while others grew independently.
This section provides the key leaders from a
number of regions, to offer comparative insights
into developments across the ancient world.

ANCIENT CHINESE MONARCHS

This list concentrates on emperors with at least some proven legitimate claim and dates are approximate. Where dates of rule overlap, rulers either ruled jointly or ruled in opposition to one another. There may also be differences in name spellings between different sources.

THREE SOVEREIGNS OR PRIMEVAL EMPERORS, AND FIVE PREMIER EMPERORS (c. 2852-2070 BCE)

These are generally thought to be mythological figures. The history of China's rulers begins with a group of three *huáng* ('sovereigns') and a group of five *di* (emperors). There is much diversity over who the three sovereigns and five emperors actually were, and the dates they ruled.

Fuxi (Heavenly Sovereign)	18,000 years
NuWa (Earthly Sovereign)	11,000 years
Shennong (Human Sovereign)	45,600 years
Yellow Emperor (Xuanyuan)	100 years
Zhuanxu (Gaoyang)	78 years
Emperor Ku (Gaoxin)	70 years

Emperor Yao of Tang (Yiqi, Taotang or Fangxun)	100 years
Emperor Shun of Yu (Yao, Youyu or Chonghua)	42 years

XIA DYNASTY (c. 2070-1600 BCE)

This dynasty was thought to be established after the legendary Shun handed his throne to Yu the Great, also a legendary leader, whose historicity is debated.

Yu the Great	2150–2106 BCE
Qi of Xia	2106–2077 BCE
Tai Kang	2077–2048 BCE
Zhong Kang	2048–2036 BCE
Xiang of Xia	2036–2008 BCE
Shao Kang	1968–1946 BCE
Zhu of Xia	1946–1929 BCE
Huai of Xia	1929–1885 BCE
Mang of Xia	1885–1867 BCE
Xie of Xia	1867–1851 BCE
Bu Jiang	1851–1792 BCE
Jiong of Xia	1792–1771 BCE
Jin of Xia (Yin Jia)	1771–1750 BCE
Kong Jia	1750–1719 BCE
Gao of Xia	1719–1708 BCE
Fa of Xia (Hou Jin)	1708–1689 BCE
Jie of Xia (Lu Gui)	1689–1658 BCE

SHANG DYNASTY (*c.* 1600–1046 BCE)

Tang of Shang	1658–1629 BCE
Wai Bing	1629–1627 BCE
Zhong Ren	1627–1623 BCE
Tai Jia	1623–1611 BCE
Wo Ding	1611–1592 BCE
Tai Geng	1592–1567 BCE
Xiao Jia	1567–1550 BCE
Yong Ji	1550–1538 BCE
Tai Wu	1538–1463 BCE
Zhong Ding	1463–1452 BCE
Wai Ren	1452–1437 BCE
He Dan Jia	1437–1428 BCE
Zu Ji	1428–1409 BCE
Zu Xin	1409–1393 BCE
Wo Jia	1393–1368 BCE
Zu Ding	1368–1336 BCE
Nan Geng	1336–1307 BCE
Yang Jia	1307–1290 BCE
Pan Geng	1290–1262 BCE
Xiao Xin	1262–1259 BCE
Xiao Yi	1259–1250 BCE
Wu Ding	1250–1192 BCE
Zu Geng	1192–1185 BCE
Zu Jia	1185–1158 BCE
Lin Xin	1158–1152 BCE
Geng Ding	1152–1147 BCE
Wu Yi	1147–1112 BCE
Wen Wu Ding	1112–1102 BCE

Di Yi	1101–1076 BCE
King Zhou of Shang	1075–1046 BCE

ZHOU DYNASTY (c. 1046–256 BCE)

Western Zhou (1046–771 BCE)

King Wu of Zhou	1046–1043 BCE
King Cheng of Zhou	1042–1021 BCE
King Kang of Zhou	1020–996 BCE
King Zhao of Zhou	995–977 BCE
King Mu of Zhou	976–922 BCE
King Gong of Zhou	922–900 BCE
King Yi of Zhou (Jian)	899–892 BCE
King Xiao of Zhou	891–886 BCE
King Yi of Zhou (Xie)	885–878 BCE
King Li of Zhou	877–841 BCE

Gonghe Regency (827–827 BCE)

King Xuan of Zhou	827–782 BCE
King You of Zhou	781–771 BCE

Eastern Zhou (770–256 BCE)

Spring and Autumn Period (770–476 BCE)

King Ping of Zhou	770–720 BCE
King Huan of Zhou	719–697 BCE
King Zhuang of Zhou	696–682 BCE
King Xi of Zhou	681–677 BCE
King Hui of Zhou	676–652 BCE

King Xiang of Zhou	651–619 BCE
King Qing of Zhou	618–613 BCE
King Kuang of Zhou	612–607 BCE
King Ding of Zhou	606–586 BCE
King Jian of Zhou	585–572 BCE
King Ling of Zhou	571–545 BCE
King Jing of Zhou (Gui)	544–521 BCE
King Dao of Zhou	520 BCE
King Jing of Zhou (Gai)	519–476 BCE

Warring States Period (475–221 BCE)

King Yuan of Zhou	475–469 BCE
King Zhending of Zhou	468–442 BCE
King Ai of Zhou	441 BCE
King Si of Zhou	441 BCE
King Kao of Zhou	440–426 BCE
King Weilie of Zhou	425–402 BCE
King An of Zhou	401–376 BCE
King Lie of Zhou	375–369 BCE
King Xian of Zhou	368–321 BCE
King Shenjing of Zhou	320–315 BCE
King Nan of Zhou	314–256 BCE

QIN DYNASTY (c. 221–207 BCE)

Qin Shi Huang declared himself emperor rather than king, and this period is often thought to mark the beginning of Imperial China.

Qin Shi Huang	221–210 BCE

Qin Er Shi	209–207 BCE
Ziying	207 BCE

HAN DYNASTY (c. 202 BCE–9 CE, 25–220 CE)

Western Han (202 BCE–9 CE)

Emperor Gaozu of Han	202–195 BCE
Emperor Hui of Han	195–188 BCE
Emperor Qianshao of Han	188–184 BCE
Emperor Houshao of Han	184–180 BCE
Emperor Wen of Han	179–157 BCE
Emperor Jing of Han	156–141 BCE
Emperor Wu of Han	140–87 BCE
Emperor Zhao of Han	86–74 BCE
Marquis of Haihun	74 BCE
Emperor Xuan of Han	73–49 BCE
Emperor Yuan of Han	48–33 BCE
Emperor Cheng of Han	32–7 BCE
Emperor Ai of Han	6–1 BCE
Emperor Ping of Han	1 BCE–5 CE
Ruzi Ying	6–8 CE
Interregnum (9 CE–23 CE; see Xin dynasty below)	
Gengshi Emperor	23–25 CE

XIN DYNASTY (c. 9–23 CE)

Wang Mang; possible usurper	9–23CE

Eastern Han (25–220 CE)

Emperor Guangwu of Han	25–57 CE
Emperor Ming of Han	58–75 CE
Emperor Zhang of Han	76–88 CE
Emperor He of Han	89–105 CE
Emperor Shang of Han	106 CE
Emperor An of Han	106–125 CE
Emperor Shun of Han	125–144 CE
Emperor Chong of Han	144–145 CE
Emperor Zhi of Han	145–146 CE
Emperor Huan of Han	146–168 CE
Emperor Ling of Han	168–189 CE
Prince of Hongnong	189 CE
Emperor Xian of Han	189–220 CE

THREE KINGDOMS (c. 220–280 CE)

Cao Wei (220–266 CE)

Cao Pi	220–226 CE	Cao Mao	254–260 CE
Cao Rui	226–239 CE	Cao Huan	260–266 CE
Cao Fang	239–254 CE		

Shu Han (221–263 CE)

Liu Bei	221–223 CE
Liu Shan	223–263 CE

Eastern Wu (222–280 CE)

Sun Quan	222–252 CE	Sun Xiu	258–264 CE
Sun Liang	252–258 CE	Sun Hao	264–280 CE

JIN DYNASTY (c. 266–420 CE)

Western Jin (266–316 CE)

Emperor Wu of Jin	266–290 CE
Emperor Hui of Jin	290–306 CE
Emperor Huai of Jin	307–313 CE
Emperor Min of Jin	313–317 CE

Eastern Jin (317–420 CE)

Emperor Yuan of Jin	317–322 CE
Emperor Ming of Jin	322–325 CE
Emperor Cheng of Jin	325–342 CE
Emperor Kang of Jin	342–344 CE
Emperor Mu of Jin	345–361 CE
Emperor Ai of Jin	361–365 CE
Emperor Fei of Jin	365–371 CE
Emperor Jianwen of Jin	371–372 CE
Emperor Xiaowu of Jin	372–396 CE
Emperor An of Jin	396–418 CE
Emperor Gong of Jin	419–420 CE

SIXTEEN KINGDOMS (c. 304–439 CE)

Han Zhao (304–329 CE)
Northern Han (304–318 CE)

Liu Yuan	304–310 CE
Liu He	7 days in 310 CE
Liu Cong	310–318 CE
Liu Can	a month+ in 318 CE

Former Zhao (318–329 CE)

Liu Yao   318–329 CE

Cheng Han (304–347 CE)
Cheng (304–338 CE)

Li Te	303 CE
Li Lui	several months in 303 CE
Li Xiong	303–334 CE
Li Ban	7 months in 334 CE
Li Qi	334–338 CE

Han (338–347 CE)

Li Shou	338–343 CE
Li Shi	343–347 CE

Later Zhao (319–351 CE)

Shi Le	319–333 CE	Shi Zun	183 days in 349 CE
Shi Hong	333–334 CE	Shi Jian	73 days in
Shi Hu	334–349 CE		349–350 CE
Shi Shi	73 days in 349 CE	Shi Zhi	350–351 CE

Former Liang (320–376 CE)

Zhang Mao	320–324 CE	Zhang Zuo	353–355 CE
Zhang Jun	324–346 CE	Zhang Xuanjing	355–363 CE
Zhang Chonghua	346–353 CE	Zhang Tianxi	364–376 CE
Zhang Yaoling	3 months in 353 CE		

Former Yan (337–370 CE)

Murong Huang	337–348 CE	Murong Wei	360–370 CE
Murong Jun	348–360 CE		

Former Qin (351–394 BCE)

Fu Jian	351–355 CE	Fu Pi	385–386 CE
Fu Sheng	355–357 CE	Fu Deng	386–394 CE
Fu Jian	357–385 CE	Fu Chong	394 CE

Later Yan (384–409 CE)

Murong Chui	384–396 CE	Murong Sheng	398–301 CE
Murong Bao	396–398 CE	Murong Xi	401–407 CE

Later Qin (384–417 CE)

Yao Chang	384–393 CE	Yao Hong	416–417 CE
Yao Xing	394–416 CE		

Western Qin (385–400 CE, 409–431 CE)

Qifu Guoren	385–388 CE	Qifu Chipan	412–428 CE
Qifu Qiangui	388–400 CE, 409–412 CE	Qifu Mumo	428–431 CE

Later Liang (386–403 CE)

Lü Guang	386–399 CE	Lü Zuan	399–401 CE
Lü Shao	399 CE	Lü Long	401–403 CE

Southern Liang (397–414 CE)

Tufa Wugu	397–399 CE	Tufa Rutan	402–414 CE
Tufa Lilugu	399–402 CE		

Northern Liang (397–439 CE)

Duan Ye	397–401 CE	Juqu Wuhui	442–444 CE
Juqu Mengxun	401–433 CE	Juqu Anzhou	444–460 CE
Juqu Mujian	433–439 CE		

Southern Yan (398–410 CE)

Murong De	398–405 CE	Murong Chao	405–410 CE

Western Liang (400–421 CE)

Li Gao	400–417 CE	Li Xun	420–421 CE
Li Xin	417–420 CE		

Hu Xia (407–431 CE)

Helian Bobo	407–425 CE	Helian Ding	428–431 CE
Helian Chang	425–428 CE		

Northern Yan (407–436 CE)

Gao Yun	407–409 CE	Feng Hong	430–436 CE
Feng Ba	409–430 CE		

NORTHERN AND SOUTHERN DYNASTIES (c. 386–589 CE)

Northern Dynasties (386–581 CE)

Northern Wei (386–535 CE)

Emperor Daowu of Northern Wei	386–409 CE
Emperor Mingyuan of Northern Wei	409–423 CE
Emperor Taiwu of Northern Wei	424–452 CE
Tuoba Yu	452 CE
Emperor Wencheng of Northern Wei	452–465 CE
Emperor Xianwen of Northern Wei	466–471 CE
Emperor Xiaowen of Northern Wei	471–499 CE
Emperor Xuanwu of Northern Wei	499–515 CE
Emperor Xiaoming of Northern Wei	516–528 CE

Yuan Zhao	528 CE
Emperor Xiaozhuang of Northern Wei	528–530 CE
Yuan Ye	530–531 CE
Emperor Jiemin of Northern Wei	531–532 CE
Yuan Lang	531–532 CE
Emperor Xiaowu of Northern Wei	532–535 CE

Eastern Wei (534–550 CE)

Emperor Xiaojing of Eastern Wei	534–550 CE

Western Wei (535–557 CE)

Emperor Wen of Western Wei	535–551 CE
Emperor Fei of Western Wei	552–554 CE
Emperor Gong of Western Wei	554–557 CE

Northern Qi (550–577 CE)

Emperor Wenxuan of Northern Qi	550–559 CE
Emperor Fei of Northern Qi	559–560 CE
Emperor Xiaozhao of Northern Qi	560–561 CE
Emperor Wucheng of Northern Qi	561–565 CE
Gao Wei	565–577 CE
Gao Heng	577 CE
Gao Shaoyi	577–579? CE

Northern Zhou (557–581 CE)

Emperor Xiaomin of Northern Zhou	557 CE
Emperor Ming of Northern Zhou	557–560 CE
Emperor Wu of Northern Zhou	561–578 CE
Emperor Xuan of Northern Zhou	578–579 CE
Emperor Jing of Northern Zhou	579–581 CE

Southern dynasties (420–589 CE)

Liu Song (420–497 CE)

Emperor Wu of Liu Song	420–422 CE
Emperor Shao of Liu Song	423–424 CE
Emperor Wen of Liu Song	424–453 CE
Emperor Xiaowu of Liu Song	454–464 CE
Emperor Ming of Liu Song	465–472 CE
Emperor Houfei of Liu Song	473–477 CE
Emperor Shun of Liu Song	477–479 CE

Southern Qi (479–502 CE)

Emperor Gao of Southern Qi	479–482 CE
Emperor Wu of Southern Qi	482–493 CE
Xiao Zhaoye	493–494 CE
Xiao Zhaowen	494 CE
Emperor Ming of Southern Qi	494–498 CE
Xiao Baojuan	499–501 CE
Emperor He of Southern Qi	501–502 CE

Liang Dynasty (502–557 CE)

Emperor Wu of Liang	502–549 CE
Emperor Jianwen of Liang	549–551 CE
Xiao Dong	551–552 CE
Emperor Yuan of Liang	552–555 CE
Xiao Yuanming	555 CE
Emperor Jing of Liang	555–557 CE

Western Liang (555–587 CE)

Emperor Xuan of Western Liang	555–562 CE

Emperor Ming of Western Liang	562–585 CE
Emperor Jing of Western Liang	585–587 CE

Chen Dynasty (557–589 CE)

Emperor Wu of Chen	557–559 CE
Emperor Wen of Chen	559–566 CE
Emperor Fei of Chen	566–568 CE
Emperor Xuan of Chen	569–582 CE
Chen Shubao	583–589 CE

SUI DYNASTY (c. 581–610 CE)

Emperor Wen of Sui	581–604 CE
Emperor Yang of Sui	605–617 CE
Yang You	617–618 CE
Yang Hao	618 CE
Yang Tong	618–619 CE

TANG DYNASTY (c. 618–690 CE, 705–907 CE)

Emperor Gaozu of Tang	618–626 CE
Emperor Taizong of Tang	627–649 CE
Emperor Gaozong of Tang	650–683 CE
Emperor Zhongzong of Tang	684 and 705–710 CE
Emperor Ruizong of Tang	684–690 and 710–712 CE
Emperor Shang of Tang	710 CE
Emperor Xuanzong of Tang	712–756 CE
Emperor Suzong of Tang	756–762 CE

Emperor Daizong of Tang	762–779 CE
Emperor Dezong of Tang	780–805 CE
Emperor Shunzong of Tang	805 CE
Emperor Xianzong of Tang	806–820 CE
Emperor Muzong of Tang	821–824 CE
Emperor Jingzong of Tang	824–826 CE
Emperor Wenzong of Tang	826–840 CE
Emperor Wuzong of Tang	840–846 CE
Emperor Xuanzong of Tang	846–859 CE
Emperor Yizong of Tang	859–873 CE
Emperor Xizong of Tang	873–888 CE
Emperor Zhaozong of Tang	888–904 CE
Emperor Ai of Tang	904–907 CE

Wu Zhou (690 – 705 CE)

Wu Zetian (only female considered legitimate)	690–705 CE

Huang Qi (881–884 CE)

Huang Chao	881–884 CE

FIVE DYNASTIES AND TEN KINGDOMS (c. 907–979 CE)

Five Dynasties (907–960 CE)
Later Liang (907–923 CE)

Zhu Wen	907–912 CE
Zhu Yougui	912–913 CE
Zhu Zhen	913–923 CE

Later Tang (923–937 CE)

Li Cunxu	923–926 CE
Li Siyuan (Li Dan)	923–926 CE
Li Conghou	933–934 CE
Li Congke	934–937 CE

Later Jin (936–947 CE)

Shi Jingtang	936–942 CE
Shi Chonggui	942–947 CE

Later Han (947–951 CE)

Liu Zhiyuan	947–948 CE
Liu Chengyou	948–951 CE

Later Zhou (951–960 CE)

Guo Wei	951–954 CE
Chai Rong	954–959 CE
Chai Zongxun	959–960 CE

Ten Kingdoms (907–979 CE)
Former Shu (907–925 CE)

Wang Jian	907–918 CE
Wang Zongyan	918–925 CE

Yang Wu (907–937 CE)

Yang Xingmi	904–905 CE
Yang Wo	905–908 CE
Yang Longyan	908–921 CE
Yang Pu	921–937 CE

Ma Chu (907–951 CE)

Ma Yin	897–930 CE
Ma Xisheng	930–932 CE
Ma Xifan	932–947 CE
Ma Xiguang	947–950 CE
Ma Xi'e	950 CE
Ma Xichong	950–951 CE

Wuyue (907–978 CE)

Qian Liu	904–932 CE
Qian Yuanguan	932–941 CE
Qian Hongzuo	941–947 CE
Qian Hongzong	947 CE
Qian Chu (Qian Hongchu)	947–978 CE

Min (909–945 CE) and Yin (943–945 CE)

Wang Shenzhi	909–925 CE
Wang Yanhan	925–926 CE
Wang Yanjun	926–935 CE
Wang Jipeng	935–939 CE
Wang Yanxi	939–944 CE
Wang Yanzheng	943–945 CE

Southern Han (917–971 CE)

Liu Yan	917–925 CE
Liu Bin	941–943 CE
Liu Sheng	943–958 CE
Liu Chang	958–971 CE

Jingnan (924–963 CE)

Gao Jixing	909–928 CE
Gao Conghui	928–948 CE
Gao Baorong	948–960 CE
Gao Baoxu	960–962 CE
Gao Jichong	962–963 CE

Later Shu (934–965 CE)

Meng Zhixiang	934 CE
Meng Chang	938–965 CE

Southern Tang (937–96 CE)

Li Bian	937–943 CE
Li Jing	943–961 CE
Li Yu	961–976 CE

Northern Han (951–979 CE)

Liu Min	951–954 CE
Liu Chengjun	954–968 CE
Liu Ji'en	970 CE
Liu Jiyuan	970–982 CE

ANCIENT JAPANESE EMPERORS

This list is not exhaustive and dates are approximate. Where dates of rule overlap, emperors either ruled jointly or ruled in opposition to one another. There may also be differences in name spellings between different sources.

MYTHOLOGICAL FIGURES AND THE AGE OF THE GODS

The first descendants of Japan are the mythological deities or *kami*. There were seven generations of *kami*, including Izanagi (Izanagi-no-Mikoto) and Izanami (Izanami-no-Mikoto), who are generally thought of as the creator deities of Japan. Among their many offspring are the Three Precious Children: Amaterasu (sun goddess), Susanoo (storm god) and Tsukuyomi (moon god). Ninigi, a grandson of Amaterasu, was sent to earth to rule. His great-grandson was the first Emperor, Jimmu.

IMPERIAL HOUSE OF JAPAN

Early History

Emperor Jimmu (Hikohohodemi; presumed
  mythological and thought descended from

Amaterasu, the sun goddess)	660–585 BCE
Emperor Suizei (Kamununakawamimi; presumed mythological)	581–549 BCE
Emperor Annei (Shikitsuhikotamatemi; presumed mythological)	549–511 BCE
Emperor Itoku (Ōyamatohikosukitomo; presumed mythological)	510–477 BCE
Emperor Kōshō (Mimatsuhikokaeshine; presumed mythological)	475–393 BCE
Emperor Kōan (Yamatotarshihiko*kuni*oshihito; presumed mythological)	392–291 BCE
Emperor Kōrei (Ōyamatonekohikofutoni; presumed mythological)	290–215 BCE
Emperor Kōgen (Ōyamatonekohiko*kuni*kuru; presumed mythological)	214–158 BCE
Emperor Kaika (Wakayamato Nekohiko Ōbibi; presumed mythological)	157–98 BCE
Emperor *Sujin* (Mimaki; presumed mythological but possibly existed)	97–30 BCE
Emperor Suinin (Ikume; presumed mythological)	29 BCE–70 CE
Emperor Keikō (Ōtarashihiko; presumed mythological)	71–130 CE
Emperor Seimu (Wakatarashihiko; presumed mythological)	131–190 CE
Emperor Chūai (Tarashinakatsuhiko; presumed mythological)	192–200 CE
Empress Jingū (Okinagatarashi; presumed mythological, not officially counted as Emperor)	201–269 CE

Kofun Period (*c.* 300–538 CE)

Emperor Ōjin (Homutawake; deified)	270–310 CE
Emperor Nintoku (Ohosazaki)	313–399 CE
Emperor Richū (Ōenoizahowake)	400–405 CE
Emperor Hanzei (Mizuhawake)	406–410 CE
Emperor Ingyō (Oasatsuma Wakugo no Sukune)	411–453 CE
Emperor Ankō (Anaho)	453–456 CE
Emperor Yūrayaku (Ōhatuse no Wakatakeru)	456–479 CE
Emperor Seinei (Shiraka)	480–484 CE
Emperor Kenzō (Woke)	485–487 CE
Emperor Ninken (Oke)	488–498 CE
Emperor Buretsu (Ohatsuse no Wakasazaki)	499–506 CE
Emperor Keitai (Ohodo)	507–531 CE
Emperor Ankan (Magari)	534–535 CE
Emperor Senka (Hinokuma-no-takata)	536–539 CE

Asuka Period (*c.* 538–710 CE)

Emperor Kinmei is the first emperor for which historical evidence exists.

Emperor Kinmei (Amekunioshiharakihironiwa)	540–571 CE
Emperor Bidatsu (Nunakura no Futotamashiki)	572–585 CE
Emperor Yōmei (Tachibana no Toyohi)	586–587 CE
Emperor Sushun (Hatsusebe)	588–592 CE
Emperor Suiko (Nukatabe)	593–628 CE
Emperor Jomei (Tamura)	629–641 CE
Empress Kōgyoku (Takara; first reign)	642–645 CE
Emperor Kōtoku (Karu)	645–654 CE
Empress Saimei (Takara; second reign)	655–661 CE
Emperor Tenchi (Kazuraki)	662–672 CE

Emperor Kōbun (Ōtomo)	672 CE
Emperor Temmu (Ōama)	673–686 CE
Empress Jitō (Unonosarara)	687–697 CE
Emperor Monmu (Karu)	697–707 CE
Empress Genmei (Ahe)	707–715 CE

Nara Period (c. 710–794 CE)

Empress Genshō (Hidaka)	715–724 CE
Emperor Shōmu (Obito)	724–749 CE
Empress Kōken (Abe; first reign)	749–758 CE
Emperor Junnin (Ōi)	758–764 CE
Empress Shōtoku (Abe; second reign)	764–770 CE
Emperor Kōnin (Shirakabe)	770–781 CE
Emperor Kanmu (Yamabe)	781–806 CE

Heian Period (c. 794–1185 CE)

Emperor Heizei (Ate)	806–809 CE
Emperor Saga (*Kamino*)	809–823 CE
Emperor Junna (Ōtomo)	823–833 CE
Emperor Ninmyō (Masara)	833–850 CE
Emperor Montoku (Michiyasu)	850–858 CE
Emperor Seiwa (Korehito)	858–876 CE
Emperor Yōzei (Sadaakira)	876–884 CE
Emperor Kōkō (Tokiyasu)	884–887 CE
Emperor Uda (Sadami)	887–897 CE
Emperor Daigo (Atsuhito)	897–930 CE
Emperor Suzaku (Yutaakira)	930–946 CE
Emperor Murakami (Nariakira)	946–967 CE
Emperor Reizei (Norihira)	967–969 CE
Emperor En'yū (Morihira)	969–984 CE

Emperor Kazan (Morosada)	984–986 CE
Emperor Ichijō (Kanehito)	986–1011 CE
Emperor Sanjō (Okisada)	1011–1016 CE
Emperor Go-Ichijō (Atsuhira)	1016–1036 CE
Emperor Go-Suzaku (Atsunaga)	1036–1045 CE
Emperor Go-Reizei (Chikahito)	1045–1068 CE
Emperor Go-Sanjō (Takahito)	1068–1073 CE
Emperor Shirakawa (Sadahito)	1073–1087 CE
Emperor Horikawa (Taruhito)	1087–1107 CE
Emperor Toba (Muhehito)	1107–1123 CE
Emperor Sutoku (Akihito)	1123–1142 CE
Emperor Konoe (Narihito)	1142–1155 CE
Emperor Go-Shirakawa (Masahito)	1155–1158 CE
Emperor Nijō (Morihito)	1158–1165 CE
Emperor Rokujō (Nobuhito)	1165–1168 CE
Emperor Takakura (Norihito)	1168–1180 CE
Emperor Antoku (Tokohito)	1180–1185 CE

Kamakura Period (c. 1185–1333 CE)

Emperor Go-Toba (Takahira)	1183–1198 CE
Emperor Tsuchi*mikado* (Tamehito)	1198–1210 CE
Emperor Juntoku (Morinari)	1210–1221 CE
Emperor Chūkyō (Kanenari)	1221 CE
Emperor Go-Horikawa (Yuahito)	1221–1232 CE
Emperor Shijō (Mitsuhito)	1232–1242 CE
Emperor Go-Saga (Kuninito)	1242–1246 CE
Emperor Go-Fukakusa (Hisahito)	1246–1260 CE
Emperor Kameyama (Tsunehito)	1260–1274 CE
Emperor Go-Uda (Yohito)	1274–1287 CE
Emperor Fushimi (Hirohito)	1287–1298 CE

Emperor Go-Fushimi (Tanehito)   1298–1301 CE
Emperor Go-Nijō (Kuniharu)   1301–1308 CE
Emperor Hanazono (Tomihito)   1308–1318 CE

Nanbokucho Period (c. 1336–1392 CE)

Emperor Go-Daijo (Takaharu; first emperor of
the Southern Court)   1318–1339 CE

Emperor Kōgen (Kazuhito; first emperor of the
Northern Court   1331–1333 CE

Emperor Kōmyō (Yutahito; second emperor of
the Northern Court)   1336–1348 CE

Emperor Go-Murakami (Noriyoshi; second
emperor of the Southern Court)   1339–1368 CE

Emperor Sukō (Okihito; third emperor of the
Northern Court)   1348–1351 CE

Emperor Go-Kōgon (Iyahito; fourth emperor of
the Northern Court)   1352–1371 CE

Emperor Chōkei (Yutanari; third emperor of the
Southern Court)   1368–1383 CE

Emperor Go-En'yu (Ohito; fifth emperor of the
Northern Court)   1371–1382 CE

Emperor Go-Komatsu (Motohito; sixth and final
emperor of the Northern Court)   1382–1392 CE

Emperor Go-Kameyama (Hironari; fourth and
final emperor of the Southern Court)   1383–1392 CE

Muromachi Period (c. 1392–1573 CE)

Emperor Go-Komatsu (Motohito)   1392–1412 CE
Emperor Shōkō (Mihito)   1412–1428 CE
Emperor Go-Hanazono (Hikohito)   1428–1464 CE

Emperor Go-Tsuchi*mikado* (Fusahito)	1464–1500 CE
Emperor Go-Kashiwabara (Katsuhito)	1500–1526 CE
Emperor Go-Nara (Tomohito)	1526–1557 CE
Emperor Ōgimachi (Michihito)	1557–1586 CE

ANCIENT INDIAN MONARCHS

This list takes up after the mythological Lunar dynasty (Chandravamsha), into which the Hindu god Krishna was born. Descendants include the god Budha (not to be confused with the Buddha). From his son, Pururavas, came several of the communities of India, including the Magadha dynasty founded by Brihadratha.

The list is not exhaustive and dates are approximate. Where dates of rule overlap, monarchs either ruled jointly or ruled in opposition to one another. There may also be differences in name spellings between different sources.

MAGADHA DYNASTY (c. 1700–38 BCE)

The following kings and dates of their rule are uncertain.

Brihadratha Dynasty (c. 1700–730 BCE)

Brihadratha (founded the Brihadratha dynasty, the earliest dynasty to rule Magadha)	c. 1700 BCE
Jarasandha (son of Brihadratha)	?
Sahadeva (son of Jarasandha)	?
Somadhi	1661 BCE
Srutasravas	1603 BCE

Ayutayus	1539 BCE
Niramitra	1503 BCE
Sukshatra	1463 BCE
Brihatkarman	1405 BCE
Senajit	1382 BCE
Srutanjaya	1332 BCE
Vipra	1292 BCE
Suchi	1257 BCE
Kshemya	1199 BCE
Subrata	1171 BCE
Dharma	1107 BCE
Susuma	1008 BCE
Dridhasena	970 BCE
Sumati	912 BCE
Subala	879 BCE
Sunita	857 BCE
Satyajit	817 BCE
Viswajit	767 BCE
Ripunjaya	732 BCE

Pradyota Dynasty (c. 682–544 BCE)

Pradyota Mahasena (dethroned Ripunjaya)	682 BCE
Palaka	659 BCE
Visakhayupa	635 BCE
Ajaka	585 BCE
Varttivarddhana	564 BCE

Haryanka Dynasty (c. 544–413 BCE)

Bimbisara (dethroned Varttivarddhana)	544 BCE
Ajatashatru	491 BCE

Udayin	461 BCE
Anirudha	428 BCE
Munda	419 BCE
Darshaka	417 BCE
Nagadasaka	415 BCE

Shishunaga Dynasty (c. 413–345 BCE)

Shishunaga (dethroned Nagadasaka)	413 BCE
Kalashhoka	395 BCE
Kshemadharman	377 BCE
Kshatraujas	365 BCE
Nandivardhana	355 BCE
Mahanandin	349 BCE

Nanda Dynasty (c. 345–322 BCE)

Mahapadma Nanda (illegitimate son of Mahanandin)	345 BCE
Pandhukananda	340 BCE
Panghupatinanda	339 BCE
Bhutapalananda	338 BCE
Rashtrapalananda	337 BCE
Govishanakananda	336 BCE
Dashasidkhakananda	335 BCE
Kaivartananda	334 BCE
Karvinathanand	333 BCE
Dana Nanda	330 BCE

Note: this period was marked by Alexander the Great's invasion of parts of India, which was only halted after the Battle of the Hydaspes in 326 BCE when Alexander's troops revolted and refused to fight onwards.

Maurya Dynasty (*c.* 321–187 BCE)

Chandragupta Maurya (founder of first imperial dynasty)	321 BCE
Bindusara	297 BCE
Ashoka	268 BCE
Dasharatha Maurya	232 BCE
Samprati	224 BCE
Shalishuka	215 BCE
Devavarman	202 BCE
Shatadhanvan	195 BCE
Brihadratha	187 BCE

Shunga Dynasty (*c.* 185–73 BCE)

Pushyamitra Shunga (dethroned Brihadratha)	185 BCE
Agnimitra	149 BCE
Vasujyeshtha	141 BCE
Vasumitra	131 BCE
Bhadraka	124 BCE
Pulindaka	122 BCE
Ghosha	119 BCE
Vajremitra	108 BCE
Bhagabhadra	94 BCE
Devabhuti	83 BCE

Kanva Dynasty (*c.* 73–28 BCE)

Vasudeva Kanva (dethroned Devabhuti)	73 BCE
Bhumimtra	64 BCE
Narayana	50 BCE
Susarman	38 BCE

SATAVAHANA DYNASTY (*c.* 228 BCE–217 CE)

This dynasty governed the Deccan region in southern India.

Simuka (dethroned Susarman)	228 BCE
(note that some sources say Simuka ruled from around 30 BCE)	
Krishna	205 BCE
Sajakarni I	187 BCE
Purnotsanga	177 BCE
Skandhastambhi	159 BCE
Satakarni II	141 BCE
Lambodara	85 BCE
Apilaka	67 BCE
Meghasvati	55 BCE
Svati	37 BCE
Skandasvati	19 BCE
Mrigendra Satakarni	12 BCE
Kunatala Satakarni	9 BCE
Satakarni III	1 BCE–1 CE
Pulumavi I	1 CE
Gaura Krishna	36 CE
Hala	61 CE
Mandalaka (Pulumavi II)	69 CE
Purindrasena	71 CE
Sundara Satakarni	76 CE
Chakora Satakarni	77 CE
Shivasvati	78 CE
Gautamiputra Satkarni	106 CE
Vasisthiputra (Pulumavi III)	130 CE
Shiva Sri Satakarni	158 CE

Shivaskanda Satakarni	165 CE
Sir Yajna Satakarni	172 CE
Bijaya Satakarni	201 CE
Chandra Sri Satakarni	207 CE
Pulumavi IV	217 CE

GUPTA DYNASTY (c. 240–750 CE)

Imperial Gupta Rulers (c. 240–540 CE)

Gupta (Srigupta)	240 CE
Ghatotkacha ('Maharaja')	300 CE
Chandragupta I (first emperor and founder of the Gupta empire)	320 CE
Samudragupta	325/350 CE
Chandragupta II	376 CE
Kumaragupta I	415 CE
Skandagupta	455 CE
Purugupta	467 CE
Kumaragupta II	470/472 CE
Budhagupta	475/479 CE
Narasimhagupta	496/515 CE
Kumaragupta III	530 CE
Vishnagupta	540 CE

Later Gupta Rulers (c. 490–750 CE)

While the Later Guptas succeeded the Imperial Guptas, they seem to be descended from different families.

Krishna-Gupta	490–505 CE
Harsha-Gupta	505–525 CE
Jivita-Gupta I	525–550 CE
Kumara-Gupta	550–560 CE
Damodara-Gupta	560–562 CE
Mahasena-Gupta	562–601 CE
Madhava-Gupta	601–655 CE
Aditya-Sena	655–680 CE
Deva-Gupta	680–700 CE
Vishnu-Gupta	dates unknown
Jivita-Gupta II	dates unknown

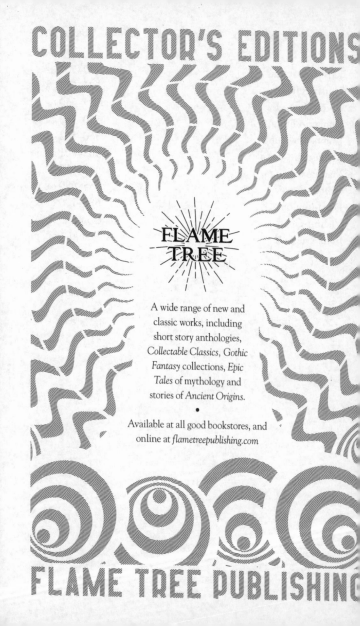